TRANSFORMING THE HEART

THE BUDDHIST WAY TO JOY AND COURAGE

TRANSFORMING THE HEART

THE BUDDHIST WAY TO JOY AND COURAGE

A Commentary to the Bodhisattva Togme Sangpo's
The Thirty-seven Practices of Bodhisattvas

by
Geshe Jampa Tegchok

edited by
Thubten Chodron

Snow Lion Publications
Ithaca, New York

Snow Lion Publications
P. O. Box 6483
Ithaca, New York 14851 USA
607-273-8519

Printed in Canada

ISBN 1-55939-099-9

Library of Congress Cataloging-in-Publication Data

Jampa Tegchok, Geshe, 1930-

    Transforming the heart : the Buddhist way to joy and courage : a commentary to the Bodhisattva Togme Sangpo's The thirty-seven practices of Bodhisattvas / Geshe Jampa Tegchok ; edited by Thubten Chodron.

    p.   cm.

    Includes bibliographical references.

    ISBN 1-55939-099-9

    1. Rgyal-sras Thogs-med-dpal Bzan-po-dpal, 1295-1369. Rgyal ba'i sras kyi lag len sum cu so bdun ma. 2. Enlightenment (Buddhism) - Requisites. 3. Spiritual life—Buddhism. I. Thubten Chodron, 1950-   . II. Rgyal-sras Thogs med-dpal Bzan-po-dpal, 1295-1369. Rgyal ba'i sras kyi lag len sum cu so bdun ma. III. Title.

BQ4399.R463J36   1999

294.3'444—dc21   98-54865

                                                          CIP

070500-1316T8

CONTENTS

PREFACE

The Thirty-seven Practices of Bodhisattvas, by the Tibetan monk Gyalsay Togme Sangpo, is a text popular in all schools of Tibetan Buddhism. Studied by old and young, monastics and lay followers, it describes, in thirty-seven short verses, the essential practices leading to enlightenment. Gyalsay Togme Sangpo (1295-1369) was renowned as a Bodhisattva in Tibet and revered for living in accordance with the Bodhisattva ideals and practices that he taught. He continuously practiced exchanging oneself with others and transforming adverse circumstances such as sickness and poverty into the path to enlightenment, and in this way inspired not only his direct disciples but also generations of practitioners up to the present day.

In the late 1980s, while he was abbot of Nalanda Monastery in France, Geshe Jampa Tegchok, who is currently the abbot of Sera-je Monastic University in India, gave a commentary on *The Thirty-seven Practices of Bodhisattvas*. Born in 1930, Geshe Tegchok became a monk at the age of eight. He studied the major Buddhist treatises at Sera-je Monastic University in Tibet for fourteen years before fleeing his homeland in 1959 following the abortive uprising of the Tibetans against the Chinese communist occupation of their country. After staying in the refugee camp at Buxa, India, Geshe Tegchok went to Varanasi, where he obtained his Acharya (Master) Degree and taught for seven years. He then began teaching in the West—three years in England and ten years at Nalanda Monastery in France. In 1993, His Holiness the Dalai Lama appointed him as abbot of Sera-je Monastic University in India.

I had the good fortune to study with Geshe Tegchok for three years in the early 1980s and was delighted when he asked me some years later to prepare his oral teachings for publication. Having received teachings almost daily from Geshe-la, I know that he teaches very clearly and with deep care and compassion for his students. While teaching, he often explores a topic in detail, revealing aspects that would remain hidden in a more cursory teaching. This commentary is no exception.

Geshe Tegchok teaches in a very strict, yet relaxed manner. He never waters down the meaning to make it more acceptable to our ego. For me, a good spiritual mentor is one who challenges my preconceptions, who makes my ego squirm with discomfort when its games are exposed. At the same time, Geshe-la is relaxed and jovial, laughing with his students as we study and discuss a text together. But his good humor doesn't prevent him from introducing us to a very subtle type of analysis. He reveals multiple layers of meaning inside seemingly simple concepts.

As editor, I was repeatedly faced with deciding what to include and what to delete from Geshe-la's oral teachings. He went into some topics in depth—especially in chapters nine and thirteen—introducing vocabulary and concepts found in the philosophical texts studied in the great monastic universities. These terms and concepts may not be familiar to the general reader, and it may require a stretch of the mind to understand their subtleties. It would have been easy to remove these topics from the manuscript, resulting in easier reading in some sections. However, I think this would have been a great loss. Where else could the average reader receive these explanations? How else could we be challenged to go deeper? My own experience in studying the Buddha's teachings is that I need to be exposed to certain topics repeatedly, knowing that I will not understand them the first few times. However, through familiarity everything becomes easier. If I constantly avoid the difficult subjects, then my practice will remain superficial. So I am happy to "plant seeds" in my mind by repeatedly hearing these topics, knowing that by making some effort, understanding will gradually come. The great masters have said that as we purify our negativities, and accumulate positive potential, we will be able to understand things that were previously obscure to us.

In chapter eleven, Geshe-la went into detail when describing the taking and giving meditation. I have heard teachings on this many times before, but find his explanation here especially captivating and stimulating. Just reading the material created a sense of joy in my mind, so when editing, I decided to include all the details in the hopes that the reader would benefit from this precious teaching.

However, if a particular explanation is too detailed or too complex for your needs, please feel free to go on to the next section. Each person's needs and ways of learning and practicing are unique and need to be respected.

As in most explanations of the Bodhisattvas' practices, the ideal is presented. Often we in the West feel that we should be able to understand and practice everything immediately. However, learning the Dharma is different from learning secular subjects, and we are not expected to be able to put everything into practice at once. Rather, we practice according to our present needs and abilities. That enables us to progress gradually, so that later we will have the ability to do practices that initially were too difficult for us. Even though some practices may seem too advanced for us now, we can still appreciate and respect those who are able to engage in them and know that one day we, too, will be find these practices within our range.

The Thirty-seven Practices of Bodhisattvas is found at the end of this volume, and an outline of the text is included as an appendix. This outline gives an overview of the text and shows how the various topics fit together. The glossary contains the general meanings of Dharma terms found in this book. Please note that these are not translations of the definitions found in philosophical texts. The section on recommended reading lists resources that complement the teachings in this book.

A few comments about language usage are needed. In an attempt to be gender inclusive, "he" and "she" have been alternately used in situations that, in fact, include people of both genders. The term "our mind" does not mean that we share one mind. We each have our own mindstream. It simply means "one's mind" or "your mind."

Geshe Tegchok taught *The Thirty-seven Practices* in Tibetan, and Thubten Sherab Sherpa did the oral translation. This was checked and retranslated when necessary by Ven. Steve Carlier. In preparing this book, I also drew on the teachings Geshe Tegchok gave on *Mind Training Like Rays of the Sun* by Namkha Pel, which were translated by Ven. Steve Carlier, and included them in appropriate areas in this book. This serves to depict the Bodhisattvas' practices more completely. The translation of the root text was done by Ruth Sonam and excerpted with permission from *The Thirty-seven Practices of Bodhisattvas* by Geshe Sonam Rinchen, translated and edited by Ruth Sonam (Ithaca NY:

Snow Lion Publications, 1997). I would like to thank Ven. Steve Carlier for making final corrections on the content, Dan Black for his editorial suggestions and for proofreading the manuscript, and Peter Green for doing the illustrations. All errors are my own. Many thanks also to the monks of Nalanda Monastery for making these teachings possible and to the members of Dharma Friendship Foundation in Seattle who supported me while I edited this book. May this book contribute towards alleviating the suffering of sentient beings and enabling them to discover and develop their good qualities and joy.

Thubten Chodron
Seattle, USA

INTRODUCTION

THE BUDDHIST WORLD VIEW

by Thubten Chodron

While some readers may be familiar with the Buddhist world view, and in particular, the world view of those following the Tibetan Buddhist tradition, some may not. Geshe Jampa Tegchok's commentary on *The Thirty-seven Practices of Bodhisattvas* presupposes the reader's familiarity with this tradition, and for that reason a brief overview could be helpful.

Shakyamuni Buddha lived in ancient India over 2,500 years ago. Born as a prince, he began to question the meaning of life upon seeing aging, sickness and death. This led him to devote his life to investigating suffering, its causes, their cessation and the path to that cessation. Once he attained liberation from suffering and its causes by following the path, he gave his first teaching on these four noble truths.

The teaching on the four noble truths is set against the backdrop of the Buddhist notion of the mind. Here the term "mind" does not refer to the brain—for that is part of the body—nor merely to intellect, but to all the conscious aspects of us. The mind is formless, unlike the body, which is composed of atoms. Yet, it is an existing phenomena, and its presence or absence marks the difference between a living being and a dead body. The mind is what experiences, perceives, thinks, and feels. In other words, our mind or heart perceives objects through our senses, thinks conceptually, feels emotionally, experiences pleasure and pain, and so forth.

Interrelated, our mind and body affect each other. When our health is poor, it is easy to be in a bad mood. When we are depressed mentally, our physical health may also decline. However, the body and

mind are two different continuums, the body being physical, the mind being formless and conscious. Life occurs while the body and mind are interrelated, while death marks the separation of these two continuums. The body becomes a corpse which is buried or cremated, and the mind, being formless, goes on to take another rebirth. Which rebirth we take is influenced by our actions, or karma.

Thus, our present life does not exist in isolation from the past and the future. Just as our body has causes—the sperm and egg of our parents—our mind at the time of conception also has a main cause, the previous moment of mind. Habits and imprints from actions we did in previous lives influence our present life, and our present thoughts, choices, and actions create habits and imprints which will influence what we will experience in the future. Thus, events and experiences are not predetermined or fated to happen. They simply arise due to causes and conditions. Knowing this, we can pay attention to our choices, actions, and the causes we create.

In the four noble truths, the first two—suffering and its causes—describe our present situation, while the last two—cessation and the path to it—describe our vast human potential. The Buddha emphasized that we must understand both our present situation as well as our potential. If we gloss over and ignore our present experience, our spiritual practice will not be grounded. On the other hand, if we ignore our potential and think that our present circumstances are unchangeable, we become like a beggar who does not recognize that the stone in his pocket is actually a jewel.

With the first noble truth, the Buddha pointed out that we have numerous problems in life. We age, fall ill, and die without choice. Though we seek pleasure, fulfillment and success, we remain dissatisfied even when things seem to be going well. When we get what we want, fear of losing it often sets in, preventing us from enjoying what we have. Although we try to protect ourselves from undesirable experiences, we cannot control everything that happens to us. We fear not having enough or not being good enough, and so never find lasting happiness or security. This is the human condition. It is the situation in which we all live. This is usually called the truth of suffering, but here the word suffering has a wider connotation than its usual meaning in English. It refers to the fact that we have difficulties and encounter unsatisfactory circumstances in that we cannot control our body, our emotions, our life experiences in the way that we would like.

With the second noble truth, the Buddha asks us to search for the cause of these unsatisfactory experiences. Although happiness and suffering seem to come from external objects—our environment, our society, other people—if we examine our lives more closely, we realize that our attitudes greatly influence how we experience what we encounter. Mental states such as clinging attachment, anger, arrogance, jealousy, and confusion disturb our mind and life. Clinging attachment makes us think that we cannot be happy unless we have the right relationship, job, or house. We then want those things so desperately that what we do to get them often creates more problems for us later. Anger makes us think that our perception of a situation is the only right one and may lead us to see harm where there is none. It impedes our ability to listen and discuss solutions. Attempting to hide our insecurity, our arrogance causes us to see others as inferior. We thus become isolated, and the connections which we seek with others elude us. With jealousy we compare ourselves negatively to others, and thus become unable to rejoice at the happiness and goodness in the world. Confusion inhibits our ability to understand things clearly and make wise decisions. Choices made under the influence of these disturbing attitudes further complicate things and often make us act in ways that harm others or ourselves. The effects of these thoughtless actions are many. For example, later we may experience deep remorse or even guilt. In addition, our choices and actions—or karma—influence the situations we will find ourselves in and our experiences in the future.

The disturbing attitudes—clinging attachment, anger, arrogance, jealousy, confusion, and the rest—are rooted in ignorance, which misinterprets how we, others, and all phenomena exist. Ignorance makes us see everything as solid and existing in its own right and under its own power. Seeing ourselves, others, and all phenomena as concrete prevents us from understanding that things are fluid and dependent, and we forget that change is possible. Fortunately all these disturbing attitudes can be eliminated because they arise from ignorance's misconstrual of reality.

With the third noble truth, the Buddha guides us to see our potential. The nature of our mind is pure and clear, like the open sky. The disturbing attitudes of ignorance, anger, clinging attachment, arrogance and jealousy are like clouds, obscuring that pure nature. Anxiety, fear, and self-preoccupation are not our inherent nature. Just as the clouds and the sky are not the same nature and the clouds can be dispelled, our real nature is not the disturbing attitudes, which can be eliminated. Therefore, it is possible to end all unsatisfactory experiences and the disturbing attitudes and negative actions which cause them. We can arrive at a state of lasting happiness because the basic, deeper nature of our mind is untainted. Knowing this gives us a firm basis for self-confidence and hope.

The fourth noble truth is the path leading to this happiness. The Buddha provided a road map to develop our potential and recognize inner beauty. Since ignorance and self-centeredness are the two chief causes of our ills, we must develop attitudes which counteract them. Ignorance is remedied by becoming wise and understanding the reality of how we and all things exist. This involves realizing emptiness, the lack of independent existence of all phenomena. Whereas ignorance makes things appear solid and insurmountable to us, the wisdom realizing emptiness knows that things do not exist in that way. Emptiness does not mean total non-existence. Rather it means that things arise dependently, and thus are flexible and changeable. The development of this wisdom is assisted by meditative stabilization, the ability to focus our minds on constructive objects for as long as we wish. Meditative stabilization, in turn, is facilitated by ethical conduct, which involves living in a way that avoids harming others and ourselves. These three—ethical conduct, meditative stabilization, and wisdom—are known as the "three higher trainings," which lead us to liberation from cyclic existence, the cycle of constantly recurring problems that we currently experience.

Love, compassion, and the altruistic intention

Along with ignorance, another obstacle we encounter on the path to full enlightenment is self-centeredness, or self-preoccupation, which makes us believe that our happiness and our suffering are more important than anyone else's. Obscuring our love and compassion, self-preoccupation, in its gross form, imprisons us in a lonely, alienated mental state, making us immune to seeing the kindness all around us. In its subtle form, self-preoccupation makes us concerned with only our own spiritual practice and liberation and inhibits our ability to be of greatest benefit to all beings.

To dissolve self-centeredness we cultivate compassion and love. The former wishes that all beings be free from suffering and its causes, the latter wishes them to have happiness and its causes. Buddhism contains many meditation techniques to help us gradually cultivate genuine patience, love and compassion which extend impartially to all beings. Herein lies the key to mental peace.

For example, when faced with harm, we often react with anger and hatred, which in turn breed physical and verbal violence against others. This incites others to retaliate, and we find ourselves trapped in a spiral of unkindness and cruelty which destroys the happiness of all concerned. To react wisely when confronted with harm or suffering, we need a clear mind, free from the turbulence of resentment and rage. While anger certainly gives us a lot of energy, we cannot use that energy wisely. From a Buddhist perspective, compassion can be an even more powerful force than anger to motivate wise action. A compassionate person is patient—undisturbed in the face of harm or suffering—and yet is powerfully engaged in the situation. For example, His Holiness the Dalai Lama, the spiritual and political leader of the Tibetan people, has remained firm in his compassionate and nonviolent approach to the occupation, repression, and destruction his country and his people have undergone in the last four and a half decades. Yet, he is not seen as weak and his cause has gained attention worldwide; his compassionate approach has saved thousands of lives.

When we brood and hold on to our resentment, who suffers— ourselves or the other? Forgiving our enemies simply means letting go of our hatred and anger towards them. We do not need to forget the harm, but we can react to it with compassion for everyone concerned—victims, perpetrators, and bystanders. In this way, we are able to clearly seek solutions.

We cannot dispel our anger and resentment simply by telling ourselves not to be angry. However, if we can look at the situation in a different way, the anger will dissolve by itself. Thus, Buddhism encourages us to realize that our enemies' harmful behavior stems from their own internal pain and chaos, which lead them to use harmful methods in an attempt to secure their happiness. By seeing the situation from the other's point of view, we automatically can have more understanding and compassion. This does not mean that we respond passively, but that our minds are clear and can actively choose appropriate methods to stop the harm.

Learning to understand and work compassionately and wisely in real life is one purpose of the Buddha's teachings. That is, the Buddha's teachings and our own spiritual practice are not divorced from our daily experiences. The Dharma is not to be merely intellectually understood, but actually applied so that it transforms the quality of our life.

Although the Dharma certainly applies to our daily life, it covers much more than our day-to-day interactions and emotions. Both scientists and the Buddha talk about the vastness of the universe and things existing in it that we do not or cannot perceive at this moment. Thus, it is also important to stretch our minds and consider other realms and states of existence.

Sentient beings and their worlds

In the Buddhist view, life is not restricted to the planet Earth, nor is existence restricted to what we can perceive through our five senses, which are indeed limited. For example, dogs can smell some odors that we cannot; birds can see some things that we cannot. Thus, it is incorrect to think that things exist only if we perceive them and that they do not exist simply because we have not experienced them directly.

With this in mind, let's look at the Buddha's description of the six realms of sentient beings—beings who have mind but who are not enlightened Buddhas. In addition to human beings and animals, there are gods (celestial beings), demigods, hungry ghosts and hell beings. How do these various realms come into existence? They arise due to the functioning of cause and effect. Specifically, our actions, or karma, create the causes for us to be attracted to these various types of rebirth, and our actions influence what we experience and encounter during these lives. From the Buddhist perspective, there is no external creator either of the universe or of the beings in it, nor is there a supreme being who determines what happens to sentient beings. Acting under the influence of disturbing attitudes, we remain trapped in cyclic existence, being born again and again in the six realms. Acting wisely and compassionately, we create the causes for happiness, both the temporal happiness of fortunate rebirths and the ultimate happiness of liberation and enlightenment.

Cyclic existence means being caught in the cycle of uncontrollable rebirth, taking one body after another under the influence of disturbing attitudes and karma. Liberation, or nirvana, is the ceasing of this unproductive and suffering cycle, and one who attains liberation is called a foe destroyer or arhat. There are two vehicles leading to arhatship: the vehicle of the hearer (Skt. *shravaka*), one who hears the Buddha's teaching and then passes them on to others; and the vehicle of the solitary realizer (Skt. *pratyekabuddha*), one who attains liberation at a time when no Buddha is present in the world. To attain the liberation of a hearer or a solitary realizer, one must eliminate the deluded obscurations which cause cyclic existence. However, there are still subtle imprints on the mindstream, called obscurations to omniscience, and when they are removed, full enlightenment is attained. The determination to be free motivates us to seek liberation and the altruistic intention (Skt. *bodhichitta*), which is concerned with the welfare of all sentient beings, motivates us to attain full enlightenment. One who attains enlightenment is called a Buddha, and as a Buddha, one has unlimited abilities to benefit others.

All sentient beings can become Buddhas because each of us already has the Buddha nature, the factors which allow us to become a Buddha, as the nature of our mind. Thus, underlying whatever pain or confusion we may experience, there is always reason for hope. Those who have entered the path to Buddhahood are called Bodhisattvas, people who are deeply motivated to attain enlightenment in order to benefit others most effectively.

A Buddha is omniscient and has unlimited abilities to help others. However, Buddhas are not omnipotent; they cannot control all that happens in the world, nor can they control the minds of sentient beings. They teach, guide, inspire and help us in a variety of ways, but we must engage in and accomplish the spiritual path ourselves. We cannot hire someone to do it for us. That would be like asking someone to eat for us and thinking that we would be full afterwards! Because of this the Buddha encouraged personal responsibility. On the other hand, we are not alone in a cold universe, devoid of help. All of those who have traversed the path before us and accomplished its goals can help us. Thus, we can rely on (or take refuge in) the Three Jewels: the Buddhas, the Dharma and the Sangha. The Buddhas are the fully enlightened beings who taught the path; the Dharma refers to the last two noble truths, true cessations and true paths. These two are the real refuge, for once our mind has transformed into these, we will experience suffering no more and will have incredible opportunities to benefit others. The Sangha is any person who has understood reality directly, and is thus engaged in removing once and for all the various levels of disturbing attitudes which cause cyclic existence.

How to approach the path

The Buddha emphasized that we need to develop discriminating wisdom and not accept the path he has outlined on blind faith. Thus, we are encouraged to question, research, reason, and most importantly, apply the Dharma teachings to our own life and see through our own experience whether or not they work. When we have examined them and then tried them out and found them effective in transforming our mind and life, our faith or confidence in these teachings will be based on solid evidence, not fanciful belief.

Thus, it is essential for us to think deeply over a period of time about what we read here. In teaching the Dharma, Buddhist teachers do not expect students to understand everything immediately. Learning a spiritual path is different from studying subjects at school. It involves much introspection, and we need to give ourselves time and space to digest the information, contemplate it, test it out, and integrate it in our lives. Merely knowing the teachings is very different from living them. Since many aspects of the Dharma may be opposite to our habits and usual ways of thinking, time and patience are essential. For example, we may intellectually understand the chapter on transforming unfavorable circumstances into the path, but when we come in contact with a disagreeable person at our workplace, we may forget the teaching. Or we may think that this teaching is nice, but it does not apply to our situation because we definitely are right and therefore our anger is justified!

We also need time and patience to gain an understanding of emptiness, the ultimate or deeper nature of existence. The vocabulary and concepts used to explain this are generally unfamiliar to us at the beginning, and we may be tempted to say, "This doesn't make sense, so forget it," or "This is too difficult, so I won't bother." It is helpful to remember that knowledge, wisdom, and internal transformation occur gradually and that we must persevere with joy, knowing that we can make progress. When a child in kindergarten gets frustrated because he cannot yet read after only a few days of school, we tell him that this is normal. He must practice over time, and then he will be able to read and understand easily.

The Thirty-seven Practices of Bodhisattvas describes methods for dealing with our disturbing attitudes and for developing our inner potential, love, compassion, and wisdom. Although this text was written many centuries ago in Tibet, it contains instructions that are relevant to our modern lives, for human nature and human potential are basically the same no matter the time or place. In his commentary on this text, Geshe Jampa Tegchok unpacked and amplified the meaning of the root text by the Bodhisattva Togme Sangpo. What follows is an overview of the book, which will help you to see the relationships of the various topics and to have a sense of delight in what is to come.

In chapter 1, Geshe-la explains the setting: how to listen to the teachings and how to cultivate a good motivation for listening. He then begins the text with Togme Sangpo's homage and promise to compose. In chapter 2, we are led to reflect on the freedom and fortune that our present, precious human life affords us. Often we take our life and the situation we have for granted or we focus on a few undesirable or disappointing circumstances. This perspective can lead to depression and to wasting a wonderful opportunity. Thus, it is important for us to recognize our fortunate circumstances and utilize them. How? By listening to the Dharma, thinking about it and meditating on it, as explained in chapter 3. To do this, we first need to create a conducive environment, the subject of chapter 4. However, the opportunity we have to practice won't last forever. Why? Chapter 5 explains that death comes to everyone and we will not have this wonderful opportunity to progress spiritually forever. In addition, our actions and attitudes in this life will influence how we die and in what circumstances we will be reborn. Reflecting on impermanence enables us to discern more clearly what is important in our lives, and to set our priorities accordingly so that at the time of death we will have no regrets. To follow a spiritual path, it is essential to have a teacher or mentor, someone who is wise, compassionate, knowledgeable, trustworthy, and patient, to lead us on the path. Chapter 6 explains the qualities to look for in a spiritual mentor and then how to rely on him or her so that our wisdom and compassion will grow. Our spiritual mentor will teach us about the Three Jewels—the Buddhas, the Dharma, and the Sangha—as explained in Chapter 7, so that we will have faith in and be committed to the path and those who taught it and practice it. The causal refuge or causal Buddha, Dharma, and Sangha are those that exist now in other persons. The resultant Buddha, Dharma, and Sangha are those which we will become through our steadfast and sincere practice.

One way to explain the path to enlightenment is according to three levels of spiritual practitioner—the initial, middle, and advanced. We must go through all three phases because the subsequent ones are built on the foundation of the former ones. At the initial level, we learn to observe karma and its effects. This makes us more aware of our choices and actions and helps us to distinguish those which are constructive from those which are destructive. Observing karma and its effects enables us to stop our gross negative behavior and speech. This is the first step on the spiritual path. Without a solid ethical foundation, without applying the teachings to the basic daily interactions we have with others, any other spiritual practice is like trying to build a castle in the air. This is the topic of chapter 8.

The middle-level practitioner gains a deep understanding of the four noble truths, thus developing a strong determination to be free from cyclic existence and to attain liberation. This is explained in chapter 9. Chapter 10 then introduces the trainings of an advanced practitioner. Here we generate the altruistic intention, or bodhichitta, the loving and compassionate intention to become a Buddha in order to benefit all sentient beings most effectively. There are two techniques for generating this mind, and they are taught in chapters 10 and 11. In chapter 12, we see how to apply these teachings on love, compassion, and altruism to unfavorable circumstances we may encounter, thus transforming them into the path to enlightenment. These instructions are particularly valuable because we continually encounter distressing situations, difficulties, changes in fortune, and things we like and dislike. As long as we do not know how to transform these experiences into the path, we are buffeted around by our habitual, emotional patterns that make ourselves and others miserable. This teaching is very practical and can be easily implemented in our daily life.

Chapter 13 beckons us to look into the nature of existence. What is the deeper mode of existence of persons and phenomena? Here we learn how to develop the wisdom realizing emptiness. Emptiness does not mean nothingness; it means a lack of solid, independent existence. Whereas things appear to exist in their own right, independent of mind and of other factors, in fact they exist dependently. This chapter will require careful reading (or re-reading). It contains specific vocabulary and concepts that may be new to us. However, beginning to question how things appear to us and looking more deeply at the nature of existence is both exciting and worthwhile.

In chapter 14, we learn how to apply the altruistic intention and the wisdom understanding the deeper nature of existence to the Bodhisattvas' trainings. We are given practical instructions regarding how to practice in daily life in a sustained and joyous manner. Although we must go through all three levels of practice, we can learn about and begin to train in advanced practices while we are still a beginner. In other words, we do not have to wait until we have mastered the first two levels before being generous! The more we know about the latter trainings, the more we will value the opportunity present in our precious human life. Although we may not be able to do the latter practices perfectly at the moment, we will be inspired by seeing the direction in which we can grow. If we begin the latter practices now according to our present capacity, and at the same time lay a firm foundation with the initial and middle-level practices, the path will develop gradually and smoothly within us.

CHAPTER ONE

SETTING THE STAGE

The Thirty-seven Practices of Bodhisattvas is a short text, but it covers vast topics. It contains the essential points and summarizes the meanings of such great texts as *The Supreme Tantra, Ornament of the Scriptures of the Universal Vehicle, A Guide to the Bodhisattva's Way of Life,* and *The Bodhisattva Stages.* It also contains all the topics from the Gradual Path, explaining the practices of the three levels of practitioners as well as thought transformation. All of these are practices of a Bodhisattva, a person who has generated the altruistic intention (*bodhichitta*) aspiring to become a Buddha in order to benefit sentient beings most effectively.

Before beginning the text, it is helpful to understand how the spiritual mentor should teach, how the student should listen, and what both need to do at the conclusion of the teaching.

At the start, it is important for both the teacher and the student to cultivate a good motivation. Without this, we may think we are great spiritual practitioners, but our actions may in fact be far from pure Dharma. Looking back, many yogis and scholars discovered that although they had studied and meditated for a long time, in the beginning their motivation was not that good, and as a result all that they had done was not really Dharma. Seeing that, they felt great sadness and anguish.

If we do a spiritual practice thinking, "I want to gain spiritual powers, then others will respect me and I will lead a group with many appreciative followers. They will give me things and provide for me

well. Others will hear of me, invite me to conferences, and want to interview me for their publications," then our action has very little to do with Dharma. Our motivation is ordinary—wishing for wealth, praise, and reputation for ourselves. Although we may outwardly look like we are doing a spiritual practice, in fact we are not.

An initial-level practitioner studies and meditates motivated by the thought, "How wonderful it would be if I could be reborn as a human being or a god in my next life." Such a motivation is a step up from the previous one in which we were focused solely on our own present egotistical happiness. Nevertheless, this motivation is not vast, and actions done for this reason will ripen in a good rebirth, but nothing more.

A middle-level practitioner is motivated by the thought, "Even if I attain a good birth as a human or god, I will still be in cyclic existence, with a life characterized by problems. Whatever pleasures I may experience in that life will be without essence and at the time of death, I will not be any better off than I am now. How wonderful if I could be free of cyclic existence and attain the peace of liberation!" All actions motivated in this way are the Dharma and will result in liberation.

If we recollect the kindness of sentient beings when they were our parents in previous lives and even when they were not, it seems so limited to want to attain liberation for our own benefit alone. How could we be satisfied with securing just our own happiness and leaving others to the wind? Thus, an advanced-level practitioner is motivated by the thought, "I definitely want to work for the welfare of all sentient beings. Not doing so would be awful. But at the moment I do not have the full ability to do so because I lack the necessary qualities and I am limited by my faults. The Bodhisattvas have not yet fully purified and enhanced their mindstreams, nor have the hearer and solitary realizer arhats. If I became a Buddha, free from all faults and possessing all good qualities, I would be able to use methods suitable to the dispositions, thoughts, and interests of sentient beings. Therefore, for the sake of all sentient beings I must attain the state of Buddhahood." All actions done with this motivation are the Dharma. These actions may not necessarily look like spiritual practice, as does the study of scriptures, recitation of prayers, and meditation on the Dharma. They could be actions that benefit our community or others in general. They could also be daily activities such as washing, cooking, cleaning, going to work, talking with people, and so forth. The value of any action is determined primarily by the motivation propelling it, and for this reason it is very important to check our motivation before engaging in any action and to deliberately cultivate a Dharma motivation.

It is difficult, even during teachings, for the person teaching and the people listening to have this kind of pure motivation all the time. But we should persist, being careful and mindful of the fact that if our motivation is not good, it is disastrous. As Lama Tsong Khapa said, "If our motivation is good, our path and our level of practice will be good. If our motivation is bad, our path and level of practice will be bad. Everything depends on our motivation." In other words, to know whether our actions of body, speech, and mind are beneficial or not, we should examine our motivation.

If our motivation slips into concern for self-centered aims of this life, it will be difficult for our action to be virtuous and benefit our future lives, let alone lead to liberation or enlightenment. Thus we must be aware of whether our actions are motivated by attachment to the eight worldly concerns. Among these eight, four stem from attachment to happiness of only this life and four come from aversion for unhappiness in this life. The four pairs are:

1. Being pleased when we have money and material possessions, and displeased when we do not have these

2. Being pleased when we have a good name, reputation, and image, and displeased when we have bad ones

3. Being pleased when we have the pleasures of this life—pleasant sights, sounds, smells, tastes, and tangible objects—and displeased when we encounter unpleasant objects

4. Being pleased when we receive praise and approval, and displeased when we receive blame, criticism, or disapproval

These varying emotional states of happiness and unhappiness arise due to our attachment to money and material possessions; name, reputation and image; objects of the five senses; and praise and approval. Any action motivated by attachment to these eight worldly concerns is not Dharma. It is polluted with limited, self-centered interests that keep us bound in dissatisfaction, frustration, and suffering. When our motivation is mixed with the thought of the eight worldly concerns, even if we work very hard, sleep very little and undergo great hardships in our practices, they will not go well. There is a solution: transforming our motivation. Through understanding, our future lives become more important to us than this one. Our present life is not stable. Our lifespan decreases moment by moment and eventually we must die. Therefore it doesn't make sense to work only for the happiness of this life, which is so fleeting and brief, and neglect to prepare for future lives. Our future lives will continue for a long time and are more certain to come than old age in this life. Therefore, they are more important than this life. Having cultivated this motivation, we enter into the initial level of practice.

Some people wonder, "If we always think about future lives, then we are not living in the present." In fact, when we are concerned with future lives, we will appreciate the present more. Why? Our mind will not be disturbed by anger, attachment, pride, jealousy, and laziness—attitudes that commonly fill our mind and make us live in the past and the future. Thus, we will be more mindful of what is valuable, more aware of our actions, and more concerned about others. All of these attitudes will enhance the experience of this life and enable us to create positive karma to accomplish our spiritual aims.

Having a good motivation is extremely important for Dharma practitioners, and for all beings. It is important to remember this, and for this reason we talk a lot about motivation. If we consider our motivation to be of little consequence, we will get up in the morning in a slipshod fashion, immediately thinking how to get as much happiness as possible for ourselves during that day, regardless of the effect on others. We will live on automatic, with little or no awareness of what we are thinking, feeling, saying, or doing, and thus may deliberately or inadvertently harm others. If we reflect and develop a good motivation when we first wake up, our entire day will go better. There is an enormous difference between these two ways of starting the day.

Merely repeating the words, "I must attain enlightenment for the sake of all sentient beings, therefore I am going to do this," with no feeling is not without merit, but it is not of great benefit. We need to unite the meaning of the words with our mind, so that we feel it as much as possible. We need to encourage ourselves by determining from the depths of our hearts, "If I live my life in distraction, it will be a great loss. I must progress towards enlightenment and serve other sentient beings. Therefore I am going to do this." Prayers to this effect remind us of the attitudes we want to cultivate and feel in our hearts. Reciting prayers without thinking of their meaning is not totally without benefit, but it is not of great benefit. We need to use the words to remind us and make the attitude they describe heartfelt.

Having heard of the faults of attachment to the eight worldly concerns, we may wonder why there are Buddhist practices to attain long life and wealth. To attain Buddhahood in order to benefit sentient beings, we need to purify our negativities and complete the two accumulations of positive potential and wisdom. If we have a short life, we will not be able to do this. Doing the meditation to accomplish long life with an altruistic motivation is fine. If we wish to benefit sentient beings widely, and see that we would be more capable of doing so if we had wealth and possessions, then doing a practice to gain wealth is suitable. Of course, if our real motivation is to have these things so we will be rich and powerful, and we mask this motivation with lots of words about working for the benefit of others, then our actions are hypocritical and polluted by the eight worldly concerns. If we lack a strong positive motivation, wealth practices could still bring wealth, and long life practices could bring long life, but they would not be Dharma practices.

We may also wonder, "If the highest aim is to become fully enlightened, isn't it selfish to be motivated simply by the desire for a good rebirth?" In one way it is, because we are operating from self-concern. On the other hand, this motivation is definitely better than that of seeking our personal happiness of only this life. In addition, we could aspire to become a Buddha and still wish for a good rebirth, because if we do not attain enlightenment in this life, we need good rebirths to continue practicing the path in the future. Certainly, even a precious human life with the freedom and fortune to practice the Dharma is still a birth in cyclic existence, characterized by suffering, and therefore is ultimately to be abandoned. Nonetheless, it is a necessary aid to accomplish the ultimate goal of enlightenment. Lama Tsong Khapa said if we have a precious human life with all the freedoms and fortunes, we will be able to quickly develop the enlightened qualities of a Buddha. Without such a birth we will not be able to progress quickly.

If we ask ourselves or if someone else ask us, "Why do you want to attain enlightenment?" we should know the answer. From deep inside ourselves, we should know the reasons. Of course, as newcomers to the Dharma, it will take us a while to understand the path, but we should know what direction we are going in and what qualities we want to develop.

There is no need to be discouraged when cultivating a good motivation, and think, "How can I possibly be enlightened? How can I ever benefit all sentient beings?" The great practitioners say that in our motivation at the beginning and our dedication at the end we need to be assertive—almost arrogant. This means that our motivation and dedication must be vast. It may seem arrogant to say, "I will make all sentient beings have happiness and its causes. I will make them free from suffering and its causes," for we are promising to do something that we are not in a position to do. However, generating these wishes helps us to develop a very vast motivation and dedication. If we do not have the motivation to do something, we will never even approach that. A vast motivation and dedication will encourage us to go in that direction and give us the courage and fearlessness to do that. Without a courageous attitude, we will have difficulty accomplishing even something easy that we are fully capable of doing.

The Kadam lamas say, "There are two actions, one at the beginning and one at the end." This applies to the motivation and dedication. At the beginning of whatever action you do—meditating, listening to teachings, going to work, and so forth—take time to reflect and generate a good motivation as described above. Then do the action, and at the end, dedicate, sharing the positive potential you have created with all sentient beings. Even though the motivation and actual practice might go well, if we do not make good dedication prayers, anger can destroy whatever virtue we have created or impede it from ripening. Therefore, we should dedicate, "May all positive potential I have created act as a cause for all sentient beings to attain Buddhahood. May the Buddha's teachings last for a long time. May sentient beings live together in peace and help each other along the path." We can add other prayers and dedications as we wish.

Our commentary explains this text in three parts, called "the three virtues":

> Part I: the virtue at the beginning, the preliminaries to the
>   text
>
> Part II: the virtue in the middle, the core of the text
>
> Part III: the virtue at the end, the concluding practices

PART I: THE VIRTUE AT THE BEGINNING

Part I covers three points: stating the name of the text, offering of praise, and the author's promise to compose.

THE TITLE OF THIS TEXT

This text is entitled *The Thirty-seven Practices of Bodhisattvas*.

OFFERING OF PRAISE

There is a brief praise and a long praise. The brief praise is: "Namo Lokeshvaraya." "Namo" literally means "I prostrate." "Lokeshvaraya" means "to the protector of the world" and refers to Avalokiteshvara, the Buddha of compassion. Together, the two words mean, "I prostrate to the guru, who is inseparable from Avalokiteshvara."

The long praise is:

> I pay constant homage through my three doors,
> To my supreme teacher and protector Chenrezig,
> Who while seeing all phenomena lack coming and going,
> Makes single-minded effort for the good of living beings.

"Going or coming" refers to the eight extremes of ultimately existing going and coming, and so forth. Thus, Avalokiteshvara (Chenrezig) is praised, "Your wisdom, Avalokiteshvara, sees that the multiplicity of phenomena are free of the fabrications of the eight extremes, and thus sees phenomena as they are." A phenomenon is anything that exists, and "multiplicity of phenomena" refers to conventional phenomena. The fabrications of the eight extremes are: ultimately existing cessation and creation, nihilism and absolutism, coming and going, and unity and plurality. In general, these eight do exist, in that there certainly is coming and going and so on, but there is no ultimately existing coming and going. We need to understand "no coming" to mean no ultimately existing coming, that is, no coming that is independent from all other phenomena. For example, coming depends on someone who is coming, the destination, the action of moving, and so on. Thus coming exists in dependence on other factors; it does not exist on its own, independently of other things. Coming does not ultimately exist. By holding a belief in ultimately existing coming we fall to the extreme of absolutism. Seeing that conventional phenomena are devoid of these extremes is seeing emptiness. The extreme of nihilism occurs if we think that because these eight extremes are empty of ultimate existence, they do not exist at all. This denies the conventional functioning of things and contradicts our experience that coming and so forth do, in fact, exist.

To understand in depth the emptiness which is free from the eight extremes of absolutism and nihilism involves studying the entirety of Nagarjuna's *Treatise on the Middle Way.* An extensive explanation would cover all of the points in the three *Perfection of Wisdom Scriptures (Prajna Paramita)*, known as the Concise, Middling, and Vast Mothers.

Phenomena can be classified into two categories: conventional truths and ultimate truths. The former includes all the objects and people in our world. The latter is the deeper way in which they exist. The third line of this verse indicates the spiritual guide's deep understanding and insight into ultimate truths. It also shows his or her quality of wisdom, from among the two, wisdom and method. Wisdom and method are the two aspects of the path that we develop to become enlightened. Method is the aspect of the path emphasizing the accumulation of positive potential through practices such as generosity, ethical discipline, and patience motivated by compassion. Wisdom is the aspect of the path that understands the nature of existence. Thus the third line praises the spiritual mentor, who is unified with Avalokiteshvara, for his or her insight into ultimate truth and wisdom.

The next line indicates that, although Guru Avalokiteshvara has such wisdom, he or she works one-pointedly for the welfare of sentient beings inspired by merciful compassion. This praises the spiritual mentor's qualities of understanding conventional truth and method. Having merciful compassion, which is the root from which other good qualities grow, Guru Avalokiteshvara works for all sentient beings according to their thoughts, wishes, and dispositions. While there are many beings to whom the author could pay homage, here he does so to Avalokiteshvara. *The Thirty-seven Practices* is a text of the Mahayana (Universal Vehicle). In this context, "vehicle" refers to a body of teachings or an attitude of mind that transports us somewhere. "Universal," connotes a vehicle that embraces the concerns and needs of all beings. The root of the Universal Vehicle is compassion, and because Avalokiteshvara is the Buddha of compassion and embodies the compassion of all the Buddhas, homage is paid to him.

Thus this verse indicates "I pay homage physically, verbally, and mentally to the supreme root guru, who possesses both method and wisdom, and who is inseparable from Avalokiteshvara." The root guru—one's principal spiritual mentor—is called supreme because he or she is the teacher explaining the Universal Vehicle. Here the Bodhisattva Togme Sangpo respectfully pays homage with his body, speech, and mind to the guru who is inseparable from Avalokiteshvara. He does this by expressing the guru's knowledge of method and wisdom and understanding of the two truths.

Why is this praise offered? There are two purposes: first, so that the author may accumulate positive potential in his own mindstream; secondly, to be in accordance with the custom of the sages, which is to begin a text with homage to a holy object.

THE AUTHOR'S PROMISE TO COMPOSE

Perfect Buddhas, source of all well-being and happiness,
Arise from accomplishing the excellent teachings,
And this depends on knowing the practices.
So I will explain the practices of Bodhisattvas.

For sentient beings the source of help, referring to temporary well-being, and happiness, referring to the ultimate happiness of liberation and enlightenment, is the Buddhas. The second line indicates that the Buddhas arise from correctly practicing the doctrine of the Universal Vehicle, thus developing the spiritual paths leading to enlightenment. Before becoming Buddhas, they first generated compassion, the root of the Universal Vehicle. Then they developed the altruistic intention, and motivated by that, they practiced the six far-reaching attitudes. In this way, they gradually completed the accumulations of positive potential and wisdom, and became enlightened. For those of us who wish to practice the Universal Vehicle, we must know how the Buddhas practiced when they were Bodhisattvas. What did they do? How did they think and meditate? Since those practices are important to know, Togme Sangpo now gives his word that he will explain them.

CHAPTER TWO

FREEDOM AND FORTUNE

This text contains thirty-seven verses each devoted to one of the Bodhisattva practices. The first two verses, containing the praise and promise to compose, are not counted among the thirty-seven. The first of the thirty-seven begins below.

PART II: THE MIDDLE VIRTUE

This has two parts:

1. The preliminary practices, by means of which the practitioner engages in the practice of the Dharma
2. Explanation of the paths of the three levels of practitioners

There are seven preliminary practices:

1. This life of freedom and fortune is difficult to gain
2. Giving up bad places
3. Relying on an isolated place
4. Mindfulness of impermanence
5. Giving up bad companions
6. Relying on good companions
7. Going for refuge

The difficulty of gaining a life of freedom and fortune

1   Having gained this rare ship of freedom and fortune,
    Hear, think, and meditate unwaveringly night and day
    In order to free yourself and others
    From the ocean of cyclic existence—
    This is the practice of Bodhisattvas.

Our present life, with eight freedoms and ten fortunes, is likened to a great ship which can ferry us safely across the vast and turbulent ocean of cyclic existence. It is difficult to gain, but once we have, is extremely useful because with it we can attain liberation and enlightenment. If we neglect to use it or use it for some trifling purpose, it is a great pity and a great loss. Not letting this fantastic opportunity pass us by, we should use it for freeing ourselves and others from the ocean of cyclic existence. How? By working hard and focusing our energy on hearing, thinking about, and meditating on the Dharma.

The subject of this verse is the precious human rebirth. According to the presentation in the Gradual Path, the precious human rebirth is contemplated by way of three points:

1. Identifying its freedoms and fortunes
2. Understanding the value of such a life
3. Seeing how difficult it is to gain

Identifying the freedoms and fortunes

Identifying the freedoms and fortunes of our present life involves thinking, "This basis—my present body and mind—is really extraordinary. It is amazing! It has this characteristic, this characteristic...," and so on, reflecting one by one on the eight freedoms and ten fortunes. Here, "freedom" means having the opportunity to take things easy, having spare time. "Fortune" means favorable condition. Sometimes we take our present excellent circumstances for granted; we do not recognize them. Or we focus on a single problem and neglect to see all the things going for us in life. Either way we tend to feel depressed and think we aren't good enough. This attitude becomes a huge obstacle to transforming our mind. The meditation on precious human life is designed to help us recognize, appreciate, feel happy about, and properly use the excellent circumstances we have at present.

There are eight freedoms. Each describes a situation that we are free from at present. It is helpful to imagine being born in these states, consider their disadvantages, and rejoice at our present opportunity:

1. The freedom from birth in a hellish realm. As a being experiencing intense physical suffering from heat, cold, and torture, we would have no free time, no opportunity to think of spiritual practice.

2. The freedom from birth as a hungry ghost or a spirit. Beings in this realm suffer from intense craving and frustration because their needs are not satisfied. Constantly suffering from hunger and thirst, they live without being able to satisfy their needs.

3. The freedom from birth as an animal. Here, the main difficulties are being stupid and dull-witted. In addition, many animals lack freedom and are controlled and made to labor by humans, who may abuse them, slaughter them for food, use them for experiments, or kill them for their skins and furs.

These three are called the three unfortunate realms because the basic situation is painful and confining. In addition to gross pain, there is little opportunity to practice the Dharma and thus create the causes for happiness.

4. The freedom from birth as a cognitionless god. The cognitionless god is a type of god who lives long. Besides thinking: "I have been born" at birth, and "I'm dying" at death, they have no cognition at all. Their entire life, for hundreds of thousands of years, is spent in a concentration that is very much like sleep. Thus they would never think: "I must practice Dharma. I must engage in virtue, and abandon negative actions."

5. The freedom from birth as a person in an uncivilized land, where one cannot encounter the Dharma, and consequently has no chance of practicing.

6. The freedom from having wrong view, such as believing that there are no long-term results of our actions, that it is impossible to become enlightened, or that there is no continuity to consciousness after death. Deeply entrenched in wrong views, a person would not practice Dharma even if he or she met it, because he or she holds views firmly opposed to the Dharma.

7. The freedom from birth in a period when no Buddha appears. Enlightened beings do not appear during all times, so if we were born during a time without a Buddha, there would be no teaching to follow, even if we wished to.

8. The freedom from having impaired faculties. If our sense faculties were impaired or if we were mentally impaired, it would be difficult to learn the Dharma.

To meditate on these, we go through them one by one, considering the impediments each of the eight would present to our spiritual development, and feeling happy that we are free from this situation at the present. If we think about the eight freedoms again and again, our mind will certainly experience joy.

In addition, our precious human life has ten fortunes. Five are related to ourselves and five to our external circumstances.

1. The fortune of being a human being, with human intellect and potential.

2. The fortune of being in a country where Dharma exists allowing us to encounter spiritual teachers, teachings, and communities of practitioners.

3. The fortune of having good mental and physical faculties.

4. The fortune of not having committed in this life a heavy negative karma, such as one of the five uninterrupted evil actions. These are (1) killing one's mother, (2) killing one's father, (3) killing a foe destroyer (a person who has attained nirvana), (4) causing a schism in the sangha, and (5) purposely causing a Buddha to bleed. They are called "uninterrupted" because if one does not purify them, one will definitely have an unfortunate rebirth in the next life without another life intervening or interrupting. Also included here is holding onto wrong ideas, such as thinking that there is no fault in engaging in the five uninterrupted actions or other heavy negative karma. Any of these would be a severe obstruction to attaining realizations.

5. The fortune of having faith and conviction in the teachings of the Buddha. Even if we had all the other fortunes, without faith and conviction, we would not engage in Dharma practice at all.

6. The fortune of being alive during an age when a Buddha has come. What could we do if we had been born at a time when a Buddha had not come?

7. The fortune that a Buddha has not only appeared, but has also taught an entire system of practice containing all we need to know about what to practice and what to abandon on the path.

8. The fortune that the teachings still remain and have not disappeared. The period during which Buddha's teaching lasts has not come to an end.

9. The fortune that we have started to put the teachings into practice, or at least, we have begun to think that it is good to practice them.

10. The fortune of having all the conditions we need for Dharma practice. Although we might not be wealthy, we have enough clothing and food, and we have a roof over our head. We often have small problems to face, but nothing so great that we cannot practice Dharma at all. In addition, we have qualified teachers to guide us. We have all the supportive conditions that we need.

To identify the freedoms and fortunes, we go through the eighteen one by one, seeing that we have each one; "I have this fortune. I have that fortune.... My situation is absolutely fantastic! My life is very significant and precious!" If we contemplate well, each of the eighteen will fill us with joy. Imagine a pauper who has a gem in his house and thinks it is just some old stone. If someone pointed out, "Did you know? This is worth a fortune!" he would be so pleased. He would start to imagine what he could do with it and he would feel even happier. Similarly, if we think of each of the eighteen, we too will be very happy and will start to contemplate the various avenues open to us, such as attaining liberation or enlightenment.

Not all human lives are precious human lives. Not everyone has all eighteen conditions. Some human beings have all eight freedoms but nevertheless have no chance to practice Dharma. For example, there are those oppressed by others, who are tortured or abused by others. There are those who live in places without religious freedom. In such situations, it is almost impossible for them to do anything to benefit their future lives, let alone gain realizations of the path.

At the other extreme, some people are so rich that their wealth becomes a burden to them. They spend so much time worrying about it being taken from them and fretting about what to do with it, that they lack freedom to think of benefiting their future lives. Other people spend their lives lazing around or absorbed in various distractions, and thus lack the freedom to practice Dharma even though they have the eight freedoms. Some people are so busy earning a living—farming the earth, working in a factory, traveling to sell products, working overtime on their computers—that they have hardly any time to practice or to learn about Dharma. All their time is consumed by earning a living. Others, who really want to practice, are so dull-witted that they are incapable of understanding how to practice. It is sad, for they may have so many good conditions to develop spiritually, but because they lack one, all the others cannot be fully utilized.

We should feel very happy that we are not beset by such bad conditions. This does not mean we should be proud and think we are better than others. Rather, we should consider ourselves incredibly fortunate and feel responsible to use our fortune wisely. Although each of us thinks we have problems, none of them prevents us from practicing. When we feel like a beggar finding a jewel, we have the realization from meditating on identifying the freedoms and fortunes. This joy does not come with each of the eighteen, but as the collection of the joys arising from meditating on each. We recognize that we have each of the eighteen, not just intellectually, but in our heart. This feeling of joy is a great help to our meditation for it makes us eager to practice. At this stage we have gained the realization of the first topic, and we can go on to the second, the value of a precious human rebirth.

Understanding the great value of the precious human rebirth

As the text says, this life of freedom and fortune is like a great ship. Because we do not encounter it often, we should use this opportunity to cross the ocean of cyclic existence and reach the island of liberation. Having such an opportunity and not using it to attain liberation is a great waste. It is like returning empty-handed from an island of jewels. This life with its eighteen characteristics has great potential, and taking advantage of it is called "taking the essence." According to our wishes we can use this life to take the least, middle, or great essence.

Taking the great essence means to totally awaken, or at least to generate bodhichitta, the altruistic mind that seeks full enlightenment. We can certainly do this if we put in the effort. If we are willing to work hard, we can attain Buddhahood in this very life. Many people, such as Milarepa, have done this in the past, and they did so with a precious human rebirth just like the ours. Ordinary people, on the basis of a precious human life with the eighteen qualities, have become the Bodhisattvas we regard so highly. So many people have become enlightened with the basis of a precious human life that we refer to them as "the jewel garland of practitioners who attained union." There is nothing beyond the reach of this life.

To meditate on the altruistic intention and progress along the Bodhisattva path, we need to expand our awareness to encompass the needs of all living beings. If we cannot think in such a vast way, we can use this life for our personal liberation and become an arhat or foe destroyer who is liberated from cyclic existence. This is the middle essence. If we decide not to do this, we can avoid having an unfortunate rebirth and ensure a good rebirth as a human or god, a life during which we will be able to practice the Dharma. In particular, we could try to attain a rebirth in which we can practice tantra. Definitely we should do that. This is the least we should do. At this time we have all eighteen conditions, and if we use them wisely we can extract temporary and ultimate benefit from them, according to our wish. It is very sad if we know this and still do not take advantage of this life.

Here we need to mention the meaning of "high status" and "definitive goodness." High status refers to a good rebirth as a human or god. It is called high because its causes—keeping pure ethical discipline, etc.—are high. These causes are higher than those that bring about rebirth as an animal, for example. Because the causes are high, the result is also considered good.

Definitive goodness refers to any one of the three enlightenments: the enlightenments of the hearer, the solitary realizer, and the Bodhisattva. Sometimes the enlightenments of the hearer and solitary realizer are put together and called the "enlightenment of the Individual Vehicle." These three are called definitive goodness because having attained one of them, we are forever free from the misery of cyclic existence and have attained a lasting state of happiness. Attaining the state of definitive goodness needs to be preceded by high status, that is, births which give us the opportunity to practice the path and develop the realizations. Otherwise, how can we hear, think, and meditate on the Dharma, activities we need to do to gain definitive goodness?

If possible, we should try to focus our aspirations on the supreme, most worthwhile goal, thinking, "For the sake of all embodied beings, if only I could attain full enlightenment! If only I could become a Buddha quickly!" Especially if we practice tantra or aspire to, it is necessary to have this motivation aiming at the best result. To take the great essence, we practice the universal vehicle, which entails meditating on love, compassion, and the altruistic intention. Just having the opportunity to meditate on these and to help others in various ways makes our life invaluable. To attain enlightenment quickly, we need to combine these with the practice of tantra. To take the middle essence and wish for liberation, we contemplate the four noble truths, which describe the way we enter and can leave cyclic existence, as well as the three higher trainings of ethics, concentration, and wisdom.

If in one moment a great, profound, and vast practice can take place by meditating on the altruistic intention and emptiness, what need is there to say how much can be done in a day, a month, a year, or a whole life? By meditating on love, compassion, the altruistic intention, or emptiness for even one moment we can create very special imprints on our mindstream and eradicate very powerful negative karma. If we reflect on any of those topics, the results are inexhaustible. Of course, if we do not know how to do this, such practice is impossible for us. But if we do, each moment of our life is extremely valuable, and we will grieve even one moment wasted. In *A Guide to the Bodhisattva's Way of Life*, Shantideva said: If we do not make the most of this life, we are cheating ourselves. If we idle away our time, or use it in distraction, no one has played a bigger trick on themselves. If we use this life well, we will have no regrets at the time of death. If we do not, then when the time of death arrives, we will be faced with memories of the time we wasted and will be overcome with remorse.

Whatever we want to do, it is in our hands now. The great meditators say, "If you want to know what you did in your past lives, look at your present body." This body is the basis of our precious human life. It is a good result, so it must have been preceded by good causes. Those causes were created in previous lives, so we can infer that whomever we were in past lives, we put effort into creating the virtuous causes for a precious human life. "If you wish to know your future lives, look at your present mind." Is our mind for the most part unruly, harsh, or overwhelmed by the three poisonous attitudes of attachment, anger, and ignorance or do we think kindly of others? Are we concerned for their welfare and patient with their mistakes? Our future rebirth depends on our attitudes and actions in this life. "Your past lives yielded this precious life. Don't throw the present life into an abyss in the next life." Because we created many wonderful causes and great virtue in previous lives, we now have this precious human life. We shouldn't neglect this opportunity, frittering it away, so that in the future we have unfortunate rebirths.

We can make our life meaningful in all of these ways: attaining liberation or enlightenment, preparing for a good rebirth, and making our life meaningful moment by moment by developing the altruistic intention and the understanding of emptiness. These are things we can do in this very life. We do not need to wait for a better opportunity.

To meditate on the value of our precious human life, we think, "This life of freedom and fortune is extremely valuable because this can be attained, because that can be attained...." Contemplating the ways in which we can make our life meaningful, we will be greatly inspired and aspire to do so. We have gained the realization of the value of our precious human life when we feel a sense of great loss if we waste even a moment in distraction, laziness, or meaningless activities. For example, if we were to waste all our money, we would feel a great loss, thinking, "Oh dear. That was a big mistake." It is not difficult to gain experience of either the freedoms and fortunes of a precious human life or its purpose. If we focus for about a week on each, definitely our mind will change.

Seeing how difficult it is to gain a precious human rebirth

The difficulty of gaining this life with eight freedoms and ten fortunes is considered from three points of view:

1. By nature, the eighteen are difficult to have all at one time
2. Their causes are difficult to create
3. It is as rare to happen as its examples

First, each of the eighteen characteristics is very rare. Being free from unfortunate rebirths is rare. So is the appearance of a Buddha. Universes form and disintegrate without a Buddha ever appearing in them since none of the inhabitants has the karma. It is therefore extraordinarily unusual to be born as a human during a time when a Buddha has appeared. Many times a Buddha appears, but does not teach at all. It is that much rarer for a Buddha to teach a complete path, with both sutra and tantra. It is rare to be a person who has spiritual interests, faith, and aspiration, especially in our world where most people put more value on money and material goods. In this way, we consider each of the eighteen and feel its rarity and preciousness. If we do not try to progress on the path to liberation or enlightenment on this extremely rare occasion, when will we have the chance again?

Second, the causes of a precious human life are difficult to create. They are threefold: ethical conduct which is the basis, the six far-reaching attitudes which accompany this, and pure prayers dedicating the positive potential created by engaging in the above two. The main cause of the least essence—stopping rebirth in the unfortunate realms and ensuring a good rebirth—is the practice of ethical conduct. This includes abandoning the ten destructive actions—killing, stealing, unwise sexual behavior, lying, divisive speech, harsh words, idle talk, coveting, maliciousness, and wrong views. If we look at our world, do most people abandon these ten actions or practice them? Do we know anyone who has not committed even one of them? Ethical conduct also includes taking and living in accordance with any of the eight ordinations for individual liberation (*pratimoksha*),[1] the Bodhisattva ordination, and the tantric ordination. When we take these, we commit ourselves to keeping them purely, but of course, this is difficult. If we transgress a precept, there are procedures for purifying and restoring it, and we should learn these. In other words, we need to learn how to confess, and we need to know what will happen if we do not confess. On the other hand, keeping precepts has so many advantages, such as allowing us to quickly accumulate a great deal of positive potential. To be able to take the precepts of individual liberation, Bodhisattva, and tantra is incredibly fortunate. Not many human beings in our universe have this opportunity. This is the practice of ethical conduct, and it functions as the basis for gaining an upper rebirth, as a human or god.

Through ethical conduct we are reborn as a god or human. To endow this good rebirth with all the favorable conditions for spiritual development, we must combine our practice of ethics with the practice of the remaining five far-reaching attitudes. Each of the five has its own particular result. Generosity enables us to have wealth. Without it, we will experience the problem of poverty and this will interfere with our ability to practice the Dharma. Patience brings an appearance that others find pleasing to see. Joyous effort makes us charismatic, able to influence others is a positive way, and able to successfully complete whatever we begin. Concentration results in a peaceful mind. Due to developing wisdom, we will have the understanding of what to practice and what to abandon.

In order to obtain a precious human life, one must combine ethical conduct and the practice of the other far-reaching attitudes with stainless prayers. "Stainless" here means a prayer for high rebirth or personal liberation. When our practice is mixed with a motivation of the eight worldly concerns, it is not Dharma. Similarly, when our prayers are mixed with worldly concerns—including prayers for wealth and fame—they are not considered stainless. Thus, we need to dedicate the virtue from practicing ethics and the other far-reaching attitudes so that we and other sentient beings will attain enlightenment, liberation, or fortunate rebirths.

[1] The eight ordinations of individual liberation are the three for laypeople (layman, laywoman, and the one-day ordination) and the five for monastics (male novice, female novice, probationary nun, fully-ordained monk, and fully-ordained nun).

Of all the fortunate rebirths, to be born a human is one of the best. In our world, human beings are born from the womb, possess the six elements, and are capable of experiencing the results of powerful karma created earlier in that life. Lacking all or some of these factors, the beings in other worlds cannot take the three ordinations—individual liberation, Bodhisattva, and tantra—and thus have no opportunity of observing the three types of ethical discipline connected with them.

We may also dedicate to be reborn in a pure land, a place created by the virtue of a Buddha, where all conditions are conducive for spiritual practice. However, the practice of the highest yoga tantra is not found in some pure lands, and in others, there is no practice of tantra at all. Thus enlightenment there takes an unbelievably long time. s in those lands are aware that with our womb birth possessing the six elements, enlightenment is possible in one short life in these degenerate times,[2] and they long for such an opportunity.

We need to be attentive to create the causes for a precious human life. Often, when we act in a harmful way, we create first-class negative actions, but our constructive actions are not as well thought out, executed, and dedicated. For example, when we're angry at someone, we cultivate a strong motivation to speak harshly, we make sure we do it, and we feel happy afterward. However, when there is a chance to help someone, we sometimes are tired and have to force ourselves. We do it half-heartedly, and at the end sigh, "Oh good, I'm glad that's done." From this, we can see that it is not always easy to create the causes for a precious human life. However, now that we are aware of what they are, we can be more mindful to create them.

Third, we can understand how rare it is to obtain a precious human rebirth from examples such as this one. Imagine a wooden yoke bobbing about on the surface of a vast ocean. A blind old turtle lives in the ocean and spends most of his time at the depths, surfacing only once in a hundred years. It is extremely improbable that the turtle will surface at exactly the right place and time so that his head pokes up through the hole in the yoke. Our rebirth with all eighteen characteristics is more difficult to have.

[2] Five degenerations plague our time: (1) time: wars, famine, and depletion of material resources are widespread; (2) sentient beings: beings are intolerant, hold wrong views, and often behave outrageously; (3) view: distorted views are rampant, making beings disinterested in acting constructively; (4) disturbing attitudes: negative emotions are very gross; and (5) lifespan: in general, human lifespan is decreasing due to increased danger from accidents and pollution.

We might think that many beings have attained precious human lives, but this is not the case. In comparison to animals, for example, there are very few human beings on this planet. Looking in the grass during the summer, we see thousands of insects in a small area. In addition, not all those with human lives have the opportunity to practice the Dharma. For example, human rebirths are as numerous as the blades of grass on the earth, but those with the eighteen qualities are as numerous as the blades growing on the roof of a house. A precious human rebirth, possessing all eight freedoms and ten fortunes, is extremely rare. If we look around superficially, we could easily think that everyone is the same, and that this life we have is quite common. But if we look closer, we will see that this is not the case.

We have realized the rarity of the precious human life when we have a sense of great loss if we waste even one moment of our life. This does not mean that we have to become filled with anxiety about wasting our life or push ourselves to be fanatic practitioners. Rather, wasting our life becomes like throwing all our hard-earned money down the drain. We know we will never be able to regain such a fortune, and seeing it wasted fills us with a feeling of loss. When we contemplate the value of our precious human life we feel a sense of loss at not doing something meaningful with our time. When we contemplate the rarity and difficulty of having a precious human life, we feel a sense of loss at passing up a valuable opportunity that will not be presented to us again. These three topics concerning precious human life are comparatively easy to realize. It does not take that long if we contemplate them continually.

Unlike a person who has never heard Dharma teachings, we have heard some teachings; we know how to free ourselves from cyclic existence and how to generate love, compassion, and altruism. We have these precious tools at our fingertips. Now that we have found such a good rebirth, if we do not make a habit of acting constructively, there is no one more stupid. We would be playing a terrible trick on ourselves. If we recognize that our life is so precious, but still waste time lazing around and daydreaming or by keeping ourselves frantically busy in our efforts to get and protect money, possessions, reputation, relationships, and praise, when death comes we will be full of remorse. It will also be difficult for us to have a good rebirth, which is even more cause for being upset.

We know these things, but we forget. Therefore it is helpful each morning when we awake to reestablish our motivation—our determination to be free, our aspiration to become a Buddha, our wish to make our life worthwhile moment by moment by developing a kind heart and wisdom. During the day, we then act in ways that benefit others and are attentive not to harm them, and in the evening we dedicate the positive potential from this. In this way, each day of our life can become very enriching and valuable.

With our present life we can plant the seeds for liberation and enlightenment. Even though we may not be able to complete all the causes for these exalted states, we should definitely plant the seeds for them by listening to teachings, thinking about them, meditating on them, and integrating them in our daily life. Doing this makes our life incredibly worthwhile. Many people have already practiced the Dharma a lot and planted many good seeds in their minds by taking and keeping the various levels of precepts, or by developing and acting with loving-kindness towards others. It is important to rejoice at what we have done, but not to be complacent or smug about it. We should take care in the future to habituate ourselves further with what is positive, put energy into creating more good qualities, and develop those we already have. We can do this within the framework of our day-to-day life in a way that is comfortable and rewarding.

The encouragement to practice must come from within ourselves. If we feel in our hearts that the spiritual path is very important, even if someone says, "Why are you wasting your time on that?" we won't pay attention. We will know what we are doing and why and will feel good about it. If we don't have a strong determination inside, we might practice only when someone tells us to or helps us to, but when he or she goes away, we stop. Or, if someone comes along and says, "It would be better not to do that. It's too difficult," there is a danger that we might give up our practice. This would be quite sad. Therefore, it is important that we spend time thinking about the reasons to practice the Dharma so that our inner resolve remains firm and confident.

If we are not careful now and if we do not take the essence of our lives, we will have lost a tremendous opportunity. If our money disappears without anything to show for it, we feel dismayed. We should feel the same way if, having thought about how difficult a precious human life is to find, we look back and recall months, days, or even moments that have been wasted in meaningless distraction. When we have generated the realization regarding the freedom and fortune of the precious human life, we then move on to the meditation on impermanence and death, which is discussed in the next verse.

CHAPTER THREE

LISTENING, THINKING, AND MEDITATING

The first verse says that listening, thinking, and meditating are practices of a Bodhisattva. Having attained a precious human life with the eighteen characteristics, we should listen, think and meditate upon the Buddha's teachings to bring to fruition our Dharma aims. From these three activities, we gain three wisdoms. First we develop the wisdom of listening. In dependence upon that, we generate the wisdom of thinking, and following that, the wisdom of meditating. The three wisdoms are produced gradually, in this order.

Here, listening does not simply mean letting a sound enter our ears. It involves a certain level of understanding. Suppose, for example, we hear a teaching stating that the aggregates—our body and mind—are impermanent, that is, that they change moment by moment. If we assent to that, thinking, "Yes, the aggregates are impermanent," the wisdom occurring simultaneously with that thought is the wisdom of listening.

Thinking is the process of analyzing. Here, we check to discover whether the aggregates are impermanent or not. The wisdom resulting from that analysis, an understanding that knows that the aggregates are definitely impermanent, is the wisdom of thinking.

Meditation is placing the mind single-pointedly upon the fact that has been decisively ascertained through the process of thinking. The wisdom of meditation is the wisdom occurring with that concentration. In

this example, it would be wisdom focused single-pointedly on the aggregates being impermanent.

In a slightly wider context, scripture states that first we need to abide in the ethical discipline of avoiding the ten destructive actions. On that basis, we listen to Dharma teachings and generate the wisdom of hearing. Then we think, check, and analyze to generate the wisdom of thinking. Finally, we meditate, by placing the mind single-pointedly on that meaning and thus generate the wisdom of meditation.

We need to listen well, and we must listen a lot. It is necessary to listen to teachings on a topic several times, not only once. Each time we hear, study, or read the teachings, we understand a little more and gain a broader view of them. We see the example of great lamas who are alive today: they continuously listen to the teachings of their spiritual guides and read the scriptures. Without adequate hearing, we will not be able to think very well, and of course then we will not be able to meditate well and it will be difficult to realize the Dharma and transform our mind.

Let us look at how one person can practice hearing, thinking, and meditating along an entire path. On the basis of avoiding the ten destructive actions, first she listens to the subjects that are common to all vehicles. They include the precious human life, death, refuge, and karma. Having listened well to those subjects, she thinks and meditates on them. Then should she wish for a more vast practice, she can take the Bodhisattva ordination, keep the Bodhisattva precepts, and again listen to, think about, and meditate upon the subjects connected with the Bodhisattva path, such as loving-kindness, compassion, bodhichitta, and the six far-reaching attitudes. Then, if she has an interest in the profound side, she will take the tantric ordination, keep those commitments, and listen, think, and meditate on the tantric path—the generation and completion stages. This, in general, is the order to be followed.

If it were only necessary to listen a little, why did the Buddha give eighty-four thousand teachings? Why did later Indian sages compose so many commentaries? The fact is that the more teachings we can listen to the better. If we try to climb a mountain, without hands, we cannot grab hold of anything. Trying to meditate without hearing is like that. We cannot catch hold of any grounds or paths.

Having listened to the teachings well, we will become familiar with everything that is to be practiced and we will gradually give up all faults. For example, by listening to teachings on the initial level of practice, we will understand the subjects at that level and will be free of the ignorance of not understanding them. By practicing what we learn, we will abandon the faults related to this stage.

It is said, "Through hearing, one attains liberation." From good hearing comes good thinking and good meditation. Through these we can abandon negativities, purify ourselves, and finally attain a state in which all karma has been exhausted.

What we call analytical or checking meditation is, in general, meditation. But within the three—hearing, thinking, and meditating—it is not termed meditation but thinking. In the three, meditation refers to putting the mind on a subject that has been clearly ascertained through contemplation. It is best is to put the mind on the object single-pointedly, but that is not necessary. In the three, analytical meditation is included in thinking because it is here that we decisively ascertain the meaning of a particular teaching and how to practice it.

Hearing, thinking, and meditating are to be practiced in union. That is, we should apply ourselves to all three practices of hearing, thinking, and meditating with regard to all of the essential topics, including impermanence, suffering, emptiness, selflessness, love, and compassion.

Analytical meditation

How do we know that we have gained the intended result from a given meditation? How much time should we spend on each meditation? How do we prevent the experiences we gain from deteriorating? We shall then cover the general points regarding this now, and points related to specific meditation topics will be dealt with as they arise in the root text. Analytical meditation was briefly mentioned above. We shall spend some time explaining it, since it is vital for us to understand.

Although we have heard many teachings and may be enthusiastic to teach them to others, our mind is not subdued and our qualities are not developed. What is the difficulty? We have not gained experience from meditation and have not integrated our knowledge into our experience. In other words, we know a lot, but have not meditated on it properly. Merely knowing the teachings does not constitute analytical meditation. This does not produce the internal transformation that analytical meditation does. Analytical meditation is real meditation, important meditation. It is indispensable for generating realizations.

Occasionally, strong determination to be free from cyclic existence or strong faith in the Three Jewels may arise without having meditated a lot. This is not analytical meditation. From time to time we might think, "Cyclic existence is awful. I'm off to a cave in the mountains to meditate." Or we may suddenly have a strong feeling of love for all sentient beings, but then it vanishes and we feel as we did before. Sometimes we may have a sense of the emptiness of inherent existence and think, "Now I've realized emptiness. This is fantastic!" But then the experience fades away and we think, "Oh no, I've lost the realization!" That also is not an experience arising from analytical meditation. What are these experiences then? They are a form of belief or correct assumption. They are positive, but unstable. If they were inferential valid cognitions arising from thinking, they would not deteriorate quickly. When they go, do not be unhappy. They arose due to the blessing of the spiritual teacher, the Three Jewels, or from good imprints from past lives. We should try to make them firm. To do this, we should inspect the conditions which brought them about and try to reconstruct and maintain those conditions. We should keep going and not allow them to degenerate. The way to make these sudden flashes of understanding stable is by familiarizing ourselves with them through analytical meditation. An experience that arises from analytical meditation is valid and stable. It comes from having thought about something at length so that we understand it deeply. Analytical meditation does not mean repeating the words of the teachings to ourselves or going over the points of the teachings in a dry, academic way. It means thinking deeply about the Dharma and applying it to our own lives. It involves checking the teaching to see if it is logically consistent, if it describes our experience, if it is more realistic and beneficial than our usual way of thinking.

For example, a person new to the Dharma might hear about the precious human life. She may have a strong experience regarding this, but subsequently it disappears. That strong feeling was an experience which arose from hearing and was easily lost. To make it stable, she should do analytical meditation to gain experience that arises from thinking and contemplating. Then it will be more firm and transformative.

If we have heard many teachings and have a lot to explain to others, but do not familiarize ourselves with them and experience them, we might become immune or thick-skinned towards the Dharma. This means that when hearing teachings, we sit there thinking, "Yeah, I know, I know. I've heard all that before. Why doesn't my teacher say something new and interesting?" Or we comment to ourselves, "This teacher could improve his way of speaking. His delivery is boring."

We will know when we become immune to the Dharma. Our mind becomes tougher and tougher, even though we know a lot. Instead of our mind being subdued, it becomes worse. If, by having heard a lot and knowing a lot, our mind becomes better—more flexible and open-minded, more receptive and appreciative of the teachings—then we do not have the problem of being immune to Dharma. But when our mind becomes hard or proud, it is difficult to cure. Usually the way to make the mind flexible is to know what the Buddha taught. However, in this case, we may know the meaning of the Gradual Path, but our mind has become tough. We have become insensitive to the medicine of Dharma. If a person has become immune to the Dharma, it is difficult for him or her to benefit even from a great master. Why? The spiritual master may use one reason to explain a certain point, but this student has studied a lot and thinks, "I know a better reason. I know more reasons." It is difficult to benefit someone when his or her mind has become hard like this. Therefore, we should try to avoid this happening to us.

In Tibetan monasteries, when the pupils became clever the teacher says, "Be careful, you're becoming immune to Dharma." Those who do not know much have no danger of becoming immune, so there is no need to warn them. It is those who, knowing a little, become proud of their knowledge and proud of their ability to explain it to others, who are in the greatest danger. They should be especially careful. When bad people meet Dharma their minds can easily be made good. Before, they did not know Dharma and acted destructively. Then they meet Dharma and easily become good. But if they know a lot and their minds become immune to Dharma, it is very hard to change. The experience that arises from listening is a superficial understanding. To deepen it we must practice analytical meditation. Even if we have only a little definite knowledge from analytical meditation, there is no danger of becoming immune to Dharma because the understanding has been made secure by tying it to our experience.

How do we do analytical meditation? Take the precious human life, for example. This topic includes identifying the characteristics of a precious human life, seeing its value, and knowing its rarity and difficulty to attain. We think about each of the eighteen characteristics of a precious human life one by one. We use reasons to recognize the advantages of each freedom and fortune. It is also helpful to think about quotations from the Buddha or the past sages on this topic. We also look at our own experience and recognize our potential. By familiarizing ourselves with this topic consistently over time we will begin to feel from our heart that we are unbelievably fortunate, that our life is highly meaningful, and that it would be a terrible pity to waste it on meaningless activities. This is analytical meditation. As we engage in analytical meditation, we make our understanding firmer. As a result it will not disappear easily and our mind will not doubt the value of our precious human life even if someone else disagrees. This understanding has been planted firmly in our mind.

A person who does not do analytical meditation might hear that the aggregates are impermanent. He might think, "Yes, they are impermanent." But that understanding can easily change. He might meet someone who says the aggregates do not change moment by moment and thus are permanent, and he starts to wonder, "Maybe they are permanent, after all!" This situation arises because the person did not make his initial understanding firm by thinking about it deeply and from many angles in analytic meditation.

Someone may study a little Dharma and like it, but then meet a non-Buddhist teacher who says, "The Buddha's teaching is wrong. If you devote yourself to my path, you will gain powers immediately." The person then stops her Dharma practice and adopts another path. This is because she had not yet gained her own inner experience of the Dharma. Her understanding was at the level of listening only, and she had not yet validated it and made it firm through contemplation and analytical meditation. When we experience the Dharma, whatever anyone may say will not shake us. Our understanding will be firm, not wishy-washy.

The Buddha said we should not just take his word on anything, but check for the truth of his teaching by way of three analyses. These are likened to the three types of analysis made by those buying gold. First they check for the more obvious faults by rubbing the gold, then for less obvious ones by cutting it, and finally for the subtlest impurities by burning the gold. The Buddha said, "Check my teachings in this way too. See if they are true or not. Make your understanding firm through reasoning, and do not believe on faith alone." Lama Tsong Khapa also stressed this. This instruction gives us so much freedom. It is really marvelous advice.

Glance meditation

The word "meditation," in general, includes several types of meditation. Besides analytical meditation in which we validate the points of the teachings using reasons, scriptural quotations, and by applying them to our own life, and single-pointed meditation in which we focus single-pointedly on what has been previously discerned by analysis, there is also glance meditation. Before doing analytical meditation on the topics of the Gradual Path, we need an overall idea of the entire path. Then we will be able to look at the whole path like someone who has a panoramic view of a town from a nearby hilltop. It is like having a map indicating all the countries, geographical features, and so on. In other words, we need to know the structure of the path, its outline, its main headings, the order of the meditations, the connections between them, and so on. When we know the structure of the Gradual Path clearly, we will feel confident that when we go through the meditations one by one, spending an appropriate amount of time on each, we will be able to develop the realizations. This is the purpose of glance meditation. We can do a glance meditation on the path each day, in order to leave an imprint of the entire path on our mindstream. Through this, in time we will have a thick layer of imprints and seeds for realizing the whole path.

Glance meditation is thinking briefly and succinctly about all the points of a particular meditation in their proper order. If we have studied well, glance meditation will come easily and will help us understand what we have studied. For example, we review that the meditation on precious human life has three major divisions: identifying it, seeing its value, and recognizing its rarity and difficulty to receive. The first part, in turn, has the ten freedoms which are 1, 2, 3,... and the ten fortunes which are 1, 2, 3,.... Then we go on to the next topic, impermanence and death, and do the same, and so on until we have recollected the essential points of all the meditations of the Gradual Path. Glance meditation is very worthwhile and important, for it plants seeds of the various realizations on our mindstream. However, its function is not to gain certainty on the points, for it is too brief and concise for that. It does help us to remember the points and to understand how they fit together and gradually develop in our mind. The great masters of the past have written various prayers that serve as glance meditations, for example, *The Foundation of All Good Qualities* by Lama Tsong Khapa, and the "Lamrim Prayer" at the end of *The Guru Puja* by Panchen Lobsang Chokyi Gyaltsen.

If we are new and not familiar with all the steps in the Gradual Path and with their individual points, it is helpful to meditate on them in a summarized form with glance meditation. Then, we can gradually go into it more extensively with analytical meditation. This is advised for any topic: first ascertain it in a general way. At the beginning, do not go into it extensively, thinking about each detail. It is better at first to develop a general understanding in which we know the fundamental point of each topic and the principal reasons to back it up and then progressively make our meditation more extensive by doing analytical meditation. It is like painting a picture: we make a sketch of the entire scene first and gradually fill in the details. We do not paint one corner of the canvas in all its detail, leaving the rest blank. Thus in learning the Buddha's teachings, we first learn the summarized, essential points, then learn all the topics in detail. Once we have gained experience in each topic, we can go through it in a concise way again because now it is easy and the feeling can arise in our mind quickly.

How to do analytical meditation

In daily life we often do "analytical meditation." For example, when we are attached to a certain person, our basic assertion is, "He/she is wonderful!" Then we think of many reasons to prove that. She looks good, she is intelligent. He has a good mind, he is kind. She is interesting to listen to. He is marvelous to look at. With these reasons and many more, we strengthen our feeling that this person is wonderful, and as a result our attachment fully blossoms and we think that we have to be with that person to be happy. There is no other way; we can't bear to be without him or her. This mental process is analytical meditation. If someone says otherwise, that he or she is unpleasant, not so attractive, we do not listen to a word of it because we are completely convinced. Analytical meditation is like this.

Sometimes we engage in analytical meditation on anger. We think such and such a person is bad. We confirm this with various reasons, such as remembering that he hurt us or our friends in the past and that he is talking behind our back now. We speculate on the harm he might do in the future. We also back it up with quotes, "My friend said this person can't be trusted," and so on. The more reasons we have, the more convinced we become and the more impervious we are to another's words pointing out that person's good qualities.

Similarly, there are some people to whom we are very close, who have helped us a lot, or with whom we have spent a lot of time. When they die, we think of them wherever we go. Everything we do reminds us of them. We think of them again and again, "If they were alive, we would do this and that. We would have a good time together. How wonderful it would be!" By repeatedly calling them to mind and thinking about them, we miss them even more and our suffering increases.

This is how "analytical meditation" reinforces our disturbing attitudes. Yet, we can use the same technique to reflect on Dharma topics for the purpose of increasing our constructive attitudes. To do this we repeatedly contemplate a particular topic and the reasons used to prove its various points. We should use whatever reasons and examples we can to make the meditation topic clear and convincing, and keep the topic in mind without forgetting it. As we do so, we will experience the conclusion more and more strongly, and we then hold this experience in our mind single-pointedly. When this happens, it is a sign that our analytical meditation is yielding results. For example, if we meditate on impermanence and death, we go through the three root points and the nine subsidiary points one by one: "Death is definite because everyone must die, because our lifespan is continuously decreasing and cannot increase, because we will die without having practiced Dharma if we continue wasting our time." We think about each point in depth, relating it to examples from our own life, using reasons, and applying it to our own experience. Thus the feeling dawns in our mind, "I must practice Dharma. This is really important." When this feeling arises strongly, we cease analyzing and focus our mind on it as much as possible. This has a transformative effect on our mind. After that we can go on to meditate on the second root in the death meditation. Some people associate the term "analytical" with dry, intellectual verbiage and thus think analytical meditation is intellectualizing. This is not correct. By examining the steps of the path closely, with reasons and examples, and by applying it to our own lives, very strong experiences can arise that transform our mind.

It is possible that despite continuous meditation, our mind does not seem to be noticeably changing in a positive way. In such a case, there is a danger of becoming immune to Dharma. To avoid it, we should temporarily stop our analytical meditation and focus on practices that purify karmic obscurations and accumulate positive potential for a week or two. It is also helpful to do guru yoga practices, such as Lama Tsong Khapa Guru Yoga, in which we recite the prayer requesting his inspiration. Then we can resume analytical meditation.

These practices to purify negativities and accumulate positive potential are very important to prepare our mind for analytical meditation. Our mind is like a field in which realizations grow from the seeds of listening to teachings. For a seed to grow, the earth needs to be free from adverse conditions and to have conducive conditions such as water, fertilizer, and sunshine. Purifying negativities in our mind is like freeing the earth from adversities, while creating positive potential is comparable to adding the water, fertilizer, and sunshine. When these factors are as they should be, the seeds of realizations will gradually sprout and grow. Thus, whenever we get stuck in meditation, or if we do not gain the experience from a particular meditation that our spiritual teacher said ought to come from it, it is very helpful to put more attention on practices such as guru yoga, prostrations, offerings, and so forth. Making prayers of request to the Three Jewels is also very effective.

It is not necessary to do analytical meditation on every topic in the teachings. For example, in the *Lamrim* or Gradual Path, analytical meditation is not done on the first three main sections: (1) explaining the greatness of the author, to inspire confidence in the source of the text; (2) explaining the greatness of the teaching, to generate faith in the teaching; and (3) the way to teach and listen to the teaching possessing the above two qualities. Glance meditation is sufficient for these three points. Analytical meditation is only done on topics in the fourth section, entitled "The way to lead the disciple to enlightenment through the actual lamrim teachings." This section starts with an explanation of the six preparatory practices, which are explained below, and then goes on to explain the way to follow a spiritual guide. Analytical meditation is necessary for the topics starting from "how to rely on a spiritual guide."

Through analytical meditation we gain certainty about our topic of meditation. This is the experience gained from contemplation. To gain certainty means to realize with a valid mind, and within the different types of valid mind, this refers to valid inference. The experience arising from hearing is an understanding that is merely able to echo what we have heard. That level of understanding is called correct assumption or a belief that is true. Inference is much firmer; it is an incontrovertible understanding reached through sound reasoning.

When we do analytical meditation on a topic, we reflect on the various points, making effort to understand the reasons, the quotations, and their applications to our life. Applying it to our life means checking to what extent our life experiences confirm the points in the lamrim. It also means contemplating how to use the teachings to deal with situations and difficulties we encounter in our life. When, through such meditation, we develop positive thoughts, feelings, and outlooks, this is called "experience requiring effort." At this stage, when we are thinking about the topic, the experience arises and is heartfelt, but when we stop thinking about the reasons, it fades. To make it firm, we need to habituate ourselves to the experience that was generated with effort, and by doing this, it will eventually become effortless. Whenever we think of the topic, the experience will automatically arise without doing analysis, and this is called "effortless experience." For example, if someone is very attached to something, merely by remembering it the attachment arises automatically, without having to think about many reasons. Currently our attachment is usually effortless while our Dharma understanding requires effort. However, by training our mind in the Dharma over time, the realizations of love, compassion, wisdom, and so on will become effortless, and it will take great effort to get angry or attached. Thus, first we do glance meditation to become familiar with the general layout of a topic. Then we apply effort to generate the experience of it. Finally, because our mind has become very familiar with the topic, the experience becomes effortless.

In general, we should meditate on the steps of the Gradual Path in the order they are presented. When we have gained deep experience or realization of one step, then we go on to do analytical meditation on the next. We should not neglect the previous steps, but continue to do glance meditation on them in order to keep our experience of them vibrant. Before realizing one subject, we should not move on and begin analytical meditation on the next. However, traditionally the Gradual Path begins by contemplating how to rely on a spiritual mentor. Because this topic is difficult and takes a lot of time to realize, it is not suitable to meditate only on this until we realize it. We can make it our main meditation while also doing analytical meditation on the topics that follow, which are easier. By proceeding in this way the realizations will come quicker in the long run. Thus, the advice from the lineage lamas is to carry out several series of meditations on several points along the path concurrently. This is like planting several seeds at once, and as a result having several trees with their blossoms and fruit simultaneously, instead of planting one seed, bringing that to maturity, then planting another seed, bringing that to maturity, and so on. This is the experience of past yogis.

In a meditation session, people who have received teachings on all the topics of the Gradual Path can either first do glance meditation on the entire path and then do analytical meditation on one topic, or first do analytical meditation on one topic and at the end of the session do glance meditation on the other steps of the path. Or we can do glance meditation up to the topic that we have reached in our analytical meditation, and then after the analytical meditation complete the glance meditation on the remainder of the path. We should do analytic meditation on the steps of the path in order: first relying on a spiritual mentor, then the precious human life, impermanence and death, and so on. If we neglect the meditations at the beginning of the path and meditate on love, compassion, and bodhichitta instead, it is useful, but if we do not go through the topics one by one in sequence with analytic meditation, there is no way that we can generate valid and firm realizations. If we do only glance meditation and not analytical meditation, the realizations will also not come about. Analytic meditation allows the mind to go deeply into a topic; we familiarize ourselves with it each day until a stable experience arises.

If some doubt arises while we are practicing analytical meditation, we should think it over, and if possible, discuss it with our spiritual mentor. If our teacher is not available, we can discuss it with knowledgeable Dharma friends who can give us good advice. If we do not discuss our doubts and merely brush them aside or suppress them, they can block our progress by making our mind tight and unclear. Thus it's important to seek help to resolve our doubts.

In a retreat setting when we do several meditation sessions a day, the main glance meditation of the Gradual Path is done during the first session. A brief glance meditation can also be done when we develop our motivation at the outset of each session. Reviewing the steps of the Gradual Path makes our motivation clearer and stronger. If we do three meditation sessions daily, the first could be a glance meditation on the entire path, the second on one section of how to rely on a spiritual mentor, and the third on precious human rebirth. If we do four sessions daily, the fourth could be on emptiness, so that we can develop familiarity with this very important topic.

During such a retreat, the spiritual mentor often has the meditator live nearby. That way he or she can explain how to meditate on each topic one by one. The student does the meditation and the mentor asks, "What experience did you have? What ideas came to you?" In this way, the mentor guides the disciple through the experiences by means of analytical meditation. It is not always necessary that the student stay near his or her mentor. If he or she has ascertained well the reasons to be contemplated with analytical meditation and has a solid foundation in the path, it is fine to meditate alone.

This advice on how to organize our meditation sessions is for those interested in realizations, who, like people climbing stairs, look up and see all the steps ahead. Even when busy, they keep going, meditating on whatever step they have reached, even if only for ten or fifteen minutes a day. This continuity is very important. For example, if we rub two sticks together trying to make fire, we have to continue without stopping, or else they will become cold. If we keep going, they will eventually catch fire. Similarly, in our meditation practice, we keep going so that the warmth of our experience is not lost. In this way, by doing analytical meditation, combined with practices to purify negativities and create positive potential, we will be able to have all the realizations of the Gradual Path in a step-by-step manner.

There are two basic types of meditation: stabilizing meditation to develop single-pointed concentration and analytical or checking meditation to develop deep understanding of the topics. Until one attains higher levels of the path, these two types of meditation are done alternately. We begin analytical meditation on the topics for the initial-level practitioner: precious human life, impermanence and death, unfortunate realms of existence, refuge, and karma and its effects. Then we go on to do analytical meditation on the topics for the middle-level practitioner: the four noble truths, the twelve links, and the three higher trainings. At the advanced level, analytical meditation is necessary to generate the altruistic intention. When, through analytical meditation, we gain some understanding of a topic, we then focus on that understanding with stabilizing meditation. By eliminating distractions, stabilizing meditation enables our mind to become more accustomed to the understanding we have generated through analytical meditation.

When the altruistic intention has been developed, we practice analytical meditation on the six far-reaching attitudes of generosity, ethical conduct, patience, joyous effort and wisdom and then practice them in our life. Calm abiding, which is included in the far-reaching attitude of meditative stabilization, is stabilizing meditation and does not involve analytical meditation. The wisdom realizing emptiness is sometimes generated after the altruistic intention and sometimes before. Analytical meditation is definitely required to develop it. When, with the motivation of bodhichitta, we have fully developed calm abiding and are able to do analytical meditation on emptiness without it disturbing our single-pointedness, then we will have special insight on emptiness, which is an important part of the far-reaching attitude of wisdom.

Having said all this as general advice, it is important to note that we should make sure that our meditation suits our mind. If we feel comfortable doing analytical meditation on the various topics in a progressive way, we should go ahead with it. If, on the other hand, we find it difficult and it is not compatible with our mind, we should meditate on whatever topic we like. If we enjoy meditation on emptiness, we should go ahead with this. If it suits us and we derive pleasure from meditating principally on the altruistic intention, we can emphasize this. At some point if we find that we cannot really get into whatever analytical meditation we have been doing, but doing prostrations, chanting mantra, visualizing a meditation deity, or reciting aspirational prayers brings peace and pleasure to our mind, we should do that practice.

Setting up a meditation practice

Our time can be divided into two: the times of actual meditation sessions and the break times in between. The meditation sessions have three parts: preparation, actual meditation, and conclusion. The preparation consists of six preparatory practices:

1. Clean the room and set up symbols of the Buddha's body, speech, and mind.
2. Make beautiful offerings which have been obtained honestly and through right livelihood.
3. Sit in the proper meditation position—the seven point posture of Vairochana (or however we are comfortable)—take refuge and generate bodhichitta.
4. Visualize the field of positive potential, the Buddhas and Bodhisattvas.
5. Offer the seven-limb prayer to purify and accumulate.
6. Make requests to the Buddhas and Bodhisattvas for their inspiration.

More about the preparatory practices can be learned from texts on the Gradual Path. Before beginning the actual analytical meditation, it is helpful to think, "Since beginningless time until the present, my mind has been under the control of the disturbing attitudes—ignorance, attachment, anger, jealousy, pride and so forth. They have made me act in harmful ways and have brought about the various difficulties I've experienced in cyclic existence. From now on, I must try conscientiously not to let my mind be controlled by the disturbing attitudes. I will develop flexibility and firmness of mind so that I will be able to concentrate on the object of meditation without distraction or lethargy. I will develop my good qualities, and since this depends on understanding and integrating the Buddha's teachings into my being, I will put effort in this direction during this very meditation session."

Then we do the actual meditation, which in this case is analytical meditation. We have already discussed the analytical meditation on the precious human life and will discuss analytical meditation on other topics in the upcoming verses. At the conclusion, we make dedication prayers for the happiness and enlightenment of all beings.

What we do during the time between meditation sessions when we are going about our daily activities influences our meditation sessions and vice-versa. Therefore, during the breaks it is advised to "close the doors of our sense faculties." This means we should be aware of when to speak and what to say, so that we do not talk indiscriminately about things that stir up our disturbing attitudes or harm others. Similarly, we should not listen indiscriminately because this can stimulate many negative thoughts in our mind, and should avoid looking around indiscriminately at things that could incite our craving, anger, jealousy, and so forth. Before acting, it is wise to check whether the action is appropriate or not, and if it is we should do it with awareness. Eating and sleeping in moderation are important as well, and rising early in the morning is good. Whenever we do things to care for our body—eating, drinking, washing, dressing, sleeping, and so forth—we should think it is to bring well-being to our body and mind because they are necessary for meditation. In other words, we transform our motivation for these activities from one of self-indulgence and self-centered pleasure, to one of taking care of the body and mind so that we can use them to practice the path to enlightenment for the ultimate benefit of all sentient beings.

CHAPTER FOUR

CREATING A CONDUCIVE ENVIRONMENT

Giving Up One's Native Land

2   Attached to your loved ones you're stirred up like water.
Hating your enemies you burn like fire.
In the darkness of confusion you forget what to adopt and
    discard.
Give up your homeland—
This is the practice of Bodhisattvas.

If we wish to practice purely, it is best not to live near the people we are close to, such as our friends and relatives. It is wise to leave such a place and go elsewhere, for if we live near these people, our attachment to them will continually arise. Our time and energy will be consumed by spending a lot of time with them, going here and there enjoying ourselves. In addition, we will become involved in many activities on their behalf. If others criticize or harm our dear ones, we will look for ways to avenge the offense, even if we have not been harmed personally. Instead of being able to cultivate patience, love, compassion, and wisdom, our time and energy will be consumed in attachment, anger, and actions motivated by them. This benefits neither ourselves nor others. Thus, we are counseled not to stay in a place where our anger and attachment continually and violently arise. We need a place where there is less outer hustle and bustle. In such a place, there will naturally be less inner disturbance. It is for these reasons that ordained people go to a monastery, and yogis go to the mountains or other isolated places.

Some people say that living in a secluded environment is escaping the world and running away from our problems and that we should stay where we are and confront the disturbing attitudes in our minds. If we are capable and strong in our practice, this is fine. However, most of us do not have the inner strength to continue our practice when we are surrounded on all sides by objects of our attachment, anger, jealousy, and pride. Although we may begin optimistically, thinking, "I will transform everything I encounter into the Dharma," our mind easily and quickly falls into its old habits because we have not had the time or opportunity to habituate ourselves to positive ways of thinking. If we stay in a conducive environment, however, our practice will become stronger and later we can be in a place full of hustle and bustle without our attachment and anger forcefully arising.

Relying on solitude

3   **By avoiding bad objects, disturbing emotions gradually
        decrease.
        Without distraction, virtuous activities naturally increase.
        With clarity of mind, conviction in the teaching arises.
        Cultivate seclusion—
        This is the practice of Bodhisattvas.**

The previous verse talks of abandoning places that produce the disturbing attitudes that we did not have before and reinforce those that we had before. This verse says that if we do this, our disturbing attitudes will naturally diminish. When we abandon continual contact with objects that generate our disturbing attitudes, the disturbing attitudes will not arise. This will give us the mental space to develop firm realizations of the path. Then, even if we again go to our old environment, our mind will remain virtuous and calm.

As mentioned before, we should close the doors of our senses. This means we should prevent our senses from contacting objects that provoke our disturbing attitudes. If we do, then automatically our mind will not be rocked by those thoughts. For example, if we're very attached to ice cream and once we start eating it we can't stop, then we should avoid going to ice cream parlors! We know through our experience that if we watch TV or read magazines a lot, we start craving things. Advertising convinces us that we need this or that to be happy, or that we need to look a certain way to fit in with others, and our mind flows along with those notions, even though we say that the media is deceptive.

Abandoning contacts with objects of attachment and anger, we will naturally engage in virtue without a struggle. Distractions and distorted mental states will subside and our mind will become clear. We will easily be able to deepen our understanding and experience of the Dharma.

Bodhisattvas are advised to go to an isolated place, that is, one without a lot of disturbing comings and goings. However, some people are miserable in an isolated place, however tranquil it might be. In that case, it would not make much sense for them to live there. Rather, they should find a place that suits their mind.

Does this stanza state that we definitely must abandon our homeland? No, it does not. However, a Dharma practitioner who is dedicated to actualizing the Dharma should abandon a place which causes a lot of attachment and anger to arise in him—even if it happens to be his homeland—and stay in a tranquil place.

The first stanza deals with the freedom and fortune of our precious human life. The fourth is about impermanence and death. Usually, in the Gradual Path system, these two come one after the other, and yet here there are two intervening verses describing the practices of abandoning non-conducive environments and relying on solitude. This is because when we understand the precious human life, we will decide to take one of the three essences from this life. To do so, we need to abandon staying in an environment that encourages attachment and anger and move to a conducive, less busy place. Having done this, we then reflect on our mortality in order to energize our practice.

CHAPTER FIVE

BEING MINDFUL OF IMPERMANENCE

4   Loved ones who have long kept company will part.
     Wealth created with difficulty will be left behind.
     Consciousness, the guest, will leave the guest house of the
          body.
     Let go of this life—
     This is the practice of Bodhisattvas.

It is pointless to slave all our lives for wealth instead of taking the
essence of this precious human life, because everything we accumulate has to be left behind when we die. We have no choice but to separate from the friends we care so much about, whom we have been
with for a long time. We even leave our body, which we identify with
so strongly and which has accompanied us since conception. Our consciousness is like a traveler who stays briefly in a guest house and
moves on.

Although we have this human life with freedom and richness, which
is so valuable and difficult to get, it cannot last forever. This is because
it is not permanent and is subject to decay moment by moment. This
life will eventually become non-existent because our body and mind
will separate. Although death meditation involves reflecting on the
moment by moment changing nature of our life, it principally entails
recognizing that one day it will come to a complete stop and our mind
will leave our body behind. Therefore, we must take the essence from
this life each day and try to fulfill a great Dharma purpose because we
will not have this opportunity for long.

The subject of recollecting death is dealt with in three sections:

1. The disadvantages of not recollecting death
2. The advantages of recollecting death
3. The actual meditation on death. This has three points and nine reasons. The three fundamental points are that death is certain, the time of death is not fixed, and at the time of death nothing but Dharma helps us.

The advantages of remembering death and the disadvantages of not remembering it

If we do not think of death, things will go badly now and in future lives. We will not think of what type of rebirth we are likely to take and because of this lack of concern, we will not think about giving up negative or polluted actions and developing positive attitudes and actions. When we do not think about death, we will not think about practicing Dharma. Even if we do think about practicing Dharma, we will not practice it right away or with strong conviction. And should we do some practice, it will probably be influenced by the eight worldly concerns, wanting to have a good image and reputation or wanting to receive financial compensation. In general, it is difficult to act in a way that is not at all mixed with the aims of this life. Those who stay up in the mountains for years say it is comparatively easy to let go of attachment to food and clothing, but it is very difficult to give up concern for our reputation and image. We wonder if the local people think about us, "Oh, he has been meditating in the mountains for so many years. He must be a great meditator with high realization." Remembering death enables us to abandon these attachments and concentrate on our practice.

When we are advised to give up attachment to the happiness of this life, it does not mean that we have to become beggars or that Dharma practitioners should forget all worldly activities. Rather it means that we should abandon the gross levels of attachment to the pleasures of this life: food, nice holidays, a good sex life, recognition at our job. It means we must emphasize the next life above the concerns of this life. In fact, the less we cling to the things of this life, the happier we will be, both now and in the future. We will be less obsessed with things that we cannot control and more satisfied with what we have.

Before doing any meditation practice, we should take care to generate a good motivation at the beginning. A strong recollection of death helps us to see what is important in life and to have a pure motivation for our spiritual practice. We shouldn't rush our recollection of death, but take as long as is necessary. Then the rest of the practice will go well. We will have fewer distractions, and it will be easier to concentrate.

What is Dharma practice? If something is an antidote to our disturbing attitudes and faults, it is Dharma. If it is not an antidote, it is not Dharma. An antidote to the disturbing attitudes does not have to make them totally non-existent. If it at least erodes them, that is good. For example, if it causes the more obvious and grosser forms of attachment to diminish a little, it is an antidote to attachment and is therefore Dharma. If, on the other hand, it does not work against the defilements at all, it is not useful and we cannot say it is Dharma. Any way of thinking or behaving that increases our ignorance, anger, and attachment is the opposite of Dharma.

Some people are attached to food, clothes, and reputation, some to two of them, and some to only one. Different people have different intensities of attachment. But for everyone, recollecting impermanence again and again will gradually diminish their attachment. When we have only a little attachment to food and so on, and tend to feel that wealth is more trouble than it is worth, we may be surprised that, one way or another all the things we need will come our way. Sometimes people will simply come up to us and give us things. Similarly, there are people like the Buddha and the masters of the past who had no interest in having a big name, yet became famous and well-respected.

Unless we recollect death, we will not stop our attachment to the pleasures of this life, and this will create many problems. For the sake of these pleasures, we may kill, steal, have extramarital affairs, lie, cause disharmony, or speak harshly to others. Then, eventually we will have to face the suffering that these actions produce. Thus, it is very beneficial to recollect death.

Milarepa said, "Previously, I had to experience death and birth without choice, under the control of disturbing attitudes and karma. My mind was always distressed about this, so out of distress I involved myself in Dharma more and more. At last, with wisdom I saw the Dharma directly. I saw the way things are and became an *arya*. Therefore, I no longer fear a death controlled by disturbing attitudes and karma, and at long last can relax."

When we don't think about death, we are overwhelmed by attraction to the appearances of this life. We have all the arguments and strife that come from a mind that is partial and segregates the world into friends to whom we're attached and disagreeable people whom we dislike. Having lived like this, when we reach the threshold of death and look back to evaluate our life, we will be horrified and will die with remorse and even terror. On the other hand, now, before we die, if we remember death we will remember the Dharma. Then, when we are about to die, we will not be afraid. The best practitioners, such as arya Bodhisattvas, can face death happily. They think, "Having an old body like this is so tiresome. You want to do something, but you can't." These practitioners, through their positive potential and prayers, can control where they are born and in which family. They don't have to take birth without choice under the control of disturbing attitudes and karma. In this way they can die happily. An intermediate practitioner has collected strong karma for birth in a pure land, or for a precious human life with freedom and fortune. They do not mind dying, although they are not happy to die since they still have a birth controlled by disturbing attitudes and karma to look forward to. An ordinary practitioner thinks, "I have done my best to purify and abandon negativities and to practice positive acts. In any case, there is no way to avoid death; everyone has to die. I practiced the best I could, so I have no regrets."

The fear of death is shared by both those who are familiar with the Dharma and those who are not, but in each case this fear has a different cause. Ordinary Dharma practitioners know that what happens to them after death and where they are reborn are under the control of disturbing attitudes and karma. We are concerned about the possibility of having an unfortunate rebirth, one that lacks not only happiness, but the freedom and opportunities to practice the Dharma. Those who do not know about Dharma are afraid of death because their body and mind will have to separate. Even animals fear it and flee when their lives are threatened. Humans worry even more because they will leave their possessions, parents, relatives, land, children, and so on. Well-trained Dharma practitioners, however, do not have that concern.

When we are about to die, there is no point in being afraid of death, but if we are concerned about death now it is quite useful. This concern will propel us to practice the methods which benefit our future lives and progress towards enlightenment. This is the advantage of thinking about death now.

In general, no one who is born under the influence of disturbing attitudes and karma is beyond death. No matter how much we may fear death, there is nothing which can prevent it. Why are we afraid? We see we are going to die without having accomplished a goal which will benefit our future lives. People who have accomplished a goal which benefits their future lives and progress on the path do not feel afraid of dying. Whether they die today or tomorrow they do not mind, they are not afraid. On the other hand, if we have not managed to transform our mind and act constructively, and if we have done many destructive actions, we will fear death because we know that we have not created the causes for a good future.

Some people say, "If we think about death it is too upsetting, so we should not think about it. If we just forget about death and have a good time, then we'll be okay." This is really not true. They do not know how to think about death in a constructive way. If we know the purpose of thinking about death and know how to think about it properly, it is very useful. It helps us put aside petty problems and focus our attention on developing a kind heart. It enables us to have a pure motivation to help others when we meditate and when we do work for the community and people in general. If we do not remember death, we will let our mind be distracted by food, clothing, reputation, relationships, and other things of this life. In this way, we will not put our mind on anything that benefits the next life. By remembering death, we will put our mind into Dharma, which provides happiness at the time of death and in future lives. Remembering death also helps us clarify our priorities in life and focus on what is important.

If we have the opportunity to do a long retreat, it is advantageous to spend seven or eight days at the beginning thinking of the many advantages of remembering death, and an equal period thinking of the disadvantages of not remembering death. This will clear away obstacles and enable us to practice with enthusiasm. In their daily lives, people like us do not have a lot of time to meditate on these topics. Nevertheless, it is helpful to do so even for a short time whenever we can.

The way to meditate on death

There are three fundamental points, nine reasons, and three conclusions in the meditation on death. In addition, there is a meditation on the aspect of death, in which we imagine our own death. The three fundamental points are:

1. Death is certain.
2. The time of death is uncertain.
3. At the time of death, nothing but Dharma is of any use.

It is said that realizing the first and third is relatively easy, but gaining a realization of the uncertainty of the time of death is more difficult.

To ascertain that death is certain we contemplate three reasons. The first is that death is certain to come, and nothing can stop it. No matter what kind of body we have, we are not beyond death. The Buddhas, Bodhisattvas, hearers, and solitary realizers of the past have all died. None has lived forever. If such holy beings have had to die, of course ordinary people like ourselves will have to. Great figures of the past—heroes, authors, doctors, the rich, famous, and powerful—have all died. They are only history now. All those who are currently living and who will be born in the future are likewise not immune to death. In short, there is no rebirth that we can take and be assured "Now I will not have to die."

Similarly, wherever we are born we have to die. There is no place of which we can say, "If I were born there I would not have to die." Whether we are born in the city, the countryside, under the ocean, in the sky, or on a mountain, we will still one day have to die. The very nature of life in cyclic existence is that we die.

In some ways this is obvious to us already. However, there is a big difference between intellectually knowing that death is certain and understanding it in our hearts so that it transforms our life. By thinking about these reasons again and again, we will become familiar with them and a deep understanding will grow. This will be very useful for our mind.

As sentient beings caught in cyclic existence, we are subject to illness, decline, aging, and death. We cannot prevent ourselves from ever falling ill, nor can we prevent the decline of the youthful splendor of our bodies. We cannot prevent ourselves from aging or from dying. Even now before the time of our death, we cannot bear losing our good looks or physical strength. Although we may try hard to avoid the effects of aging, we will all end up looking like we are wearing a monkey's mask! Aging destroys youth. Sickness destroys health. Decline destroys our splendor. Death destroys our life itself. When these four occur, nothing can free us. An athlete cannot run away from them; a hero cannot conquer them; an eloquent speaker cannot talk her way free; an attractive person cannot charm his way free; nor can the wealthy buy their way free. No medicine, mantra, or magical substance will help. Death will definitely come, and nothing can stop it.

To summarize, the way to meditate on this reason is, "Death is definite, because the time of death definitely will come and nothing at all can stop it. Aging, sickness, decline, and death will definitely come to me, and neither wealth, strength, beauty, heroism, nor eloquence can prevent them." As with all the teachings we meditate on, we should apply this to our own lives and our own situation. Glance meditation such as this is not intellectual; it is very personal.

Secondly, death is certain because our lifespan cannot be extended and is constantly shortening. We can hardly expect to live to be one hundred. People seldom do. Thus, right from the start we do not have much time. As the days, months, and years go by, the time we have left to live decreases. When we keep pulling away the strands of a piece of cloth, eventually the cloth will disappear; likewise, as each moment goes by, we approach death.

As an animal is being led down the road to slaughter, each step it takes brings it nearer to its death. Similarly, each day, month, and year that passes brings us nearer to our death. From our birth, moment by moment we travel along the road to death. Our life is getting shorter and there is no way to stop it.

A drawing done on water disappears in a moment. A design in earth is more enduring, and one etched in stone is the most durable. However, the life of a human being is like a drawing on water. It quickly perishes. Our life is like an autumn cloud that quickly dissipates. It resembles a flash of lightning that endures but a moment. Water descending a very steep mountain quickly reaches the plains. So too does our lifespan decrease.

To meditate on the second reason, think, "Death is certain because our lifespan cannot be extended and is constantly being reduced. It will quickly come to an end, like a drawing on water, an autumn cloud, a flash of lightning, and water rushing down a mountainside." Thinking about each example helps bring the point home to us.

If there is no way of increasing our lifespan, why are there longevity practices? Do they increase our life? No, they do not. If we originally have a lifespan of sixty years, for example, an unfortunate circumstance could occur which could stop us from living out the full sixty years. Long life practices are for eliminating such unfortunate conditions.

Among the many meditational deities for long life, three are well known: Ushnishavijaya (Namgyalma), White Tara (Drolkar), and Amitayus (Tsepagmay). With Ushnishavijaya, we practice making thousands of offerings to avert ominous conditions. With White Tara, we do the long life practice involving meditation on the self-generation ritual. With Amitayus, we practice the meditation on vase breathing and so on. In the practice of other deities, such as Yamantaka, there is the vajra recitation practice, and this too is excellent to prolong life. Nevertheless, someday we must leave this body. It is impossible that it will remain forever.

The life of a tree, for example, requires compost, moisture, sunshine, and many other conditions. Similarly, in order to live and to avoid the separation of body and mind that death entails, many conditions must be assembled. Generally speaking, death can come about in one of three ways or in any combination of them: our lifespan being used up, our merit being exhausted, or the sudden ripening of negative karma. If our life is threatened by one or two of these, there are means whereby we can restore the status quo before death can occur. If all three of them occur at once, there is nothing that we can do. It is like a candle which has a natural duration of three hours. If the wind blows, or water falls on it, or it is knocked over, it will go out. If it is protected, it can last three hours, but no more.

The third reason for the certainty of death is that if we continue to live our life on automatic, we will die without having practiced the Dharma. Actually this reason does not prove that death is definite, but it does remind us that we will definitely die without having practiced the Dharma if we continue on as we are now. Why? Because even while alive, we have hardly any time to practice. When we are young, we do not think of practicing Dharma, and when we are elderly we may wish to practice but not be able to because our physical faculties are worn. In the middle of our lives, when we are healthy adults, it hard to find time to practice. We have to spend a lot of time working, eating, sleeping, washing, taking care of errands, and attending to social obligations. When we do practice, we have to ask ourselves how much time is spent in good practice and how much in distraction? Sometimes our motivation is not good, sometimes we are not focused, and sometimes our dedication is weak. If we take all this away, only a very short time of actual practice remains.

Looking at my own life, this is very clear. I have been a monk since I was eight and feel like I have been practicing Dharma a long time. However, although I spent a lot of time memorizing and reciting texts when I was young, my motivation was not a Dharma motivation. I knew that if I did not memorize well, my teachers would punish me. When I went to the rituals with the monastic assembly, my motivation was not like that explained in the Gradual Path. Now, at the age of sixty-two, the intensity with which I can practice has definitely diminished compared to what it was when I was in my thirties and forties. I get tired easier, and my body is not as healthy. If I look at that middle period of my life and take away the time spent sleeping and doing other activities, there is not much time when I can say I really practiced well.

The environment and inhabitants of the world do not stay long; they are not constant. Therefore, it is pointless to cling to them, to be attached to them, to crave them. Beautiful flowers bloom in the spring and summer and soon die. Now they are here, now they are gone. In each moment they are fading and are unable to remain a long time. Like that, we too are here for a brief time. Right now we are aging and heading towards death. Now we are here, now we are not; alive this morning, dead this evening; alive tonight, dead tomorrow morning. So many people die suddenly. Knowing this yet planning to be around a long time is ludicrous.

Throughout history people have been annihilated by death, yet we do not feel that death will befall us. Instead, we lose ourselves in distractions, in pleasure, in having a good time, in attachment to the transient goals of this life. This is not wise. Innumerable people in the past have been born and right away have had to face the suffering of birth. Then, as they lived, they experienced the sufferings of illness and aging, of not getting what they desired, meeting things and situations that they did not like. Finally they died, tormented by the suffering of death and in a pathetic state went on to the next life. That is how our life too, began, how it has been up to now, and how it will continue to be unless we transform ourselves. Some of this we know through experience, some we know intellectually, but in our heart we do not think death will happen to us. Living in denial, we spend our lives in distraction, filling each available moment with constant busyness. Knowing that she faces unretractable aging, sickness, and death, and that she will have to go on to a future life alone, in a pathetic state, without companions, a wise person could never be happy letting life slip by consumed by meaningless activities that are only for the sake of this life. Knowing that our death is certain and unavoidable, we should not get lost in purposeless activities and pleasures, but try to develop our good qualities and purify our faults as much as possible. Before death strikes, we should try to prepare for our future lives and work towards liberation and enlightenment.

In our adult years when we are able to practice the Dharma to transform our mind, we often postpone it, thinking, "I'll do it later. First I have to complete this project. I have to be financially secure. I want to live my dreams while I'm able." There is no meaner trick than the procrastinating attitude, and with it we will never get around to practice. There is no end to the work that we could do. Work only really ends when we die, and we have to practice Dharma now.

If we think about this, our daily behavior and attitudes will improve. We will recognize what is important in life and set priorities in our life. Then, it will be easier to practice the Dharma, to control our temper, to let go of obsessions and fears about the things of this life. Things that used to bother us a lot will cease to seem important, and we will become more tolerant. As a result, our negative behavior and harmful actions towards others will diminish. Our motivation for spiritual practice will improve, and we will not have as much internal conflict between what we want to do and what we think we should do.

When we reflect that death is certain and dwell upon the three points to explain it, our outlook will change. A lot of needless worry and stress will vanish. In my own case, when I think my death is definite but its time is not certain, much useless anxiety stops. If I thought I would live long, let's say until eighty, then I would worry, "I am only sixty-two now but already my body is not in a good state. Already I cannot do everything for myself. When I am eighty what will I do? Soon my health will make it so that I can no longer teach at Nalanda. Will the monks keep me here? If I go back to Sera Monastery in India, I'll be too old to be much good, so what's the point in going there? Who will help me and look after me? How will I get food?" This creates a lot of anxiety. But if I think that death is certain and the time of death is uncertain, I do not think about these things. Instead, I think that if, due to the kindness of the Buddha, Dharma, and Sangha, I live another year, it will be marvelous because that will give me a chance to do some real, pure Dharma. Anyway, if we live to the age of eighty, things will work out, one way or another. Thinking in this way stops useless worries from disturbing our inner peace of mind.

The time of death is uncertain

Here, too, there are three reasons to help us ascertain that the time of death is uncertain. First, there is no fixed lifespan in our world. People die at all ages: some in the womb, some at birth, some in infancy, some in childhood, some in their youth, some in middle age. We have many reasons for thinking we won't die soon: "I'm still young. My health is good and my mind is clear. The sick, aged, and senile die first. I will die when I'm old, after I've lived a full life." However, there is no guarantee that this will be the case. Not everyone who dies is old. In fact, we have known people who died young, and many were younger than we are at present. Being young and healthy does not mean that we will not die soon. Some people who are chronically ill and continuously complain about their health live long, while others who are vibrant and healthy die young, suddenly. Some people die while playing, some while eating, some while talking. Some people die in a sudden calamity, some in a car accident while driving along listening to music. When we consider this, our daily actions will improve. When serving others, we will think of benefiting them, and love and compassion will arise more easily. When meditating, our motivation will be better and our prayers more pure.

The second reason that the time of death is uncertain is that the conditions for death are many and the conditions for life are few. Many factors can provoke death—illness, accidents, and so forth. Even some of the things that we rely on to keep us alive can become a cause of death. For example, we can choke on our food or eat food that makes us ill. If medicine is not used properly, or if we have an allergy to it, it can kill us. Our home, which was built to protect us, can collapse in an earthquake and kill us. Cars, designed to make life easier, can become the agents of our death. When the four inner elements—earth, water, fire, and air—which form our body are harmoniously balanced, we are well. However, if they are thrown out of balance, we may die suddenly. Our life is like a candle in the wind, in danger of going out at any moment. It is fragile like a water bubble on the surface of a pond; it does not last long and perishes quickly. The fact that we remain alive between one out-breath and the next in-breath is amazing. We are ready to die at any moment. Since the time of our death is uncertain, we should practice right now what we will need at that time— the Dharma. There is no time to waste.

Third, the time of death is uncertain because our body is very feeble. Our bones break easily, our skin is punctured without much effort. Our internal organs wear out and malfunction; tiny viruses we cannot even see can kill us. It is extremely easy for our body to perish.

Death comes suddenly. Yet many people who are ill in the hospital and who will be dead by tonight do not think that they will die today. We have a strong, innate feeling that death will come later, when we are ready, when we are prepared. However, this is not the case. We should not postpone practicing the method which will help at the time of death. We must do it now. If we keep postponing Dharma practice— that is, if we put off transforming our mind and heart—death will reach us before we are prepared, and that will be disastrous. At the conclusion of the first point, we made up our minds to practice Dharma because our death is definite and Dharma is what will benefit us at that time. Now, at the conclusion of the second point, we make up our minds to practice right now. Why is there such a hurry? Because the time of death is not certain.

When we are constantly aware that there is no certainty which will come first, tomorrow or the next life, that is a sign that we have realized that the time of death is not certain. The first point is easier to realize than this one, but if we persist, the understanding will come, and with it, all the benefit it brings to our life.

At the time of death, nothing except the Dharma is of use

Here, too, there are three points to contemplate: at the time of death, our possessions will not be of any use to us; our friends and relatives will not be able to help us; and even our body will become a burden. It is clear that none of these things can prevent our death and none can come with us at the time of death. At the time of death, only our Dharma practice and the actions we have done to benefit others are of any use. Therefore, while we are alive we should have a healthy relationship with our possessions, our dear ones, and our body, not a relationship of clinging, possessiveness, attachment, and fear. If these things are ultimately of no value at the time of death, what is the sense of spending our lives creating negative karma to obtain and protect them? Developing a healthy relationship does not mean that we should have aversion for and angrily reject wealth, dear ones, and our body, but that we should relate to them wisely and not be bound by obsessive attachment to them.

When the time of death comes, this precious human life possessing the eight freedoms and ten fortunes will be left behind. Usually our body goes everywhere with us, but at the time of death, it will not be there. What will accompany us to the next life are the karmic imprints left on our mindstream from actions we have done in the past. Mental habits from both our positive and negative ways of thinking will go with us. For example, if a robber were to attack us when we are traveling and take all of our possessions—our clothes, our shoes, our money, our credit cards—we would be in a very sorry state. Similarly, when we reach the time of death, our parents, siblings, spouse, children, friends, and wealth all have to be left behind and we go on alone. If we are wise, we will be mindful of this, and think about what will help us at that time.

When we are about to die and in our future lives, all the virtue and Dharma practice we have done will help. Nothing else can help because it is impossible for anything else to go with our mindstream into another life. Therefore now, while we are not dying, we should cut as much as possible our attachment to those objects. It is important to remember that freeing ourselves from attachment does not mean we have to scornfully reject these things. Rather we need to develop a balanced attitude towards them. Of course, we have our basic needs: we need to keep our body healthy and well; we need a certain amount of money and possessions; we need friends and companions. The point is to begin now to cut through the gross levels of attachment to things that seem attractive, cause us to create negative karma and are of no benefit to us at the time of death. By letting go of our attachment, we will be able to relate to other people and things in a healthy and beneficial way. The verse in the root text is specifically connected to the third point.

Having contemplated the third point, we conclude, "Nothing but the Dharma helps at the time of death. Therefore, I must practice it purely without excessive attachment, anger, or distraction to friends and relatives, wealth and possessions, or my body." Combining the conclusions of the three points, we think, "I definitely must practice Dharma right now, because the time of death is not certain, and because nothing helps at the time of death except Dharma." Even if we know this, it is helpful to keep reminding ourselves of these points.

When we travel along an unknown path, we need a guide to show us the way. To travel the path of death, which we do not know, we have the Dharma as our guide. To take a long journey, we need a fund to draw on to cover our expenses. That also is the Dharma. When we are alone in a dangerous place, without a single friend, we need a protector. The Dharma is also our refuge and protector while we are in cyclic existence. Therefore, we are wise to entrust our mind solely to the Dharma. Doing this does not mean we become stilted religious fanatics who are obsessed only with our own beliefs. It is important to remember that practicing Dharma means transforming our mind. Letting go of attachment and clinging; pacifying hatred, resentment, and anger; developing a kind heart, wisdom, and skillful compassionate means to help others; avoiding actions that harm others; extending a smile and a helping hand whenever possible—all these are the Dharma.

Imagining our death

In the Gradual Path, the meditation on the aspect of death is explained after the three roots and nine reasons. However, according to the oral instructions of the lamas, we meditate on it before meditating on the three fundamental points and nine reasons. First we imagine ourselves about to die. Then we think, "My death will certainly come, but I don't know when. Nothing else but the Dharma can help me at the time of death."

Meditating on the aspect of death involves imagining what it would be like to die. We have seen or heard of others dying in many ways. Now we think of ourselves dying in one of those ways. For example, we imagine we are ill and check into a hospital. Lying in the impersonal room, our cheeks and nostrils sunk in, lips drawn apart and coated with scum, eyes watering, we hear the doctors say in hushed voices, "There is no more hope. There is nothing else we can do." Our friends or relatives are afraid. It is hard for them to see us in this state and we can feel them withdrawing from us. We should imagine what it would be like to be in such a pathetic situation, and reflect, "This will happen to me." We will be afraid at the thought of dying because we have actualized so little of the Dharma in our mind and nothing but the Dharma can give us strength and clarity at the time of death when we are separating from everything and everyone else. When this situation appears so clearly to us that our heart trembles, we have the realization of the certainty of death. After this, the decision easily comes, "I must practice Dharma. In particular, I must do things that benefit others. I must meditate on love, compassion, and bodhichitta. There is nothing else more important than helping others and acting with a good motivation."

Meditating on impermanence is very important. The Buddha's first teaching was on impermanence, and it is the first point discussed in the four noble truths. It was also his last teaching, when he gathered his disciples around him and said, "Come! Look! The Tathagata is about to die!" In the beginning, thinking about impermanence activates us to practice Dharma. We start to think, "I am going to die, so I must practice Dharma." Then, while we are practicing Dharma, thinking about death invigorates our practice so it becomes better and better. At the end, reflecting on death inspires us to complete our practice and attain enlightenment. Thus this reflection is important in the beginning, middle, and end.

First we think about the value of our precious human rebirth with freedom and fortune, its purpose and meaning, and how rare and difficult it is to have this wonderful opportunity. Then we consider that it will not last long. Thinking like this helps us to value our life and to make use of the opportunity it affords us, without taking it for granted. It also helps us curtail attachment to our personal welfare in just this life. We will not spend a lot of time planning for the future, dreaming of wonderful pleasures to procure, places to go, things to do, recognition and appreciation to have, and ways to prove ourselves to others. We see that no matter how much we may come to possess, all of it will be left behind when we die. It is not worthwhile to get excited about wealth, good reputation, popularity and so on. Understanding this, we will be satisfied with having just enough to eat, drink, and wear.

If we think we will live a long time, we easily become obsessed with worries about the future, "Will I have enough? What will happen to me? What if this or that happens?" The lamas say, "Don't make problems in your mind repairing something that is not broken!" Assuming as certain that which is uncertain is mistaken. It is better to think about what is really certain. This is that we are going to die, although we do not know when. Only Dharma practice is of any use at that time, so it is important to focus on that. Acting in a way that is clear, honest, and not deceitful makes what we do Dharma. It is fruitless to create hardships for ourselves by thinking we will definitely live long, when this is not certain. If we do live long, things will work out. For example, if someone had asked me when I was thirty what provisions I had made to live until I was sixty, I would have said that I had nothing—no money or anything. In fact, things have worked out. If we live a long time, things do work out. Dharma practitioners and people with experience in Dharma should think like this.

Concerning our personal situation, we should not think we will be here a long time and emphasize arranging circumstances for a long stay. However, in considering the community, country, and world in which we live, it is different. Here we have to project a long way ahead, thinking that once we have died someone else will come along, so we have to plan good conditions for them. We should not abuse resources that others will need in the future and we should arrange as good circumstances for them as we can.

To take the essence from this life, the lineage lamas generally recommend that we put effort into whichever Dharma practice we like. That is, we should focus on doing whichever practice makes our mind happy and at ease. Because different people have different dispositions and interests, some are happier doing tantric practice, some are happier meditating on emptiness, some contemplating love, compassion, and bodhichitta, some in making prostrations, offering mandalas, and so on. If our life passes doing the practice we find most meaningful, it is very good. We should take the essence out of this life by putting effort into the practices we are more attracted to and find more beneficial for our mind.

It is said that offering just one meal to the Buddha and his disciples creates enormous positive potential. Still greater positive potential is generated during a good meditation on impermanence. Why is that? Meditating on impermanence weakens and destroys the delusion of permanence. For example, our laziness and reluctance to practice the Dharma is due to the belief in permanence, thinking that since we are here for a long time, "I'll practice! I'll meditate, and do retreat..., but not right now. For the time being, I have other things to do." This thought usually continues until the time of death and thus very little transformation of our mind is accomplished. But if we meditate well on impermanence and death, we will see that death is definite, when it will happen is completely uncertain, and only the Dharma helps at death. Then we will practice right away because it energizes us to practice and turns our mind towards what is meaningful and worthwhile in life. Meditation on impermanence is said to create immense positive potential.

It is not that making offerings to the Buddha and his disciples yields no positive potential. On the contrary, the positive potential is immense. But if we know how to meditate on impermanence and meditate accordingly, the results are even greater. It is said that it is better to meditate on emptiness than to do a three-year retreat on a tantric deity. If a person spends three years in such a retreat, just reciting mantra and not spending much time in contemplation, that is still very good. In fact, the positive potential and benefit of that is beyond words. But when a person meditates on emptiness in a proper way, she gathers even greater positive potential because meditating correctly on emptiness directly counteracts self-grasping ignorance, which is the root of samsara. Doing a tantric retreat does indeed reduce self-grasping and the other disturbing attitudes, but not in the same way that meditation on emptiness does.

Meditating on the three points of the precious human rebirth is comparatively easy, while meditating on impermanence and death is more difficult. In the Gradual Path, the meditation on the suffering of the unfortunate realms follows the meditation on death. This is because after we die we will not become non-existent. We go on to another life, and we should be concerned about our rebirth. In the root text, we are advised to first meditate on giving up unwholesome friends and relying on spiritual friends. After this, we are told to meditate on refuge, and then in order to encourage us to take refuge in the Three Jewels, we consider the sufferings of the unfortunate rebirths.

CHAPTER SIX

SPIRITUAL FRIENDS

Giving up bad company

5 **When you keep their company your three poisons increase,**
Your activities of hearing, thinking, and meditating decline,
And they make you lose your love and compassion.
Give up bad friends—
This is the practice of Bodhisattvas.

What is a bad friend? It is someone whose influence has a negative effect on us. When being close to someone makes our attachment, anger, ignorance, and negative actions increase, that person is considered a bad friend. This type of friend is like a poisonous tree. Once it has taken root, its leaves, branches, and fruit come this year, next year, the year after, and so its poison spreads. Through keeping company with this type of person, the virtuous qualities that we have built up of listening, thinking, and meditating on the Dharma and serving sentient beings will deteriorate, and new virtues will not grow. Although we may enjoy someone's company and he may even wish us well, if our disturbing attitudes increase due to his influence, they cut the root of our liberation and we create negative karma which will only bring us suffering in the future. The impartial love and compassion which we have developed through much effort will degenerate and we fall

back into helping only our friends and harming the people we don't like because of our attachment to self. Should we have an unfortunate rebirth due to the karma we create as a result of the influence of bad company, how can we be of benefit to sentient beings?

Even if being around a person who acts and thinks negatively does not directly cause our good qualities to decrease, other people will still develop a bad impression of us and this will impede our endeavors to help others. When a person goes around with people who act against the laws of a country, for example, others will think she is also a criminal. Everyone in the group gets the same bad name.

The Kadam masters used to say that they would not fear walking with a mad elephant, but they would fear keeping the company of a bad friend. Although a wild elephant can cause our death, its negative influence is limited to taking this life; it cannot harm our future lives. But a bad friend harms many of our lives because of the negative karma we create under his influence. The sage Drom Tonpa asked the great Jowo Atisha, "Who is the worst of enemies?" Atisha replied, "The evil friend." We may have a sincere wish to transform our minds, but at present our determination is relatively weak and our physical, verbal, and mental actions are not powerful in virtue. If we meet a bad companion and follow his advice, we have no chance. We are finished.

Keeping our distance from bad friends does not mean we consider them inherently bad people and lack concern or compassion for them. It simply means we recognize our own weakness and how easily we can be influenced in negative ways and thus decide not to cultivate close friendships with these people. We can still be polite when we meet them and include them in our meditations on love and compassion, but we should have firm boundaries about how close we get to them. In the short term, they may be upset that we remain at a distance, but in the long run, it will be best for everyone.

Included among bad companions are teachers who teach us wrong views and practices, or present a wrong system of basis, path, and result. Although we may meditate on and work hard at practicing what they teach, since from the beginning the path is mistaken, we will only go on to more confusion in the future. They teach us a wrong view, and thinking it correct, we exert ourselves to practice accordingly. That leaves thick negative imprints on our mind, the results of which are felt for a long time. We will have difficulties in many future lives due to those imprints. For this reason it is very important to check the qualities of a spiritual teacher before deciding to rely upon him or her. It is easy to meet and follow a bad one. If we rely on good spiritual friends our virtuous qualities will increase like the waxing moon.

There are varying degrees of good friends. The best is someone who can lead us to omniscience or, if not that, to liberation. A good friend, at the very least, encourages us to practice virtue. We may not have found a friend who can lead us to liberation and enlightenment, but if we rely on someone who has good ethical discipline, talks gently, and has a kind heart, we benefit greatly. Even if this person is not very learned, if he or she is humble and good-natured, that is very good. By spending time with such people, our good qualities will naturally grow. Even if they don't actively encourage us, their example will influence us in a virtuous direction.

Not all bad companions have the same traits. However, they share some general characteristics we should beware of. Someone who continuously criticizes and judges others, seeing only bad things in them, is a bad friend, as is someone who laughs at the mistakes of others and ridicules them. A bad friend ascribes bad motivations to others and negates their positive actions. She may encourage us to drink, incite our lust, or get us involved in her negative way of thinking and acting. Whenever we try to do something positive, such as go to Dharma teachings or retreat, or make donations to a charitable organization, a bad friend criticizes us, saying, "Why waste your time and money doing that? It's better to enjoy life!"

We cannot tell a bad friend from his external appearance. Bad friends don't have horns or even an evil-looking face. As often as not, this person will talk pleasantly and with a smile on his face, tell interesting stories, and invite us out. In this way we are deceived, fooled into thinking that he is a good friend. This person may or may not have ulterior motivations. Even if he wishes us well, because he does not understand the Dharma, his advice and influence may not be good because he is thinking only of the happiness of this life and only of his own personal happiness. It can be difficult to distinguish good from bad ones. A reliable way to check is to see if what they do corresponds to the teachings and if their values are based on non-harmfulness and compassion.

It is impossible to find a friend without any faults. Only a fully awakened Buddha can fit that requirement. If staying with a person over a period of time harms our practice, makes disturbing attitudes grow, or makes our precepts deteriorate, gradually we should put ourselves at a distance from her.

For example, someone may tell a monastic, "You should not be a monastic. Life is so short! You have no freedom. You can't have a good time. Your mind becomes closed. You stay there with all your suffering inside. It's better if you give up your ordination and enjoy yourself. Be open!" Such a person is a bad friend. She may even seem to be motivated by compassion, but we should not be fooled. A bad friend might say, "It's all right to drink alcohol and take recreational drugs. Alcohol is good for your health, and drugs expand your mind. People all over the world drink, and you're just being self-righteous if you don't." Thus, if we have taken the precept to abandon intoxicants, we should avoid becoming close friends with someone who thinks like this.

In a similar vein, there are people who argue that because the spiritual path is a union of wisdom and method, and since according to tantric Buddhism the female is wisdom and the male is method, we definitely need to be in a relationship. Otherwise, we are repressing our sexuality and the spiritual path is not complete according to tantra. These people are missing a vital point. Although in tantra there is the possibility, at a very high level, of transforming desire into the path, there is no way that we are able to do that now. We must choose a life style, monastic or lay, that suits us best now, and within that avoid unwise sexual behavior. We should not use tantra as an excuse for unrestrained or even harmful sexual relations. People who hold such wrong views about tantra are another example of bad companions. Although they may seem well-intentioned, it is better not to keep their company because they may try to influence us with their misinterpretations and wrong views.

Relying on good friends

6   When you rely on them your faults come to an end
     And your good qualities grow like the waxing moon.
     Cherish spiritual teachers
     Even more than your own body—
     This is the practice of Bodhisattvas.

Relying on good companions helps us and enables us to help others. Among good companions, the supreme is the virtuous spiritual guide, or guru. We need to know the proper way to rely upon such a person, since devoting ourselves to the spiritual guide is the foundation of the path. By being around a virtuous spiritual friend for a long time, our faults decrease and our virtuous qualities continuously increase like the moon growing full.

Good companions also include our fellow Dharma students at our Dharma center or monastery. We listen to the teachings, discuss the teachings to eliminate doubts, and meditate and practice together. By supporting us along the path and encouraging us when we feel discouraged, our Dharma friends help us transform our minds in a positive way and progress on the path to enlightenment. Even if they do not have great positive influence over us such that they cause our faults to decrease and our qualities to increase greatly, we are still inspired by seeing them get up early each morning to meditate, go to teachings regularly, and study and practice to the best of their ability. Their example gives us confidence that we can do the same.

The main subject of this verse is how to rely on a spiritual guide so that we benefit from the relationship and are open to his or her help and inspiration. The spiritual guide is very important on the path. We need teachers for worldly skills like auto mechanics, so we definitely need instruction from those who are wiser and more compassionate than us to correctly learn the path to enlightenment.

We should check, "What I need are the qualities of hearing, thinking, and meditating on the Dharma, for these are the methods for attaining liberation and enlightenment. If I rely on this person, will he or she guide me to these qualities?" We should only rely on a person who can guide us in this way. Thus, we need teachers with vast and excellent qualities of hearing, thinking, and meditating in regards to sutra and tantra. They should understand clearly what to practice and what to abandon on the spiritual path. They should be able to alleviate our doubts. If they cannot clearly explain the things we need to know to generate the qualities of hearing, thinking, and meditating, we should not rely on them.

It is therefore important to choose our spiritual teachers carefully. We should examine their qualities over a period of time before deciding to take them as our teachers. In the meantime, we can attend their classes and observe their conduct. It is no use looking for a person who is well known, from a high family, who looks impressive or is entertaining. Those of us wishing liberation and enlightenment need to know what to practice and what to abandon. We need to know how we enter into cyclic existence and how to emerge from it. We need to know how to subdue our disturbing attitudes and develop our good qualities. Therefore we need teachers who can explain these topics clearly.

We should choose spiritual guides who teach with the thought of benefiting others. They should have compassion for their students, be patient with them and enthusiastic to help them. Our teachers should have good ethical conduct, meditative experience, and wisdom. They should be knowledgeable in many aspects of the Dharma, humble, and good-natured. If we rely on a person with these qualities, we will naturally become like him or her, just as a log of ordinary wood, when placed in a pile of sandalwood, picks up the smell of sandalwood. If we cannot find a fully qualified guide, at least the person should have more good qualities than bad ones, cherish others more than self, and be more concerned with future lives than the present one.

Some people, without checking the qualities of a person, immediately take him or her to be their teacher. Later they see that the person is lacking in good qualities and may even have many bad ones, and they become very confused about what to do. Therefore, it is wise to go slowly and to understand what qualities to look for in a spiritual teacher.

We may have few or many spiritual guides. This depends on whom we choose to form this relationship with. We may be closer to or see some more often than others. Our "root spiritual mentor" is the one we feel the closest to. This may be the teacher who first introduced us to the Dharma or the one who made the Dharma come alive for us in a special way. Ideally, we should rely on all of our spiritual guides correctly, seeing them all as equal. Still, when we meditate on this topic, we will most likely find there is one teacher that we feel closer to and have a greater respect for. It is often easier to do the meditation first in relationship to that spiritual mentor and later to extend that feeling to the others.

In addition to looking for qualified spiritual mentors, we should try to make ourselves into good disciples. A good student is one who is genuinely interested in the Dharma, who is open-minded, intelligent, and thinks about what she has learned, and who is sincere and tries to practice. The more we develop these qualities in ourselves, the more we will benefit from contact with our teachers.

Once we have chosen someone as our spiritual guide, we should rely on him or her properly so that we can derive benefit from the relationship. Properly relying on a spiritual mentor does not mean that we idolize him or her like a movie star, expect him to fulfill our emotional needs, or give up our wisdom with some romantic idea of "surrendering to the guru." The purpose of the relationship is to increase our wisdom and compassion and to enable us to benefit ourselves and others.

There are four topics to consider when contemplating how to rely on a spiritual guide:

1. The advantages of properly relying on a spiritual guide
2. The disadvantages of not relying on one or relying on one incorrectly
3. How to rely on one by means of our thoughts
4. How to rely on one by means of our actions

The advantages of properly relying on a spiritual guide

To meditate on the advantages of properly relying on a spiritual guide and the disadvantages of not properly relying on him or her, we should think about each benefit and drawback and thus build up our wish to rely on a virtuous friend correctly. In general, we do not need to spend many weeks thinking about these points. After we have captured their sense, we can go on to meditate on how to rely on our spiritual guides through our thoughts and actions. There are eight advantages of properly relying on a spiritual guide:

1. We will approach enlightenment. The main way to rely on our spiritual guides is to practice the teachings they give us. The essence of these teachings is to avoid what should be avoided and to practice what needs to be practiced by a person seeking enlightenment. Enlightenment can be attained in one life through tantric practice. This is mostly due to the strength of our reliance on our mentors. On the sutra path as well, the time required to attain enlightenment is much shorter when we properly rely on our spiritual guides.

2. We will please all the Buddhas. We cannot communicate directly with the Buddhas, so they help us through our spiritual mentors, who are their representatives. If we practice our teacher's instructions, they will rejoice because we are creating the causes for happiness.

3. We will not be adversely affected by evil spirits and misleading friends. By practicing what our teachers instruct, we build up positive potential that is a strong force protecting us from receiving harm from such beings. In addition, our wisdom will grow and we will be more confident; thus we will not be as prone to follow the bad advice of misleading friends.

4. Our disturbing attitudes and the negative actions that arise from them naturally decrease. This occurs because we practice our mentors' teachings on how to subdue our disturbing attitudes and avoid negative actions.

5. We will develop higher paths, meditative experiences, and stable realizations. This comes about not only by meditating, but also by creating extensive positive potential. We can create great positive potential by serving our spiritual guides: running errands, cleaning their rooms, and performing other mundane activities. Atisha had one disciple who was a great meditator, one who was his cook, and Drom Tonpa, who was his attendant and translator. Neither the cook nor Drom Tonpa had much time to meditate. Since the meditator was rather proud of his accomplishments, one day Atisha called the three together to examine who had the most spiritual attainments. It turned out that Drom had the most, then the cook, and last of all the meditator.

6. We will be cared for by a spiritual guide in all our future lives. Following the spiritual guide correctly leaves imprints on our mindstream that yield various good results in future lives. One of these results is to meet with spiritual masters like Manjushri and other enlightened beings, and to be cared for by them. This point is very important, for if we do not meet qualified teachers in our future lives, how will we learn the Dharma? If we don't learn the Dharma, we will not be able to practice it or to attain its wonderful results.

7. We will not have unfortunate rebirths. By following our mentors' teachings, we will purify actions leading to these rebirths and avoid doing such actions in the future. When our mentors sometimes scold us or give us a hard time, they are helping us, out of compassion, to purify negative karma and thus avert bad conditions.

8. We will gain all our temporary and ultimate goals. This summarizes the above seven.

The underlying point of these eight advantages is that if we have a good attitude towards our spiritual guides, we will take what they teach us seriously, value it, and put it into practice. Our practice of creating positive attitudes and actions and avoiding negative ones brings about everything good that we experience. On the other hand, adoring our teachers but not practicing what they teach does not bring about these excellent results. Making idols of our teachers is not what is meant by properly relying upon them.

When we think about the first advantage, for example, we decide to rely correctly on our spiritual mentor because by doing so we will approach enlightenment, and by not doing so we will not approach enlightenment. The other seven should be thought about in a similar way. The disadvantages of not relying on a spiritual guide are the opposite of the eight advantages. Here, we contemplate that if we do not correctly rely on our spiritual guide, we will miss out on the eight advantages.

The disadvantages of not relying correctly on a spiritual mentor

Those who teach the Dharma show us great kindness, for they reveal to us the path to liberation and a lasting state of happiness. If we then angrily despise, scorn, criticize, or reject them, there is the danger that we will abandon our Dharma practice and the path to enlightenment as well, and that would be disastrous for us. If we reject someone who teaches us with compassion, who will we rely on to guide us on the path? If we dismiss those who are wise, who can help us clarify our doubts and subdue our disturbing attitudes? We can see that rejecting our spiritual guide is detrimental to us in this life and plants the seeds to not meet qualified spiritual guides in future lives. Thus the main things to avoid in relating to our spiritual mentors are anger, resentment, and belligerence. However, should these attitudes arise in our mind or be expressed through our words and actions, we can apply the four opponent powers of purification in order to avoid the negative consequences.

We are human beings and conflict and misunderstandings are bound to arise among us. When they do, we should seek to resolve them through communicating respectfully with the other person. If we see the importance of having a good relationship with our teacher, we avoid projecting preconceived expectations on our teacher and engaging in the dysfunctional ways we have of resolving conflict. Instead, because we value the relationship, we will try to subdue any disturbing attitudes that arise towards our teachers and to find more beneficial ways of working through misunderstandings.

The main points to understand here are how correctly relying on our spiritual mentors benefits our practice and how incorrectly relating to them puts obstacles in our way. In meditation, we can contemplate each advantage and disadvantage until we gain a powerful feeling for it. In that way we will be enthusiastic to develop a good relationship with our teachers through our thoughts and actions.

How to rely on our spiritual mentors through thought

Relying on our mentors through thought involves cultivating two attitudes: faith (confidence) and respect (gratitude). The first is developed by seeing our spiritual mentor as the Buddha, the second by remembering his or her kindness. These points, especially the first, are very difficult to gain experience of, and confidence arises only after meditating on them for a long time. As we gradually work on these points, without pushing ourselves or rushing, it is important to try to always see our spiritual mentors in a positive light, not to pick faults or feel superior. Such critical attitudes can easily arise if we notice that we know more about science, politics, and computers than they do or if they don't agree with our ideas of how things should be done.

When our confidence and gratitude become stronger and stronger, it is a sign that our analytic meditation on these topics is working. In the beginning, we can do glance meditation on relying on a spiritual mentor. Here we recognize what properly relying on him or her means, what points to reflect on to do this, and their order. After our glance meditation, we slowly reflect on each point. When great unshakable confidence in the spiritual guide arises, feeling that he or she is not separate from all the Buddhas and is kinder than all the Buddhas, then the experience is said to be effortless. It may take us a long time to generate these feelings, depending on past prayers, imprints, the thickness of negativities and obscurations, and our karmic relationship with our spiritual teacher. However much we can generate them, they will inspire and give energy to the rest of our Dharma practice, enabling us to integrate the Dharma in our mindstream with ease and joy.

Training ourselves to have confidence in our spiritual mentors has three parts:

1. The reason it is necessary to see the mentor as Buddha
2. The reason we are able to see the mentor as Buddha
3. The way of looking at the mentor as Buddha

It is important to see our mentors as Buddhas because will we only profit from this attitude. The eight advantages of properly relying on a spiritual guide enumerated above show the benefit we will receive. Seeing our teachers in this way helps us to practice. For example, if we see our teachers as ordinary persons, when we listen to teachings, we may think, "What do they know? Why should I practice this? They're just saying this because they think they're important or because they want me to offer them something." With such an attitude, we clearly will not be motivated to practice what they teach. On the other hand, if we realize that even if Shakyamuni Buddha himself were here at this very moment teaching us, he wouldn't say anything different from what our mentor is saying now, we will pay close attention, and be interested and enthusiastic to practice what our mentor teaches. By developing the confidence that regards our spiritual guides as Buddhas, then whether or not they are, we profit from the relationship in the same way as if they were. It all depends on our own attitude.

This practice of seeing the spiritual guides as Buddhas is done with those whom we have chosen to be our teachers. We do not have to think of everyone who is a Buddhist teacher as a Buddha.

We can see our spiritual teachers as Buddhas because it is possible to train our mind to recognize and focus on their many good qualities and to think less and less about their faults until we don't notice the faults at all. For example, when we have a girlfriend or boyfriend, we easily get into the habit of seeing only their good qualities and ignoring their faults. In the daytime, there are stars shining but they are outshone by the sun. Similarly, if we focus more and more on our mentors' good qualities, they will outshine the faults.

There are four specific reasons which help us look at our spiritual mentors as Buddhas:

1. Vajradhara, the form the Buddha took when teaching tantra, said that in future times he would take ordinary forms and manifest as spiritual masters, and that followers should regard such masters as Vajradhara himself.

2. The spiritual guide is the agent of all the Buddhas' actions. Although there are many enlightened beings, our minds are too obscured to be able to be aware them. It is through our spiritual mentors that we have access to the Buddhas' blessings, inspiration, and positive influence. For example, although the sun has enormous power, we cannot use it to burn anything. But if we have a magnifying glass, we can focus its rays and start a fire. In the same way, the spiritual guide is like a magnifying glass focusing the rays of the actions of all the Buddhas for our benefit.

3. Our spiritual guides do the work of the Buddhas and Bodhisattvas by working for sentient beings right now. All the Buddhas and Bodhisattvas have committed themselves to benefit us sentient beings and to lead us from suffering to enlightenment. We cannot recognize them around us, but there is no way that they would renege

on their word. If we examine who is doing the work the enlightened ones promised to do for us, we find that it is our spiritual mentors. They are the ones teaching us what to practice and avoid on the path. If Shakyamuni Buddha were here in front of us, he wouldn't be doing anything other than what our spiritual mentors are doing: teaching, guiding, and inspiring us on the path. Therefore, we can conclude that our mentors are the Buddha.

4. What appears to our mind is not reliable. An enlightened being can appear in many forms: as a beggar, a dog, or a queen. We cannot say, just because our spiritual guides look ordinary, that they are. Appearances are deceptive. For example, it sometimes seems that the train we are in is moving when in fact it is the train on the next platform that moves. When a torch is spun around in the dark, we see a circle of light, but it is an illusion. Our senses and mind are often deceived by what appears to them. When we feel that our spiritual guides are just ordinary people who don't know much, we should remember how easy it is to be wrong when we rely only on superficial appearances.

Sometimes people wonder, "If my teachers are Buddhas, why don't they show their clairvoyant powers and special abilities so that we will know they are Buddhas and develop faith?" First, our minds are very obscured and even if a *nirmanakaya* Buddha appeared in front of us, we would not be able to recognize that form as a Buddha. Just as our ears do not have the ability to hear some sounds that dogs can hear, our minds at present do not have the ability to see the Buddha's qualities directly. Secondly, if we did see our teachers with a body made of light and witnessed their clairvoyant powers, we might get distracted by marveling and talking about it. We might miss the point and think the path is to gain these qualities, and forget that our goal is to develop a kind heart and wisdom. By appearing in ordinary form, our teachers enable us to observe how they handle problems, and we can learn from their example. Seeing how they practice, we are inspired to do the same.

At first, it may seem strange to us to develop respect for our teachers by remembering their kindness because we think of respect arising from seeing someone's excellent qualities and gratitude arising from seeing their kindness. Yet, when we feel very grateful to someone, we do tend to admire and respect him or her. Training in respect or gratitude by remembering the kindness of our spiritual guides has four points:

1. In general, our spiritual mentors are kinder to us than all the Buddhas, and in particular, kinder even than Shakyamuni Buddha. Although all enlightened beings are equally wise and compassionate, we consider Shakyamuni Buddha to be the kindest to us because only he came to the Earth during our time and gave the teachings which benefit us to this day. But even he passed away and is not directly helping us now. Only our spiritual guides are here for us now, so they are kinder to us than even Shakyamuni Buddha.

2. They are kind in teaching us the Dharma. Our teachers show us how to avoid unfortunate rebirths, how to break free of cyclic existence, and how to attain enlightenment to make our lives the most meaningful for all beings. We should feel more gratitude for this kindness than we feel towards a doctor who cures us of a dreadful illness or towards a person who helps us out of a frightening situation. Without people to show us the path, what would our life be like? Without their having taught us the Dharma, what would happen to us at the time of death and afterwards?

3. They are kind by inspiring and blessing our mindstream. Blessing our mindstream means transforming our minds into something better. This is not accomplished only by direct teachings. When Atisha was old, Drom Tonpa used to carry his excrement out for him, and as a result he gained clairvoyant powers. Tilopa hit Naropa in the face with a sand mandala, causing Naropa to experience a deep concentration. Tilopa said that to gain results from meditation we should make requests to our spiritual guides and then the results will come easily. When we continuously and sincerely request inspiration from our spiritual guides, we definitely get results. Our mind becomes more open and we experience the Dharma more easily. Our spiritual teachers inspire us by being good role models. We can learn about the Dharma simply by observing how they practice in their daily life.

4. Our spiritual guides are kind by providing for our material needs. In the monasteries, teachers often care for the needs of their students by sharing the offerings they receive. However, for lay students, this is not the case because they have jobs and incomes. Though our teacher may not be kind to us in this way, we should remember that he or she takes care of us by teaching us Dharma, and that this is infinitely more valuable than material goods. Their gift of Dharma is the supreme gift.

How to rely on our spiritual mentors through action

There are three ways of relying on our spiritual guides through our actions:

1. Making offerings. Due to their excellent qualities and their kindness to us, our teachers are powerful objects for creating good karma, so it helps our practice to give them offerings. In addition, our teachers need food, clothes, shelter, and medicine. If we students do not provide for them, they would have to get jobs, and it would be difficult for them to find the time to teach us.

2. Offering service and respect. Our teachers often need help with their various projects to benefit others. Thus we serve sentient beings by serving our spiritual guides. When we offer help, it allows our teachers to do what they're good at—teaching and counseling people in the Dharma.

3. Practicing the Dharma in accordance with their instructions. This is the supreme offering to make. Our spiritual guides teach us the Dharma for our happiness. When we practice what they instruct, they are delighted because they know that we are helping ourselves and others by doing this.

When we have strong confidence, trust, respect, and gratitude for our spiritual guides, the path is generated more quickly in our mindstream. That is the purpose of developing confidence and gratitude. As mentioned above, gaining realization of these is difficult. When we feel that there is no mentor apart from the Buddha, and there is no Buddha apart from our mentor, that is, when the two seem inseparable, then we have gained this realization.

If we have received teachings from many spiritual guides, we should first train with the one we have the most faith in, the one who seems to us to be the best, our root mentor. Then, when we have some feeling of confidence and gratitude towards him or her, we spread it to the others. We develop the thought that all our spiritual teachers are the same, that they are emanations of our root teacher. If our meditation on this topic has gone well, we see our mentors like waves of the ocean of the Dharmakaya; and when they die, seem to dissolve back into the Buddha, like a wave sinking back into the sea. If we think in this way, the realization has been well generated.

Incorrectly relying on spiritual mentors means having no confidence in them and developing wrong views about them. Here, wrong view means that when something about our teacher appears bad to us, we actually believe it to be the truth and think that he or she is bad. We should remind ourselves that the way things appear to us is not reliable. For example, if a student likes to go to bed early, he may consider his teacher making him practice until late in the evening a fault. But if a student likes to stay up late, he sees the same quality as something wonderful in the teacher. We can think of many examples from our own experience to illustrate this point. If we have studied certain philosophical texts, such as "Mind and Awareness," we know that much of the time what appears to our mind does not entirely accord with reality.

While developing our faith and respect in our teachers, we must also keep in mind that if a teacher instructs us to do something which runs counter to the general teachings of the Buddha, we should not do it. If a teacher acts in a way that is abusive or unethical, we should not follow his example. In neither case do we need to get angry. As His Holiness the Dalai Lama suggests, we can keep a respectful distance from them, yet still appreciate what they taught us that helped us along the path. In other words, we don't need to negate everything positive about the person simply because of one aspect of their character.

This discussion on how to rely on our spiritual mentors applies to all of our teachers, not just to those who are famous or those who are our vajra masters. If we practice tantra, it is important to regard our vajra masters as Buddhas. In tantra, we practice seeing all sentient beings as Buddhas and our environment as a pure land, so we certainly can't omit our vajra master from this pure view by seeing him or her as an ordinary person! Nevertheless, even for our teachers who are not our vajra masters, it is helpful to see them as emanations of the Buddha and view them as working for the benefit of sentient beings. A positive attitude makes us receptive to what they teach and inspires us to practice, and we in turn reap the good results of practice.

We cannot actually know if someone is a Buddha or not, but we can decide to view our spiritual guides in that way. We say that the Dalai Lama, for example, is a Buddha, but how can we know for sure? We are not capable of knowing. But we can recognize the benefits of having this view and decide to adopt it. Similarly, we cannot say that we do not know a Bodhisattva, nor can we say there are no dakinis in our town. Without clairvoyance and high realizations, we are not capable of knowing these things. Nevertheless, we can realize the advantage of thinking well of others and recognizing how much they benefit us. On that basis, we can decide to cultivate the attitude that they are, or at least might be, exceptional beings—Bodhisattvas, dakinis, or Buddhas.

If we have a positive attitude towards our spiritual guides, we will accomplish what we wish. For example, if we think that the room we live in is cramped, dark, and airless, we become unhappy. Thinking it is just right, nice, spacious, makes our mind happy. The room has not changed, simply our attitude has, but that makes all the difference. If we are unable to think of our spiritual guides as Buddhas, we can still consider them very important and precious. Even this is an excellent way to purify negativities, and for this reason alone it is a very important practice.

CHAPTER SEVEN

REFUGE: A SAFE DIRECTION

7   Bound himself in the jail of cyclic existence,
     What worldly god can give you protection?
     Therefore when you seek refuge,
     Take refuge in the Three Jewels which will not betray you—
     This is the practice of Bodhisattvas.

The term "worldly gods" refers principally to a group of gods called the "eight proud gods of the world," which includes Brahma and Indra. If we turn to them to free us from the suffering of cyclic existence and lead us to liberation, it is of no use because they themselves are not liberated. Still wandering in the prison of cyclic existence, they have no power to protect us, free us from samsara, or lead us to liberation and enlightenment.

Taking refuge in the Three Jewels of the Buddha, the Dharma, and the Sangha means that we are clear about our spiritual direction and entrust our spiritual guidance to them. If we seek liberation and enlightenment, we are advised to rely on the guidance of the undeceiving Three Jewels. They are undeceiving because they are free of all the fears of cyclic existence and self-complacent peace and are expert in leading others from those conditions. Because the Buddhas have eliminated all defilements in their own mindstreams, they are no longer subject to the uncontrolled rebirth of cyclic existence. Their love, compassion, and altruism are fully developed, so they are not content to rest in their own peaceful liberation, but actively work to benefit others by leading them to temporal and ultimate happiness. Many objects offer us slight or temporary refuge. For example, water temporarily frees us from thirst, food satisfies our hunger, an umbrella shelters us from the rain, and clothes protect us from the cold. Here, however, we have a final, completely reliable refuge, one which can show us the way to liberation and enlightenment. We shall discuss the subject of refuge in five points:

1. The benefits of refuge
2. The reasons or causes for going for refuge
3. Identifying the objects of refuge
4. The way of going for refuge
5. Guidelines to follow after taking refuge

The benefits of refuge

If we clearly understand the purpose or benefits of taking refuge, we will be inspired to do so. The benefits of refuge are:

1. When we have taken refuge, we become a Buddhist.

2. Taking refuge is the basis of the path and needs to precede any other ordination. All the various ordinations—individual liberation (lay precepts and the various levels of monastic precepts), Bodhisattva, and tantric ordinations, are all taken on the basis of taking refuge. Without refuge, none of them can be generated. If we generate the wrong view in our mind, deciding that the Three Jewels are not a perfect refuge, it would destroy our refuge and at the same time any ordinations we have received would become non-existent. If we again cultivate faith in the Three Jewels, refuge is again generated, but our ordinations do not automatically come back. We need to take them again.

3. Each time we take heartfelt refuge—not merely say the words—our negativities and obscurations diminish.

4. We will not have unfortunate rebirths because the negative karma which causes them will be eliminated by taking refuge and practicing the Dharma.

5. If we take heartfelt refuge, we will not be harmed by spirits or other non-human beings even in this life. There many stories in the Lamrim of people being saved from fire, water, spirits, and the like by going for refuge.

6. We eventually accomplish all of our objectives. If we go for refuge to avoid an unfortunate rebirth, we will be born in the higher realms. If we go for refuge to be free from cyclic existence, we will attain liberation. If we go for refuge because we want to be saved even from the peace of liberation and to attain enlightenment, that also will happen. Therefore, we should begin every action we do—especially the important ones—with refuge and prayers to the Three Jewels. In this way our work will be successful.

7. We accumulate a great deal of merit or positive potential. If the resulting positive potential could be converted into form, the entire universe could not contain it and it would overflow.

8. In brief, through refuge we gradually attain and increase all positive qualities until we reach enlightenment.

The reasons or causes to take refuge

The depth of our refuge corresponds to the strength of our motivation for seeking it. To take refuge and to increase its strength, we reflect on the causes, or reasons, which inspire us to go for refuge. These are principally two: the first is fear of cyclic existence in general and of unfortunate rebirths in particular, and the second is faith or confidence in the Three Jewels. It is important that we understand what "fear" means in this context. It is not a panicked or paranoid fear that immobilizes us. Rather, it is a wise fear that, seeing danger, motivates us to prevent further suffering. If we are not afraid or concerned about suffering befalling us in the future, we will not look for protection from it.

After death, we do not become non-existent, but go on to a future life. What rebirth we will take depends upon the actions we have done in this and previous lives. It is helpful to evaluate how we act in this life. Do we consistently hold to our ethical standards? How much do we adjust and rationalize them when it is convenient? How often do we utter harsh words out of anger or retaliate for perceived wrongs, and how often are we able to let go of anger and resentment and find constructive ways of resolving conflicts? Self-reflection in this area is crucial. We may discover, much to our dismay, that although we have lofty ideals, it is quite difficult to live up to them and we inflict a good deal of pain on others due to our own uncontrolled disturbing attitudes and lack of skillful behavior. If this is the case, our chance of fortunate rebirth is reduced, and we should be concerned about this. Concern for this danger gives us the impetus to look for ways to prevent it and to be protected from it.

Without faith in the Three Jewels—that is, without believing that their qualities enable them to help us out of our predicament—we will not seek their guidance and will deprive ourselves of their beneficial influence. Similarly, without confidence in their qualities, we may recite the refuge prayer, but our refuge will not be firm or sincere.

Buddhism speaks of three types of faith or confidence. When we think of the qualities of the Three Jewels, our confusion and mental cloudiness clear. Our mind becomes joyful because we recognize the qualities of the Buddha, Dharma, and Sangha and admire them. This is the first kind of faith, lucid faith. The second is faith with conviction. Here, we investigate the Buddha's teachings and understand from our study that they are accurate. Because we are convinced by our own investigation of the truth of the teachings, we have confidence in the Three Jewels. The third type of faith is aspiring faith. In this case, we see the qualities of the Three Jewels and wish to attain them ourselves. Blind faith or obligation to believe a certain dogma play no part in any of these types of faith. In Buddhism, faith or confidence arises through understanding. The more our understanding grows, the deeper our confidence and trust in the ability of the Three Jewels to guide us will be.

Identifying the objects of refuge

The qualities in the mindstream of a Buddha, such as compassion and wisdom, are the supreme objects of refuge because they are completely free of faults and possess all qualities. If we search for someone who can be our refuge, we will come to see that only a fully enlightened being can really help.

We can speak of ultimate and conventional refuge when discussing the Three Jewels. Any Buddha, or enlightened being, has four "bodies." "Body" here does not refer to a physical body made of flesh and bones, but to a body or corpus of qualities. Two of a Buddha's bodies are truth bodies (*dharmakaya*). One is the wisdom truth body and is the Buddha's omniscient mind itself. The other is the nature body, which is the lack of inherent existence of a Buddha's mind and the cessation of suffering that a Buddha enjoys. These two bodies are the ultimate Buddha Jewel. The other two bodies are form bodies. One is the enjoyment body, the form in which the Buddha appears to teach *arya* Bodhisattvas. The other form body is the emanation body, the form in which a Buddha appears to those who are not *arya* Bodhisattvas.

Sometimes a Buddha appears as a human being, sometimes as a dog, and so on. The two form bodies are the conventional Buddha Jewel. They are beings that possess the ultimate Buddha Jewel in their mindstream, and thus they are called conventional Buddha Jewel.

The ultimate Dharma Jewel refers to the true paths and the true cessations in the mindstream of a superior or *arya*. These are the last two of the four noble truths. The conventional Dharma Jewel refers to the twelve divisions of Buddha's scriptures which show us the way to actualize the true paths and true cessations in our mindstream.

The ultimate Sangha Jewel includes all superiors. A superior or *arya* is any person who has direct non-conceptual realization of the nature of reality, the lack of inherent existence. The conventional Sangha Jewel refers to a group of four or more ordinary monastics who are fully ordained. Although they are not superiors, they are to be thought of and recognized as the Sangha Jewel. The founding teacher of Buddhism in this historical age, Buddha Shakyamuni, is included in the Buddha Jewel because he is a Buddha. Since he has a direct, non-conceptual perception of reality, he is a superior and is therefore also included in the ultimate Sangha Jewel.

There are also causal and resultant refuges. The causal refuges exist in the mindstreams of those who have accomplished them, while the resultant refuges are the ones that we ourselves will become as we practice the path and transform our mind. The causal Buddha refuge is those who are already Buddhas. The causal Dharma refuge is the true paths and true cessations in the mindstreams of others who have developed them, and the causal Sangha refuge refers to people other than ourselves who have become superiors. The resultant Buddha refuge refers to the Buddha that we will become, resultant Dharma refuge to the true paths and true cessations we will attain, and resultant Sangha refuge to the superior that we will become. The causal refuges are so-called because for us to become the resultant refuge, we need to take refuge in the Three Jewels that already exist in the mindstreams of others while we practice the path leading to those results. In this sense, they are causes we rely on to attain the desired result—enlightenment—in our own mindstream. Therefore the main refuge is the resultant refuge, and in particular the Dharma refuge, because once we have developed the realizations expressed in the Buddha's teachings in our own mindstream, we will have stopped our own suffering and enabled ourselves to better benefit others.

Shakyamuni Buddha is a sound refuge for us to rely on to show us the real refuge, the realizations that we will develop in our own minds. The Buddha is a suitable refuge for four reasons. First, he is beyond all fear. After becoming enlightened, the Buddha declared that he could be harmed by nothing within him and nothing in his surroundings. Some kings, naturally, doubted this, and wanted to test him. One of them sent a mad elephant with sharp knives attached to its trunk hurtling towards Buddha. Another poisoned his food. One built a camouflaged fire-pit under the path where the Buddha walked. The Buddha was not harmed by any of these. As he said, "These types of threats are external and are no problem for me, because I have pacified the inner threat of the disturbing attitudes."

Second, the Buddha is expert at freeing others from fears. In the Gradual Path texts, there are stories of many people who could not be helped by others but were helped by Shakyamuni Buddha. Gandarva Praraja was extremely proud, yet the Buddha found a way to break his pride and turn him in a positive direction. He also helped Arya Small Path, who was very stupid; Angulimala, who was full of anger; Kungawo, who was obsessed with desire; Kyimdak Pelkye, who was old, poor, and miserable; and Nyewong, who was almost devoid of positive potential.

The third reason the Buddha is a reliable refuge is that he is not partial. He does not hold some sentient beings close and others at a distance. He cherishes all, without discrimination. For example, Buddha's cousin Devadatta hated the Buddha and was forever competing with him. Once, in his arrogance, he copied one of the Buddha's extraordinary actions and as a result got very ill and almost died. Instead of allowing him to suffer, the Buddha healed him.

Fourth, the Buddha helps everyone whether they help him or not. For us, it is quite normal to help those who help us and to neglect those who don't. But the Buddha helps even those who are not kind to him and who do not help him.

How to go for refuge

To go for refuge in the Three Jewels we need to know their qualities. The Buddha's qualities of body, speech, mind, deeds, and actions are inconceivable to our ordinary mind. Nevertheless we can get some idea about them. The Buddha's physical qualities are the thirty-two signs and the eighty marks of an extraordinary being. They are physical qualities that we ordinary beings do not have—such as a crown protuberance and a hair curl at the forehead—and indicate a Buddha is a great being who is free of all faults and possesses all good qualities. The eighty marks are signs of a Buddha's qualities that even the tenth-level Bodhisattvas do not have.

The qualities of speech of the Buddha are the sixty melodious intonations and so forth. For example, by giving one teaching, the Buddha addresses each person who is listening in a way that corresponds to his or her level of mind. A Buddha's voice also soothes troubled emotions and brings joy to the minds of the listeners.

The qualities of a Buddha's mind are the twenty-one types of uncontaminated wisdom. These are clearly explained in Nagarjuna's *Precious Garland*, and in Maitreya's *Ornament of Realization*, and can be summarized into the Buddhas' wisdom and compassion. The wisdom of the Buddha simultaneously sees all things of the past, present, and future, far or distant, as clearly as we see an object in the palm of our hand. We who are not fully awakened are unable to see things far in the past and future because our minds are obscured by defilements that we have not yet purified. Since a Buddha has purified all obscurations and disturbing attitudes, all things are clearly visible to him or her.

When we are hot, cold, hungry, thirsty, and so on, we wish to be free from this suffering, but the Buddhas' compassion for us is thousands of times stronger than our compassion for ourselves. When we are miserable, we can't bear it, and when the Buddhas see us suffer, they can bear it even less. Although we ordinary beings want to be happy, our compassion for ourselves often does not extend to wanting ourselves to be free from all suffering in cyclic existence. The Buddhas' compassion for us extends that far and beyond.

The qualities of the Buddha's actions include the twelve deeds, which describe the major events in the life of the Buddha. The qualities of the Buddha's actions are reflected in his appearing in our world and turning the wheel of Dharma, thereby leading innumerable beings to enlightenment, arhatship, and the various Bodhisattva paths. He taught everyone, giving advice from the Universal Vehicle and Individual Vehicle alike, depending on the dispositions and thoughts of the audience. To benefit sentient beings, a Buddha may first display magical powers in order to inspire those without faith to enter the path of faith. Then he turns the three wheels of Dharma. Through that he matures the mindstreams of sentient beings who are not yet mature, and frees the sentient beings who are already mature. Immense good has come to our world due to the Buddha's qualities. If we continue to reflect on them, we will gradually develop faith with conviction in the Buddha's power to protect us from suffering and show us the actual refuge, the Dharma.

The qualities of the Dharma, in brief, are that by practicing it we become an enlightened being possessing the qualities described above. Dharma principally refers to the true paths and true cessations, which are the ultimate Dharma. By meditating on the true paths, we attain higher and higher true cessations in our mindstream until we reach the highest level, Buddhahood, at which point we will be able to turn the wheel of Dharma.

The qualities of the Sangha reflect the Dharma existent in their minds. Someone on the path of preparation is able to weaken the power of the manifest disturbing attitudes. Such a person may be considered the conventional Sangha. When they advance to the path of seeing and the higher paths, they become the ultimate Sangha. Those on the path of seeing abandon the intellectually acquired disturbing attitudes, and those on the path of meditation gradually abandon the innate disturbing attitudes, finally becoming a Buddha, and therefore the Buddha Jewel.

One prayer states that the qualities of the Buddha are inconceivable, the qualities of the Dharma are inconceivable, the qualities of the Sangha are inconceivable, and that by thinking with faith about the inconceivable, an inconceivable ripening result arises.

The definition of refuge is placing our trust in the Three Jewels after having developed fear of an unfortunate rebirth and the suffering of cyclic existence in general. Faith in the Three Jewels is believing them to have the ability to protect us from that suffering. Simply reciting the words "I take refuge in the Buddha, Dharma, and Sangha" is not refuge. These words are a method to induce an attitude of lucid faith and trust in the Three Jewels and to reinforce the mind of refuge. By reminding us of refuge, a prayer is an auxiliary to going for refuge, it is not the actual refuge. Refuge in the Buddhas means putting our trust in the Buddhas because we are deeply concerned about the possibility of suffering and have the confidence that they can lead us to the actual refuge, or the Dharma, which will protect us from this suffering. Refuge in Dharma is putting our trust in the Dharma as the actual refuge that will pacify the suffering and disturbing attitudes. Refuge in the Sangha is placing our trust in the *Arya* Sangha as our companions on the path.

The beings of the three levels of practice each have their own level of practicing refuge. Initial-level practitioners entrust their spiritual guidance to the Three Jewels from fear of an unfortunate rebirth and faith that they can free us from that suffering. Middle-level practitioners take refuge after considering the suffering of all of cyclic existence and recognizing the ability of the Three Jewels to guide them from that. Higher-level practitioners, unable to bear the suffering of all sentient beings, are motivated by compassion. They take refuge because they do not want to remain in either cyclic existence or the peace of nirvana without benefiting others, and they know the Three Jewels can guide them to full enlightenment.

The instructions to be followed after having taken refuge

To maintain and enrich our refuge, some actions are to be adopted:

1. Having taken refuge in the Buddha, we should not rely upon a teacher who presents a perverse system of what to practice and to abandon. If we rely upon a teacher who has an incorrect understanding of the causes of happiness and the causes of suffering, we will practice those teachings and they will not bring about the results we desire.

2. Having taken refuge in the Dharma, we should refrain from harming living beings. Of the two, view (of reality) and conduct, conduct means non-harmfulness. This a basic tenet of the Buddha's teachings. Harming others includes injuring their bodies, stealing their possessions, having unwise sexual relations with them, lying to them, causing disharmony in their relationships, speaking harshly to them, and so on. Not only do these actions harm others, they also bring suffering to us for they prevent our having a fortunate rebirth and obstruct our attaining liberation and enlightenment. Harming living beings causes only suffering; happiness will never come about from harming others. If we seek enlightenment, we need to abandon selfish concerns and to cherish others, instead of harming them. Clearly, non-harmfulness is the cornerstone of world peace.

3. Having gone for refuge to the Sangha, we should avoid bad companions, people who engage in destructive actions or who discourage us from our spiritual practice.

Some actions are to be avoided after taking refuge:

1. In terms of refuge in the Buddha, we should not say, "This Buddha is ugly, this one is beautiful," when we look at various representations of the Buddhas. Although we may comment on the artistry or the quality

of the material the image is made from, we should not say the image is ugly. All images are regarded as the form of an actual Buddha, so it is inappropriate to criticize them.

2. In terms of refuge in the Dharma, we should respect and take good care of all Dharma books which describe the path to liberation and enlightenment, no matter what language they are written in.

3. In terms of refuge in the Sangha, we should regard the *arya* Sangha, be they monastics or lay practitioners, as very important and respect them. In addition, we should consider the monastic community or even one monk or nun that is an ordinary being as precious and important. It is very important to train oneself in pure appearance in this way.

These are the main actions to practice and abandon once we have taken refuge in the Three Jewels.

Meditating on refuge

It is helpful initially to spend about a week contemplating the benefits of refuge as described above. In brief, initial-level refuge prevents us from having an unfortunate rebirth. Middle-level refuge stops birth in cyclic existence, and highest-level refuge saves us from the extremes of cyclic existence and the complacency of nirvana attained for our benefit alone. When we have meditated on the benefits of refuge, we can start to meditate on refuge itself.

Imagine the Buddhas, Dharma, and Sangha in the space in front of you. A simple visualization is to think of Shakyamuni Buddha as the embodiment of the Three Jewels: his mind is the Buddha, his speech the Dharma, and his body the Sangha. A more extensive visualization of the objects of refuge is explained in the texts on the Gradual Path and the "Jor Cho" (Preparatory Practices) meditation manual. We then imagine all beings of the six realms surrounding us. As we recite "I take refuge in the Buddhas, I take refuge in the Dharma, I take refuge in the Sangha," we imagine light and nectar radiating from them and flowing into us. The light and nectar enter through the crown of our head, purify all obscurations to actualizing the stages of the path, and fill us with all the realizations of the path. The light and nectar also flow from the Three Jewels into all sentient beings, purifying their obscurations and bringing them realizations of the path.

If our concern about the dangers of cyclic existence and our faith in the qualities of the Three Jewels is not strong, then our refuge will lack vitality. Therefore, it is helpful to contemplate the results of an unfortunate rebirth. If we think of what our experience would be if we were born in the lower realms and asked ourselves, "Could I bear this?" we will come to have a strong impulse to take refuge. Refuge will become very real and important to us.

To contemplate this, think of each realm one by one, and imagine being born there, and after each, turn to the Three Jewels for refuge. Beings in the hell realm suffer from fear, anger, and physical torment. In the hungry ghost realm they suffer from frustration, dissatisfaction, hunger, and thirst. Animals suffer from confusion and the lack of freedom. Imagining these many sufferings and feeling urgent concern that we may experience them, think of the inconceivable qualities of the Buddha, Dharma, and Sangha. Reflect that they can protect us from this suffering by teaching us the path. The Buddhas' qualities of wisdom, compassion, and skillful means, their qualities of body, speech, mind, deeds, and actions all show that they are a sound and non-deceptive refuge. If a vivid faith arises when we think of the qualities of the Three Jewels, and we confidently entrust ourselves to the Three Jewels, we have gained the realization of refuge.

Although it is unpleasant to consider the possibility of having an unfortunate rebirth, doing so energizes us to take measures to prevent it. Examining our lives, we look to see if we have created the causes to be born in those situations. Most of us have engaged in harmful actions in this life and we can assume in previous lives as well. These karmic imprints have not vanished and will bring their results if we have not purified them. If we can face this fact, then we can act to prevent such rebirths from occurring, and a very strong and pure refuge will arise in our hearts when we turn to the Three Jewels and recognize their power to guide us from such suffering to states of happiness.

This concludes the section on the preliminary practices as presented in *The Thirty-seven Practices of Bodhisattvas*. They are preliminary in relation to the practices of the three levels of practitioners. In the Gradual Path system, the topics to be meditated on at the initial level are precious human rebirth, death, the suffering of the unfortunate realms, refuge, and actions and their results. In this text, the actual practice of the initial level starts with the presentation of actions and their results, which is covered in the following stanza.

CHAPTER EIGHT

CREATING CAUSES, EXPERIENCING RESULTS

EXPLANATION OF THE PATHS OF THE THREE LEVELS OF PRACTITIONERS

The path to enlightenment can be divided into the paths of initial, middle, and advanced practitioners. Explaining the path in terms of these three levels helps us understand how to gradually develop our mind and to progress along the path in a comfortable way. Having thought about precious human life and the fact that it does not last forever, the initial-level practitioner is concerned with future lives and thus takes refuge and observes karma and its effects in order to have a good rebirth. Having considered the unsatisfactory nature of cyclic existence in general and the advantages of liberation, the middle-level practitioner generates the determination to be free and the wish to attain liberation and practices the three higher trainings of ethical discipline, meditative stabilization, and wisdom in order to attain their goal. Realizing that all sentient beings similarly wander in cyclic existence, the advanced practitioner generates love, compassion, and the altruistic intention to become a Buddha in order to benefit them. He or she then practices the six far-reaching attitudes as the path to enlightenment. We will see the unfolding of this gradual path to enlightenment in the following verses.

How to Train in the Path of the Initial-level Practitioner

8   The Subduer said all the unbearable suffering
       Of bad rebirths is the fruit of wrong-doing.
       Therefore, even at the cost of your life,
       Never do wrong—
       This is the practice of Bodhisattvas.

This verse explains how to observe karma and its effects, which is the main practice at the initial level. The Buddha's first and most important advice to us after we have taken refuge is to observe karma and its results. This subdues many problems in our daily lives, plants the seeds for fortunate rebirths after we die, and prepares a good foundation for practicing the higher levels of the path. Observing karma and its effects principally refers to practicing the ten positive actions and abandoning the ten negative actions, even at the cost of our life. Karma refers principally to volitional actions. These actions leave imprints on our mindstream, and these imprints ripen into our pleasant, unpleasant, and neutral experiences. They also influence the type of rebirth we have, our experiences during a lifetime, our habitual attitudes and behaviors, and the environment in which we are born. Since we all want happiness and to avoid suffering, we need to be concerned with the causes we create, for they bring about our various experiences. For this reason, the Buddha described the functioning of karma—our actions—and how it brings its results.

The topic of karma is presented in two parts: first, the general aspects of karma, and then the particular types of karma. In speaking of the general aspects, four points encourage us to avoid destructive actions and act constructively. They are:

1. Karma is definite. It is definite that negative actions result in suffering and positive ones in happiness. The opposite is never true. Thus, once we engage in a negative action, if we do not confess and purify it with the four opponent powers, suffering will definitely come as a result, never happiness. Similarly, if we act constructively, it will result in happiness, never suffering, unless its ripening is impeded by our getting angry.

2. Karma expands. Even a small negative action is to be refrained from, because karma increases in size, just like a great tree grows from a small seed. Similarly, small positive actions are worth doing because their beneficial results likewise grow.

3. The result of karma is not experienced if the cause is not created. If we do not act negatively, it is impossible to meet with the unpleasant

experiences that result from such actions. On the other hand, if we do not create the causes for happiness, it will not come by itself.

4. The result of karma is never lost. When we act destructively, the karma does not vanish even if we do not experience the result in this life. Even if thousands of eons pass by, we will eventually meet with the result unless we purify this negative karma. The results of positive actions also do not vanish but will bear their fruit when the conditions are ripe. We should not think that they are ineffectual just because a good result does not follow immediately.

There are three types of karma:

1. Non-meritorious karma
2. Meritorious karma
3. Unfluctuating karma

Non-meritorious karmas are of many types, but the majority of them can be included within the ten destructive actions. These are termed destructive or negative because they destroy our happiness and directly or indirectly harm other sentient beings. When this verse advises us to give up negative actions at the cost of our life, it mainly refers to these ten. These ten are to be given up by both monastics and lay people. Since we all want happiness, we should avoid or at least diminish these. The first three actions are done physically, the next four verbally, and the last three mentally.

1. Killing destroys the life of another being. The negative action of killing means intentionally taking the life of someone else. If we mistakenly kill a human being, we do not create the actual negative karma of killing, although the negative karma we collect is subsumed under the category of killing. This is also the case if we accidentally step on a bug, or if we throw a rock off a cliff and it kills someone, but neither of these carries the full negative karma of killing. If we kill an animal, the karma is less heavy than if we kill a human being because an animal rebirth is more unfortunate compared to a human one. This is because a human has the potential to attain enlightenment in that very life, while as an animal, one temporarily does not. However, taking the life of either a human or an animal creates the negative karma of killing. If we kill a fish, for example, we make the fish suffer, and just like a human being, the fish never likes to experience pain and only wants happiness. Killing our parents, who gave us our body, or killing arhats and other aryas who are highly realized beings is heavier negative karma than killing ordinary people. There are various ways

to kill, some rough and some less so. For example, killing can be done in a war, by poison, and so on. Or we may commit the action of killing by asking another person to kill for us or making another kill. Thus, if a general orders his soldiers to kill, he will receive the karma of killing as many people as they kill. If we tell someone else to kill, not only do we get the karma of killing, but so does the one who carries out our wish. Therefore, if we definitely have to kill, it is better to do it ourselves, since this prevents another person from also accumulating that negative karma.

2. Stealing refers to taking what is not given and harms others by way of their possessions. The negative action of stealing entails stealing from a human being, although stealing from an animal and so forth is also a form of stealing. The method of stealing can vary: taking by force, compelling another to give, cheating someone, not paying fines or fees, deliberately not returning things we have borrowed, or using materials at our work place for personal use without permission. We complete the act of stealing when we think, "I've got it. It's mine."

3. Unwise sexual behavior harms oneself and others. One should avoid having sexual relations with close cousins, siblings, parents, or the partner of another. Having sexual relations in front of a stupa or statue of a Buddha is inappropriate because it is disrespectful. One should not have relations when one's partner has taken the eight precepts for one day, since he or she is observing celibacy for that twenty-four hour period. Having sexual relations too many times in a day, for example, more than five times, is also unwise because it may lead to a deterioration of the body's strength, making it ineffective for other work.

4. Lying harms others by deceiving them. A lie can be explicit or implicit, or even nonverbal, such as lying by a gesture. We may say we saw what we did not, or did not see that which we saw; or we may say something is when it is not, or is not when it is. It is especially damaging to claim that we have spiritual powers and realizations that we do not have.

5. Divisive speech refers to causing conflict between people who get along well together and enhancing the conflict between people who don't get along. We may engage in divisive speech directly by speaking to one or both parties or indirectly by passing on harmful information. In either case, the result is to create disharmony among people.

6. Harsh speech is saying things that hurt the feelings of others, such as angrily criticizing, ridiculing, insulting, or shouting at them.

7. Gossip or idle talk is the last of the four negative actions of speech. This includes reading or speaking about frivolous books or films which excite lust or provoke anger. Even explaining a Dharma text while motivated by the eight worldly concerns, such as wishing to receive a good name or offerings in return, is considered idle talk. Although idle talk is the least harmful of the four destructive actions of speech, it is the one which wastes the most time and distracts us from being mindful and practicing the Dharma.

8. Covetousness is the first of the three negative actions of mind. It is a mind that is attached to the things of others, such as their body, possessions, and wealth, and wishes to possess them.

9. Maliciousness is the wish to harm others. It may arise from jealousy, which makes us unable to bear the good fortune of others and wish to destroy it. It can also be motivated by resentment, grudge, or belligerence.

10. Wrong view refers to stubbornly and cynically holding incorrect ideas about important topics. For example, we may think it is impossible to become enlightened because the Three Jewels do not exist, that there are no repercussions to our actions, or that past and future lives do not exist and thus there is no reason to live ethically. Wrong views are fixed and rigid opinions and do not refer to doubt, inquisitiveness, and open-minded exploration of ideas.

To be a complete destructive action, each of the ten must have four factors. If any of the four is missing, the action is not complete and the karma is lighter. The four factors are: basis, thought, action, and conclusion. For example, in the case of killing, the basis is someone other than oneself. The thought has three parts: recognition, intention, and disturbing attitude. Recognition means one kills the being that one intended to kill. If one kills one person when one intended to kill another, it is not the full karma of killing. Intention is the intention to kill; that is, the action was not done accidentally. A disturbing attitude—anger, attachment, or ignorance—must motivate the action. The action is the actual action of taking life, and the conclusion occurs when the other person dies before one dies oneself.

The actions, or karmas, of the ten non-virtues are called non-meritorious. Their results vary according to how heavy they are. Several factors influence how heavy both positive and negative karmas are. For example, doing the action in relation to our spiritual mentors, parents, or the poor and sick is heavier. Repeatedly acting in that way or not doing any purification makes the karma heavier, as does acting with a strong motivation. If the means of doing the action are exceptionally cruel, it is heavier. The nature of the action also makes a difference. For example, in general, killing is heavier than idle talk. If the karma is heavy, it results in rebirth as a hell being. If it is middling, it results in a hungry ghost rebirth. If it is light, the result is rebirth as an animal. It is important to keep in mind that these results are not punishments, they are simply natural outcomes of harmful actions. Similarly, the happy experiences that result from positive actions are not rewards. They, too, are the natural fruits of planting positive seeds in our mindstream.

The second category of karma, meritorious actions, are the opposite of non-meritorious karma. For example, in a situation where one could kill, the action of not killing is a positive one. Simply avoiding the ten negative actions is acting constructively. On top of that, if we save life, protect others' possessions, speak kindly, tell the truth, and so on, we create much positive karma. The result of meritorious actions is to have a fortunate rebirth as a human being or as a god of the desire realm. However, we should remember that although these are considered good rebirths, they still are within cyclic existence and are therefore unsatisfactory in the long run.

The third category, unfluctuating karma, leads to rebirth as a god of the form or formless realms. We create this karma by meditating with single-pointed concentration without having the wisdom that realizes emptiness. It is called unfluctuating because when we meditate on the meditative stabilization of the first form realm, for example, it leads to rebirth as a god of the first form realm, not another. The form and formless realm gods spend millions of years in bliss, but after that karma has been consumed, their life there ends. Then other karma created in previous lives ripens, and they again have to experience the grosser miseries of rebirth in other realms.

We can also speak of karma in terms of throwing and completing karma. Throwing karma is the karma that ripens into our future rebirths, the mental and physical aggregates we have later on. These actions "throw" or propel us into our next rebirth in cyclic existence. Throwing karma generally has all four components—of basis, thought, action, and conclusion—and can be positive or negative. Completing karma influences the specific events or circumstances of our future lives, such as the place we are born, the family we grow up in, our social status, and finances. When these karmas ripen, they "complete" our future rebirth in that once we have been "thrown" into a new body and mind, they complete what we experience.

Although karma is definite in that happiness comes only from constructive acts and suffering from destructive ones, there is still a considerable amount of flexibility as to how and when a particular karma ripens. For this reason it is important to purify any negative actions we have done and dedicate the positive ones. The ultimate purification, which prevents the ripening of a negative action and removes its imprint from our mind, is meditation on emptiness. Since emptiness is not easy to understand, in the meantime it is helpful to purify by more conventional means such as the four opponent powers. These are:

1. Regretting our mistaken actions
2. Taking refuge in the Three Jewels and generating bodhichitta
3. Resolving to avoid those actions again in the future
4. Engaging in some type of remedial action, that is, any virtuous deed such as spiritual practice, or service and generosity

Dedication prevents the power of our positive actions from being diminished or destroyed should we get angry or have cynical wrong views later. That is why at the completion of our meditation sessions or after we have done any positive actions, we should pause and dedicate the positive potential for the welfare of all sentient beings.

Contemplating karma and its effects makes us more mindful and conscientious in our daily life. By considering the long-term results of our actions, we will increase our motivation to restrain ourselves from harmful behavior and enhance our enthusiasm to act constructively. This will have a profound effect not only on our future lives, but also on the quality of our present one. Just think how much smoother our interactions with others would be if we consciously refrained from speaking harshly to them and pointed out their good qualities instead! It is no wonder that to observe our actions and their effects is the Buddha's first advice to us after we have taken refuge. Nevertheless, we must implement this gradually and continuously because it is unrealistic to expect ourselves to stop all unproductive behavior immediately. Rather, we must choose the behaviors that are the most destructive and work on those first. Then, gradually, we can refine our mindfulness and work on other actions.

CHAPTER NINE

THE FOUR NOBLE TRUTHS

Having trained our mind in the path of the initial-level practitioner, we now turn our attention to the path of the middle-level practitioner. Here, we look deeply into our present state as well as into our potential, as expressed in the four noble truths. As we come to understand these, a determination to be free from cyclic existence and to attain liberation will arise and grow in our mind. We will then have the confidence that through practicing the path taught by the Buddha, we can arrive at a state of lasting happiness.

9   **Like dew on the tip of a blade of grass, pleasures of the three
    worlds
    Last only a while and then vanish.
    Aspire to the never-changing
    Supreme state of liberation—
    This is the practice of Bodhisattvas.**

This stanza deals with the entire practice of the middle-level person, the essence of which is the four noble truths. The first line mentions the three worlds, also called the three realms of cyclic existence. These are the desire, form, and formless realms. The desire realm consists of a variety of beings: celestial gods, demigods, humans, animals, hungry ghosts, and hellish beings. It is called the desire realm because the beings there desire the objects of the five senses—pleasing sights, sounds, smells, tastes, and tangible objects—from which they derive some sense of happiness. The beings in the form realm have subtle bodies and those in the formless realm have only the four mental aggregates. They do not have bodies. These gods experience the ecstasy of the form and formless concentrations. But all these instances of happiness in the three realms are contaminated in that they are under the control of ignorance and the other disturbing attitudes. They are like a drop of dew on the tip of a blade of grass, for they do not last long and disintegrate very quickly. Since they deteriorate in a short while, they are not to be trusted. They cannot give us lasting happiness, and therefore there is no point in being attached to them. Nor should we put a lot of effort into gaining them. It is more worthwhile to put effort into attaining the unchangeable, supreme bliss of liberation and enlightenment.

The importance of understanding the four noble truths

The four noble truths are: the truth of unsatisfactoriness or suffering, the truth of its origin, the truth of its cessation, and the truth of the path to its cessation. They are called noble because they are four topics understood to be true by the noble ones, or aryas, who have directly realized reality.

We may wonder why it is important to meditate on the unsatisfactory nature of cyclic existence. To attain enlightenment requires effort. We have to traverse the ten Bodhisattva grounds to perfect the causes for enlightenment, and to do that we must first generate the altruistic intention seeking enlightenment in order to benefit all living beings. This altruistic intention must be preceded by compassion, a mind concerned about the suffering of other beings. Compassion for others can only arise if we clearly recognize and are concerned with our own suffering so that we are determined to be free from cyclic existence and attain liberation. To generate the determination to be free and the wish for liberation, we need to understand the faults of cyclic existence and the advantages of liberation. Without clearly seeing the disadvantages of cyclic existence, we will not wish to be free from it. Without wishing this for ourselves, how can we wish it for all sentient beings?

There are two methods to see the unsatisfactoriness of cyclic existence: contemplating the four noble truths and contemplating the twelve links. Here we will focus on contemplating the four noble truths. Through this we will understand how we wander in cyclic existence and how we can leave it. This will help us generate the determination to be free and the wish for liberation.

Buddha gave many teachings, all based on dependent arising, and all for the purpose of leading beings to nirvana, whether it be the hearer's nirvana, solitary realizer's nirvana, or the non-abiding nirvana of the Mahayana. These teachings were given to pacify suffering and its origin in the mindstreams of sentient beings. The four noble truths are explained in the literature of both the individual and the universal vehicles. They are also explained in the first, second, third, fourth and fifth chapters of Maitreya's *Ornament of Clear Realizations* and show the way we circle in samsara and how we can leave it. True suffering and true origin stand as one pair of cause and effect, showing how we wander in cyclic existence. True cessation and true path are another pair of cause and effect, and show how we can leave cyclic existence.

In both his middle and extensive *Expositions of the Gradual Path*, Lama Tsong Khapa said that those wishing liberation must know the four noble truths. In his *Commentary on Valid Cognition*, Dharmakirti said that it is not very important to know how many insects exist or the number of atoms in the earth, but it is important to know the four noble truths. By understanding them, we will know what is to be practiced and abandoned in order to attain liberation, and how to do this. The compassionate Buddha protects living beings from the suffering of unfortunate rebirths and cyclic existence by teaching what to practice and what to abandon if we want to realize a state of lasting happiness.

The wise and discerning who seek liberation and want to be free of cyclic existence should contemplate the four noble truths over a long time. Because they are essential to understand, the four noble truths were the first teachings the Buddha gave after he attained enlightenment. Everything we need to know about what to practice and what to abandon on the path is contained in this teaching. Those on the hearer, solitary realizer, and Bodhisattva paths all meditate on the four noble truths, gradually deepening their understanding of their profound meaning. The three higher trainings—ethical discipline, meditative stabilization and wisdom—which are included in the truth of the path, constitute the path to nirvana, and of these, the higher training in wisdom involves understanding the four noble truths and their sixteen aspects.

The four noble truths in brief

As mentioned, the Buddha's first teaching was the four noble truths, and within that, he first explained the truth of suffering. Here suffering does not refer only to overt pain but also to the unsatisfactory nature of cyclic existence. The Buddha said, "This is suffering; suffering is to be known." We do this by contemplating the three, six, and eight sufferings, some of which will be described below. True sufferings are the result of our disturbing attitudes and karma, which are the second noble truth, the true origin or cause of suffering. The root of all the disturbing attitudes is the misapprehension of a self, also called self-grasping ignorance. Based on this ignorance the root and auxiliary disturbing attitudes arise. These in turn act as the motivating thoughts for our actions, or karma, which bring about all the unsatisfactory—and often painful—experiences we undergo in cyclic existence. Thus, by meditating on true origin, we know the root of cyclic existence from which all suffering derives. In short, by meditating on true suffering and true origin we develop distress at being in cyclic existence and wish for liberation.

From what do we want to be liberated? From our disturbing attitudes and karma, which produce suffering. Liberation or nirvana is the state of these having become extinct, and this state is called true cessation, the third noble truth.

To eliminate disturbing attitudes and karma we need to practice the fourth noble truth, the path. This path is described in terms of the three higher trainings, or alternatively, in terms of method and wisdom, method being the practices we do to accumulate positive potential and wisdom being the practices which directly cut the root of cyclic existence. The two higher trainings in ethical discipline and meditative stabilization are the method side of the path, while the higher training in wisdom is the wisdom side of the path and is the actual antidote to the disturbing attitudes. To cut through the disturbing attitudes and karma and eliminate them forever from our mindstream, we need to generate an uncontaminated path, one which is not conjoined with the disturbing attitudes. The third higher training, wisdom, is just that. This also is a uniquely Buddhist assertion.

The higher training in ethical discipline includes the ethical training in the pratimoksha or individual liberation precepts, the Bodhisattva precepts, and the mantra precepts. However, here it refers mainly to the ethical discipline of abandoning the ten negative actions, which is the basic path. By following this ethical discipline, we stop the gross suffering of the three unfortunate rebirths, because its cause, the ten negative actions, is stopped.

Through the higher training in meditative stabilization we make our mind more powerful, enabling it to stay firmly on a virtuous object. The manifest disturbing attitudes are weakened through the practice of concentration, in that when a virtuous mind stays one-pointedly on its object, it blocks the arisal of non-virtuous mental states. An afflicted state of mind cannot arise at the same time as a virtuous state of mind.

In dependence upon the method, the higher trainings of ethical discipline and meditative stabilization, the higher training in wisdom cuts the very root or the fundamental cause of cyclic existence, the apprehension of a truly existing self. By cutting this, suffering and its causes are destroyed, and true cessation, which is the state of having extinguished the causes of suffering, is attained. True cessation is brought about in dependence on wisdom, specifically the uncontaminated wisdom realizing selflessness.

The hearers and solitary realizers at that point attain their respective personal liberation and become arhats, or foe destroyers, because they have totally destroyed the foe of the disturbing attitudes and karma. The great liberation which the Bodhisattvas aim for is more than a cessation of the disturbing attitudes and karma. It is also the extinguishment of all stains of the disturbing attitudes. The disturbing attitudes are often likened to onions in a pot. Once they are removed, their odor lingers on. This odor is analogous to the obscurations to omniscience which are the stains of dual appearance left on the mind even after the disturbing attitudes themselves have ceased. Once a Bodhisattva eliminates these, he or she attains full enlightenment. This is also called non-abiding nirvana, because one abides neither in cyclic existence nor in the complacent peace of personal liberation. The hearer and solitary realizer foe destroyers and the Buddha are the same in being foe destroyers, since all three have destroyed the enemy of disturbing attitudes and karma. But the method—as in method and wisdom—of the Universal Vehicle foe destroyer is the altruistic intention and the six far-reaching attitudes. This is superior to the method of the Individual Vehicle foe destroyer, the higher trainings in ethical discipline and meditative stabilization. From this point of view, a Buddha is superior to a hearer or solitary realizer foe destroyer.

There are various meanings of the term "higher" in the phrase "higher training." For example, the three trainings practiced by Buddhists are superior, or higher than, the three trainings practiced by non-Buddhists. In some cases, the practices of ethical discipline seem to be the same for non-Buddhists who also abandon killing, stealing, and so on. But there is a difference in method: the Buddhist practice is supported by a mind of pure refuge, while the non-Buddhist practice is not. Similarly, when training in meditative stabilization, both non-Buddhists and Buddhists can realize impermanence, but there is a difference in that the Buddhists' realization is held by refuge. Because they take refuge, their goal and motivation are different from non-Buddhists, and this influences the results of ethical discipline and meditative stabilization, making them the cause of liberation. Thus, they are called "higher trainings."

The order of the four noble truths

When the four noble truths are taught, sometimes the two causes— origin and path—are explained before their respective results—suffering and cessation. This order accords with the fourth chapter of *The Ornament of Realizations* and is the order in which they actually occur: first the cause happens, then the effect follows. This is referred to as "the actual cause and effect order." However, in general, the order of explanation is: true suffering, true origin, true cessation, and true path. This is the sequence the Buddha followed when he taught the four noble truths because it is very important to recognize true suffering at the beginning. In *The Compendium of Abhidharma*, Maitreya's *The Supreme Tantra*, and Vasubandhu's *Treasury of Abhidharma*, the truth of suffering is also explained first, for this is the order in which a meditator generates the realizations of the four noble truths. *The Supreme Tantra* instructs us first to know true suffering, which is like a sickness, then know its cause. This will inspire us to find the way to stop the cause.

We do analytical meditation to understand the various unsatisfactory conditions or sufferings of cyclic existence. When we gain an experience of them, we then place our mind firmly on that experience using stabilizing meditation. The more we meditate on suffering, the more we are motivated to rid ourselves of it. We will want to find out its causes and cease creating them. Thus, after contemplating true suffering, we contemplate true origin. Investigating this, we will see that suffering arises from karma, which is produced in dependence on the disturbing attitudes. These in turn are rooted in self-grasping ignorance. We will want to eliminate this ignorance, and will see that because it is a faulty attitude or misconception, it can be eliminated. Thus we will be certain that we can attain the true cessation of suffering and its origin. Through further contemplating the four noble truths, we will recognize that the way to abandon self-grasping ignorance is to meditate on the true path, since this path is principally the wisdom realizing the non-existence of the self that is adhered to by ignorance. This is the order in which the four noble truths unfold in meditation and thus is the order in which to practice them. So, although the actual order in which the four occur is first the causes and then the effects, when the Buddha taught for the purpose of practice, he explained the results first.

The truth of suffering

To generate the determination to free ourselves from all unsatisfactory circumstances or sufferings of cyclic existence, we must recognize them clearly. Here we consider the suffering of cyclic existence in general and the particular sufferings of each realm of existence. The Sanskrit word *duhkha* is often translated as suffering. When it is said that our life is permeated by *duhkha*, we might wonder, "What does that mean? I'm not suffering and in pain all the time!" That is true, and thus *duhkha* is sometimes translated as unsatisfactoriness, for it is true that our situation is by nature unsatisfactory and flawed. The general sufferings can be described in terms of the three or the six unsatisfactory conditions. The three are: the unsatisfactoriness of suffering, of change, and of the pervasive and compounded, the latter referring to the contaminated aggregates of body and mind.

The unsatisfactoriness of suffering is the feeling of pain. It is what all beings recognize as suffering: sickness, poverty, pain, depression, grief, and so on. The unsatisfactoriness of change refers to things such as good health, food, clothes, and good conditions in general that give us a feeling of physical or mental pleasure. Although this is what is commonly called happiness in the world, it is not real happiness. It is contaminated, for it is no more than an appearance of happiness due to a big suffering diminishing while, at the same time, a small suffering has just begun. It is called contaminated happiness because it is conjoined with the disturbing attitudes; it occurs under their influence. Therefore, it seems to be happiness, but it is not really, for it initiates the change into another discomfort or pain. For example, eating seems to give us pleasure, but as we keep eating we gradually become uncomfortable. What is actually occurring is that first we have the suffering of being hungry. As we eat, that suffering disappears and we call this happiness and consider it pleasurable. But at the same time as the suffering of hunger stops, the suffering of eating starts. At first that suffering is so small that we do not notice it. Gradually, as we

continue eating, the suffering grows until we definitely regard it as suffering, and we have to stop eating because we feel full or sometimes
even sick to our stomach. If eating were inherently pleasurable, the more
we did it, the happier we would be. But this is clearly not the case!

Another example is resting after a long walk. At first it seems to be
real pleasure, but it is only relief from the suffering of walking. If it
were an actual source of happiness, the more we rested, the more we
would enjoy it. Suffering would never arise and the happiness would
not change. However, eventually, we become restless and uncomfortable and want to walk again. The appearance of happiness stops and
the suffering of sitting becomes noticeable. Contaminated happiness
always changes into suffering. We can find many examples in our own
lives of this kind of situation.

The unsatisfactoriness of suffering and the unsatisfactoriness of
change are feelings. The unsatisfactoriness of suffering is an unpleasant feeling, a feeling of discontent, while the unsatisfactoriness of
change is a feeling of satisfaction and pleasure, albeit one which soon
changes to dissatisfaction.

The pervasive compounded unsatisfactoriness is more subtle. It
refers to our aggregates which are under the influence of the disturbing attitudes and karma. It is called "pervasive" because it pervades
all births in cyclic existence, and it is called "compounded" because it
comes together due to, or is compounded by, disturbing attitudes and
karma.

All living beings possess four or five aggregates that arise due to
disturbing attitudes and karma. The five aggregates are: the form aggregate, which is our physical body; the feeling aggregate, which refers to our pleasant, unpleasant, and neutral sensations; the discrimination aggregate, which discerns one object from another; the consciousness aggregate, which includes our six primary consciousnesses
(visual, auditory, olfactory, gustatory, tactile, and mental); and the aggregate of compositional factors, which includes all other aspects of
ourselves, such as the disturbing attitudes, the virtuous attitudes, and
so forth. All the beings of the desire realm and those of the seventeen
abodes of the form realm have five aggregates. The gods of the four
levels of the formless realm (infinite space, infinite consciousness,
nothingness, and the peak of cyclic existence) have four aggregates.
They do not have a body produced by disturbing attitudes and karma.
These aggregates are pervasive compounded unsatisfactoriness.

Although human and god rebirths are considered fortunate, they are full of problems. As a human being we have the sufferings of birth, aging, sickness, death, the misery of not being able to get the things we like, of being separated from the good things we have, and of encountering many situations that we dislike. Life in the god realm is also unsatisfactory. The demigods have unbearable jealousy towards the higher gods and are in constant conflict. The other desire realm gods suffer because as they approach death, their radiance fades and they are shunned by their peers. Also, during the last part of their lives, they are tormented by precognition of death and the miserable rebirth they will have afterwards.

The form and formless realm gods are still obliged to go from life to life, leaving one set of aggregates and taking a new set. They have no suffering feelings like the beings in the desire realm. Nor do they have the unsatisfactoriness of change because it is experienced only in the desire realm by persistent use of a pleasurable object so that it starts causing us pain. However, the form and formless realm gods do experience pervasive compounded unsatisfactoriness, because their aggregates are under the influence of disturbing attitudes and karma. Due to this, their happy situation eventually comes to an end, and due to previously created karma they take rebirth in a realm with grosser forms of suffering. These different forms of suffering will unfold when their karma which resulted in rebirth in the form or formless realms runs out.

We are born as a form or formless realm god due to having meditated on the actual concentrations of those realms in previous lives and being attached to the bliss of those concentrations. Through that we accumulate karma which propelled us to take form or formless realm rebirths. Although we attained calm abiding, because we did not develop the wisdom realizing selflessness which is the actual antidote to attachment and ignorance, we are still trapped in cyclic existence. When the karmic potential for those form and formless realm rebirths is exhausted, we descend again to lower forms of life. Not being beyond suffering, we are still chained by pervasive compounded unsatisfactoriness.

In previous lifetimes, we developed calm abiding, attained those concentrations and were born as form and formless realm gods many times. But these states eventually deteriorated because we neglected to take the altruistic intention and selflessness as the object of our meditation. This indicates that calm abiding in itself is not sufficient for liberation, although it is indispensable for it and is important in certain contexts.

The formless realm, in particular the gods of the realm called "Peak of Cyclic Existence," is the most subtle rebirth in cyclic existence. The realm with the grossest suffering is the hell realm. It is said that all of cyclic existence, from the top to the bottom—from formless realm god to hell being—is unsatisfactory. There is no place in cyclic existence where we will find lasting peace and happiness. As we have seen, even those with wonderful rebirths do not experience them forever and must continuously wander through the various types of rebirth impelled by disturbing attitudes and karma.

The six unsatisfactory conditions

Contemplating the six unsatisfactory conditions also strengthens our determination to be free and our wish to attain liberation. These six are:

1. Nothing is fixed. No situation in cyclic existence is fixed; things are always changing. Even within one life, we can see friends become enemies and enemies become friends. We see that someone can be wealthy one moment and destitute the next. One day the Buddha's disciple Shariputra came across what was apparently a normal family scene, a woman with her baby on her lap sitting at a table eating fish and kicking the dog as it came to beg for the fish bones. With his psychic powers Shariputra saw that previously the woman's mother and father had lived in the house. Her father used to catch fish in a nearby lake, and as a result was born as a fish there and was now served up on his daughter's plate. The woman's mother, due to her strong attachment to the house, had been reborn as a dog there, and the enemy of the family had been so attached to this woman that he had been born as her child. Shariputra thought, "How ironic! The woman is cuddling her worst enemy, chewing her mother's bones, and beating her father. Cyclic existence makes me laugh." In the same way, nothing in our lives is fixed, certain, or secure, for the nature of cyclic existence is constant change and instability.

2. No pleasure we experience in cyclic existence gives true satisfaction. In our attachment to the pleasures of life, we are like a moth who, attracted to the light of a candle, flies into the flame. Experiencing sensual pleasures with attachment is like drinking salt water: it cannot quench our thirst but only makes it worse. Who do we know

who has enough money? Everyone always wants more and better; first we want a hundred dollars, then when we have that, we want a thousand, then a million. We are never satisfied and constantly wish for something else that we think will give us more happiness.

3. Over and over we give up our life and die. No matter who we are, where we live, how powerful, famous, rich, or well-loved we are, we eventually must die.

4. Again and again we pass on to a new life. Since beginningless time, over and over again, we enter a new life, after a time it ends, and we take another rebirth. How do we know rebirth exists? Our present mind is a product both of the mind we had in a previous moment and of many other cooperative factors. However, the previous moment's mind is its perpetuating cause because that is what actually transforms into our present mind. Similarly, yesterday's mind also had a perpetuating cause, the mind from the previous day. Following this back, we see that at the beginning of this life, the perpetuating cause of our mind was the previous moment of mind which existed before this life. Thus we can establish the existence of previous lives. Since beginningless time we have been taking birth and dying and taking birth again, experiencing many problems in each lifetime. Our present life is remarkably fortunate: with it we have a chance to bring an end to this suffering. If we do not take advantage of this opportunity, we will go on life after life, with no respite from this confusion.

5. Changing from high to low. Even in this life it is possible to lose our high social position or status and be faced with a low one, to go from rich to poor, powerful to oppressed, well-respected to denigrated. Even if this has not happened to us yet, we can see many examples of it in the newspaper, and there is no guarantee it will not happen to us. In addition, from one life to the next, our status can also change radically, going from higher realm to lower realm and vice-versa.

6. Being alone. We are born alone and we die alone. We go through illness and various problems alone. No one can share these sufferings with us or experience them for us. Thus, it is pointless to be attached to friends and relatives who not only cannot take away our suffering, but cannot even prevent their own.

As we contemplate these six disadvantages of cyclic existence, our interest in continually being reborn in it will fade and our obsession to attain its pleasures will be deflated. In our mind will arise a strong wish to know the causes for such suffering and cease creating them, as well as a determination to be free from cyclic existence and to attain the lasting happiness of liberation. Interestingly, our lack of interest in remaining in cyclic existence and our focus on liberation will make our present lives more peaceful. Because we will not constantly be grasping at pleasure from people and objects, we will be able to relate to them more naturally and feel more contented.

What to practice and what to abandon

In *The Stages of the Shravaka*, Arya Asanga explains positive and negative karma and through this, we can understand what to practice and what to abandon on the path. Of the four noble truths, we need to practice or adopt true cessation and true path, and we need to abandon true suffering and true origin. Because all rebirths in cyclic existence are ultimately unsatisfactory, Asanga says that all karma that causes them is negative and to be avoided. From this viewpoint, not only non-virtuous karma but also virtuous throwing karma—karma which propels us into fortunate rebirths as gods or humans—are considered negative. They are negative in that they are to be avoided because they make us take birth in cyclic existence. On the other hand, all causes for liberation are considered positive karma in this context.

When we discussed karma before, it was said that certain karma is virtuous or positive because it brings fortunate rebirths. But here, for that same reason, Asanga counts it as negative: it produces happy rebirths as a human or god, but it also keeps us bound in cyclic existence. For Asanga any action resulting in rebirth in cyclic existence is negative. Any action destroying cyclic existence together with its results is positive. Nevertheless, karma which brings rebirth as a human or god is temporarily to be practiced because those rebirths are of temporary benefit. For the time being, we need them in order to practice the path to true liberation. However, in the long term they are undesirable and to be forsaken because they keep us chained to cyclic existence with all of its constantly recurring problems.

Similarly, we previously praised a precious human birth for its freedom and leisure. Yet now it is considered faulty, and because it is a rebirth in cyclic existence it is to be given up. We should not think that these two ideas conflict. Although a precious human life with freedom and leisure is a rebirth in cyclic existence, it also gives us the opportunity to attain everlasting freedom from rebirth in cyclic existence.

That is why we need it—temporarily. Similarly, the five obects of desire—pleasurable sights, sounds, smells, tastes, and tangible objects—are nice to experience and are the result of virtuous karma. They are worthy as a short-term goal, and the causes producing them are temporarily to be practiced because these objects bring temporary benefit. But on a deeper level, they chain us to cyclic existence. If we act constructively in this life, good results such as having access to food, clothes, and so on, will come. Receiving these objects is considered pleasurable by the world, and on that basis an action causing us to have them is called virtuous. But because our motivation for such actions is often mixed with the eight worldly concerns, they are not usually considered the cause of liberation.

Practicing ethical discipline with the wish for a good rebirth is not the cause of nirvana; it is the cause of samsara. It is a meritorious karma throwing a samsaric rebirth; therefore it is not a positive karma according to Arya Asanga's *The Stages of the Shravaka*. It is not part of reversing samsara, but of entering it. An action done with the motivation to attain nirvana is the cause of nirvana. Its final result will not come until nirvana, but its other good results will continue to come while we are still in cyclic existence.

An action done with the motivation for the happiness of this life, without the thought of liberation or enlightenment, cannot bring a human birth. Such an action is not Dharma. Only when we are motivated to attain a higher rebirth, liberation, or enlightenment does the action become Dharma. Nonetheless, if we give food to the hungry or medicine to the sick with the motivation to stop their suffering, it is a positive action. If someone dies with the wish to complete a worthwhile project, such as building a hospital, which he did not have time to finish while alive, this wish alone is not sufficient to cause a human rebirth so he can finish it. But, it will bring a good result.

The drawbacks of not recognizing suffering

Right now many of us wish for liberation, yet sometimes we cannot keep ourselves from creating the causes for cyclic existence. When we understand true suffering well, our wish for liberation will become firm. At present our resolve to reach liberation is not firm because we think of suffering, but not deeply. The deluded attitude believing that the unsatisfactoriness of change is true happiness easily arises in us because we are not yet deeply convinced that all happiness in cyclic existence is contaminated and is in fact only a variety of suffering. To remedy this, we should meditate on true suffering more often and explore its meaning deeply. Then our wish for liberation will become firm.

We consider many things—clothes, food, good health, nice possessions, financial security, the higher rebirths—as true happiness. As a result, we are attached to them and create more causes for suffering in cyclic existence in order to gain them. Thinking that the human birth is something marvelous, we work at creating the causes that propel us toward it. In fact all we are doing is creating the cause for yet another rebirth in cyclic existence, together with all the problems that such a rebirth involves.

If we understand that by its nature, cyclic existence is unsatisfactory, we will have a deep aversion to it. If we do not have a deep aversion to it, we will not be determined to be free, and therefore will not be able to destroy our self-grasping ignorance, which is the root of cyclic existence. In that case, we will not be able to attain liberation. However, when we deeply feel the extent to which we suffer in cyclic existence, we will automatically want to abandon the true origin of suffering, attain the true cessation, and meditate on the true path. Having realized true suffering, we will easily realize the other three of the four noble truths. Thus it is said: suffering is to be known. The origin is to be abandoned. The cessation is to be attained. The path is to be practiced. The determination to be free is the wish for ourselves to be free of cyclic existence. When we wish others to be free, that is compassion.

What is this cyclic existence to which we are developing aversion? In general, it is the three realms and the beings inhabiting them that have arisen from the disturbing attitudes and karma. However, cyclic existence mainly refers to the contaminated appropriated aggregates. They are considered contaminated because they are conjoined with disturbing attitudes and are called "appropriated" because we take them due to our disturbing attitudes and karma. From this viewpoint, cyclic existence is not an external place that we have to leave, but the state of again and again taking the contaminated aggregates of body and mind under the influence of disturbing attitudes and karma. These contaminated appropriated aggregates are also pervasive compounded unsatisfactoriness. They are at the root of the unsatisfactoriness of suffering and of change, and pervade them. The contaminated appropriated aggregates are called compounded because they arise from disturbing attitudes and karma, they induce all our future suffering, and they are the basis of all the suffering that we have at present. Thus they compound or collect suffering.

Aversion to the unsatisfactoriness of suffering is easy to generate. All beings in cyclic existence dislike mental and physical pain and want to be free from it. Aversion to the unsatisfactoriness of change is not as easy to generate, for we generally feel that it is happiness although it is not. If it were real happiness, the more we had of it, the more the pleasure should increase and never give way to unhappiness. It should be pleasant when produced, pleasant while it lasts, and when it finishes we should feel happy. But on the contrary, when the appearance of happiness which is the unsatisfactoriness of change comes to an end, we are not pleased. Activities such as eating, being with our friends, lying on the beach, and having sex, at the beginning seem wonderful, but if we continue doing them without respite, they become painful. Similarly, all pleasures in cyclic existence are unsatisfactory because they change and are not stable, and are thus contaminated happiness. Therefore, they are not reliable and are said to be faulty.

Aversion to the unsatisfactoriness of change alone is not the determination to be free, and the wish to be free is not the wish for liberation. Even some non-Buddhists have aversion to the unsatisfactoriness of change. For a real, profound aversion to cyclic existence to arise within us, we have to recognize pervasive compounded unsatisfactoriness and generate a deep aversion to it. Then we will have the determination to be free from cyclic existence and the wish for liberation. This determination to be free is the support for the paths of the hearers, solitary realizers, and Bodhisattvas. Developing it by meditating on the unsatisfactory nature of cyclic existence is therefore indispensable for all practitioners.

A prisoner on death row might have an influential friend who can arrange for him to receive food and not to be beaten. But though he is treated well, since he has been sentenced to death, there is no happiness in his heart. Similarly, while we still have the pervasive compounded unsatisfactoriness—a body and mind under the control of the disturbing attitudes and karma—there is no true happiness in cyclic existence. Like a person carrying a load of thorns on her back has no happiness until she reaches a place to put it down, we will have no real happiness until our pervasive compounded unsatisfactoriness has come to an end.

What does it mean to be under the control of disturbing attitudes and karma? It means that we have no freedom to have the secure happiness we wish for, and we are constantly buffeted by our misconceptions, negative emotions, and the actions we have done motivated by them. A simple example is when we try to meditate. It is difficult to sit down on our cushion, for our mind sees many other things to do that seem more important or interesting. When we do sit, our thoughts wander here and there, and it is difficult to keep our attention on the object of meditation. In addition, even though we wish to be comfortable, our knees and back hurt. After we finish meditating, we may get up and encounter an unpleasant situation that we aren't expecting. For example, someone may say something that doesn't suit our ego, and we instantly become angry or depressed. We carry that bad mood around all day, and even though we want to have good relationships with others, we are grumpy. From this example, we can see that although we wish to be happy and kind, it is very difficult to do. Our disturbing attitudes and karma constantly interfere. This is what is meant when we say we are under their control. Happily, since the disturbing attitudes are all based on ignorance, and ignorance can be eliminated through generating the wisdom realizing emptiness, the situation is not hopeless. The possibility of liberation exists.

An elaborate explanation of the four noble truths involves a discussion of the sixteen aspects, which are impermanence and so forth. Each truth has four attributes. The aggregates, which are true suffering, are impermanent, suffering, empty, and selfless. Disturbing attitudes and karma, which are true origins, are causes, origins, conditions, and strong producers. True cessation, which is a state in which sufferings and their causes have been extinguished, is cessation, peace, contentment, and definitively emerged. The true path, the wisdom realizing emptiness, is a path, suitable, establishing, and definitely emerging. Although in English the four noble truths are each generally translated in the singular—for example, true suffering, not true sufferings—in fact, each one consists of many things. That is, there are many things which are true sufferings, true origins of suffering, true cessations, and true paths.

The four attributes of true suffering

As mentioned above, the Buddha said that suffering is to be known. The way to do this is to contemplate the three sufferings and the six sufferings. True suffering mainly refers to the contaminated appropriated aggregates. In a broader sense, it also refers to the world and its inhabitants. Thus the things in our environment as well as our mental and physical aggregates are called true sufferings because they are all produced under the influence of disturbing attitudes and karma. As an illustration of true suffering, sometimes we use the contaminated aggregates and sometimes the person. In general we can select any part of the environment or its inhabitants that have arisen by the power of disturbing attitudes and karma, and the same points can be made with regard to it. What is to be known are the four attributes of true suffering: impermanent, suffering, empty, and selfless. Here, the attribute of suffering is slightly different from true sufferings, for suffering refers to the three sufferings or unsatisfactory conditions, while true sufferings refer to the world and its inhabitants—and especially our contaminated aggregates of body and mind—which are under the power of disturbing attitudes and karma.

If we do not know the four attributes of true sufferings, we will have the four contrary conceptions of apprehending true sufferings as pure, pleasant, permanent, and self-existent. These four misconceptions are disturbing attitudes and thus are included in true origin, the cause of suffering. Understanding that true sufferings are impermanent and so on is, therefore, the antidote to the cause of suffering and is included in the true path.

The four attributes of true sufferings are that they are impermanent, suffering, empty, and selfless. Of the four contrary conceptions regarding true suffering, apprehending them as pleasant focuses on the feelings in our mindstream, apprehending them as pure focuses on our body, and the apprehensions of permanence and self-existence focus on the person.

The misconception apprehending the impermanent as permanent views our aggregates as not disintegrating moment by moment. Therefore, we feel that we are permanent and unchanging. This way of thinking arises due to the imprint of previous grasping at permanence and is opposed to the first attribute, impermanence. Apprehending things as permanent, we think we will live for a long time. Then, motivated by the three poisonous attitudes of anger, attachment, and ignorance, we engage in negative actions in order to gain the good things of this life.

Understanding impermanence—specifically the gross impermanence of death—is an antidote to the wrong apprehension of permanence and the problems it creates. When we think about the three roots and nine reasons of the death meditation and they become clear to us, they block the thought that we are staying here long and we lose interest in doing a lot of unnecessary things to obtain the happiness of this life. That is how the third misconception of true sufferings, apprehending them as permanent, is opposed by understanding the first attribute, impermanence.

The misapprehension of true sufferings as pure principally concerns seeing our body as clean and pure. We also apprehend certain feelings as real pleasure—such as the feeling we have after a good meal or when we get a promotion—whereas in fact they are only the unsatisfactoriness of change. Seeing the aggregates as in the nature of suffering opposes this faulty appearance of pleasure. In actuality our aggregates are in the nature of suffering because they chain us to the three unsatisfactory conditions. Apprehending the aggregates as pure and apprehending them as pleasant are both modes that think of the aggregates as pleasing, and the aggregates appear pleasing to both of these misconceptions. By seeing the aggregates in terms of the three sufferings, they will start to appear as displeasing, and we will think of them as displeasing. In this way, understanding the suffering aspect of true suffering is the antidote to both the apprehension of the aggregates as pure and the apprehension of the aggregates as pleasant.

The last of the four contrary conceptions related to true suffering is self-grasping. It has two antidotes: understanding emptiness and understanding selflessness. Selflessness is what is to be proven, and empty of self-existence as the same or different is the reason that proves it. In the context of the four noble truths, self and selfless are generally explained according to the views of the lower philosophical tenets. But here we will explain them according to the highest—that is, the most precise and accurate one—the Prasangika Madhyamika. This will help us later in the text when we go into more depth regarding the emptiness of inherent existence. "Self-existent" means independently existent, that is, existing without depending on anything at all. For example, our gut feel of "I" is that there is a self independent of causes and conditions, parts, or a consciousness which conceives and labels "I." To prove the lack of self-existence of the person, for example, we say: the person is not self-existent because of not being self-existently the same as or different from the aggregates. When we talk of the I as not being the same or different, we are discussing its relationship with our mental and physical aggregates. Is the person inherently the same as the body or the mind? To be the same, the person and the aggregates would have to refer to the same object and have the same name. But when we examine, we find that the person and his or her aggregates are not identical in all aspects. Is the person inherently different from the aggregates? To be different, they would have to be totally unrelated and independent of each other, but upon examination we find that the person depends on his or her aggregates. If the person were self-existent, it would have to be either exactly the same as the aggregates in every way or absolutely different and totally independent from them.

Sometimes we say that the person is not self-existent because of not being self-existently one or many. In this case, we are looking at the I, or person, and examining whether there is one self-existent I or many I's. For example, if someone claims that a house is haunted, it is appropriate to ask how many ghosts there are. There must be one or many because everything exists as either one or many. Similarly, if the person were self-existent, it would have to exist as either one or more than one.

We examine: the person, for example, is not self-existent because of not being self-existently the same as or different from the aggregates which are its basis. The first part of the reason indicates that the person is not self-existently the same as the aggregates, and the last shows the person is not self-existently different from them. The reason therefore shows that the person is not self-existent as the same or different, and therefore is not self-existent at all, since there is no other way of being self-existent other than being self-existently the same as or different from the aggregates. By understanding that the person is empty of being self-existently the same or different, we understand the third aspect of true suffering, its being empty. Because the person is empty, it is not self-existent; it is selfless, and this is the fourth aspect of true suffering. This will be explained in more depth in the chapter on emptiness.

In summary, the first aspect of true suffering, impermanence, is the opponent to the third wrong conception, grasping at true sufferings, such as the aggregates, as permanent. The second aspect, suffering, is the opponent to the first and second wrong conceptions, grasping at the aggregates being pure and pleasurable; and the third and fourth aspects, emptiness and selflessness, are joint opponents to the fourth wrong conception grasping at true sufferings as self-existent. Understanding the impermanent and suffering aspects of true suffering does not actually free us from cyclic existence. However, it is an essential preliminary. Understanding emptiness and selflessness are the direct antidote to cyclic existence.

There are various levels of subtlety in describing the self that the self-grasping mind (the fourth misconception) apprehends. The coarsest level of self-grasping is believing that the self or person is permanent, partless, and independent. A subtler level is believing the self is self-sufficient and substantially existing. From the Prasangika Madhyamika viewpoint the principal antidote to the self-grasping of the person and of phenomena is understanding that they are not self-existently the same as or different from the aggregates. If we understand this clearly, we will be able to harm the conception that apprehends them as self-existent.

In brief, by understanding the four attributes of true sufferings—impermanence, suffering, empty, and selfless—we will eliminate the four misconceptions which incorrectly conceive of the aggregates as being pure, pleasurable, permanent, and self. Until we eliminate those misconceptions, we will continuously wander in cyclic existence, suffering as a result of the negative karma we create under their sway. Not realizing that true sufferings such as our possessions, our body, and our mind are impermanent, we will continue to feel that these are permanent. Consequently, we will feel that we will live for a long time and will engage in many negative actions to acquire and protect the things we think we need and want for a long stay. Not realizing these things are in the nature of suffering, we will think they are pure and pleasurable, and will engage in various destructive actions to procure and protect them.

Misconceiving the environment and the beings in it as permanent, pure, and pleasurable prevents us from disliking cyclic existence and finding it distressing. However, when we see clearly that they are impermanent, unclean, and dissatisfactory by nature, we will finally recognize that cyclic existence is dreadful and will want to be free of it and its suffering. At that point we will want to learn what causes these sufferings, and naturally we will want to avail ourselves of any method that can free us from it. We will see that the four misconceptions have no basis in reality and therefore they can be abandoned by generating the wisdom which is opposed to them.

We can examine the person in light of the four aspects. The person is impermanent because of being conditionally produced. The literal translation of "conditionally produced" is "occasionally produced," and it means that something is produced only when its causes and conditions are assembled. If something were permanent, it could not be conditionally produced. It would always remain the same, without changing. Conditional production indicates momentary existence and moment-by-moment disintegration. Permanent phenomena such as uncompounded space, true cessation, and emptiness can never be conditionally produced because they are not produced from causes and conditions. A person, on the other hand, exists only when the causes and conditions for his or her existence assemble.

An ordinary person is in the nature of suffering because of being controlled by disturbing attitudes and karma. Therefore a person is not autonomous or independent because he or she is under the influence of disturbing attitudes and karma. A person is empty and selfless because of not existing as self-existently the same as or different from the aggregates.

True origin

True origin refers to all disturbing attitudes and karma, for they are the origin or cause of true sufferings. The disturbing attitudes are divided into two categories: the six root disturbing attitudes and the auxiliary disturbing attitudes. The root disturbing attitudes are the roots of the auxiliary ones and they are the root of cyclic existence as well. They are attachment, anger, ignorance, pride, deluded doubt, and wrong views. The twenty auxiliary disturbing attitudes can be researched in texts on mind and awareness (Tib. *lo rig*), and include mental factors such as spite, belligerence, laziness, jealousy, lack of personal integrity, and lack of consideration for others. There are various ways to speak of karma as well. Some of these, such as throwing and completing karma, and meritorious, non-meritorious, and unfluctuating karma, were discussed in the previous chapter. In addition, there is karma which will definitely be experienced during the life in which it is created, karma which will be experienced in the very next life, and karma which will ripen in any lifetime following the next. All of these are the cause, or origin, of suffering.

There are four wrong conceptions connected to true origin. The first one thinks that true suffering has no cause. The last three hold that true suffering is produced from a cause that is discordant, that is, a cause which in fact is not the real cause of true suffering. These wrong conceptions prevent us from knowing that true origins are to be abandoned and that we are able to abandon them. The four misconceptions are:

1. Suffering is causeless
2. Suffering has just one cause
3. The cause of suffering is permanent and unchanging
4. Suffering is created by an external deity such as God or
   Ishvara

The four attributes of true origin are: cause, origin, condition, and strong producer. By understanding these four, we can dispel four wrong ideas about the cause of true suffering. First, true suffering has its causes because it is conditionally produced. Because it occurs only when its causes and conditions—disturbing attitudes and karma— are complete, suffering has causes. It does not exist without a cause, and it is not produced when its causes are not complete. This refutes the first wrong conception regarding true origin, thinking that suffering is causeless.

Second, when we examine deeply, we see that true sufferings have many causes. The main ones are disturbing attitudes and karma. These are the origin of suffering. Thus, all suffering in cyclic existence occurs not by chance or accident, and not just by one cause alone, but as a result of specific causes. When these causes are stopped, the resultant suffering will automatically be stopped.

Third, disturbing attitudes and karma are strong producers of suffering. They act forcefully to produce all the suffering we experience, from an upset stomach to the misery of the hell realms. Fourth, disturbing attitudes act as the immediate conditions that give rise to suffering. For example, when our minds are under the influence of a strong disturbing attitude, the stage is set for us to be miserable before very long.

The realization that true suffering is produced from disturbing attitudes and karma is a tool sufficiently powerful to eliminate all four misconceptions. Because suffering is produced by disturbing attitudes and karma, it is not causeless. There is not just one cause but many— disturbing attitudes and karma. Disturbing attitudes are impermanent and conditioned themselves, therefore the cause of suffering is not permanent. Because suffering is caused by disturbing attitudes, it is not caused by God, Ishvara, or the devil. Understanding that suffering is only produced when its causes—disturbing attitudes and karma—are present gives us the impetus to apply the antidotes to the disturbing attitudes when they arise in our daily life. It also encourages us to meditate on the true path—the wisdom realizing emptiness—in order to eliminate the disturbing attitudes and karma from our mindstream completely.

We can also understand the faults of cyclic existence by contemplating the twelve links. Although they will not be explained here, you can read about them in other texts, such as *The Meaning of Life* by His Holiness the Dalai Lama. These twelve links describe the process through which we continuously take birth in cyclic existence and the way that we can reverse this process. Seven of the links are effects, and they result from the remaining five links, which are causes. The seven effects are true sufferings, and the five causes are true origins. Thus, the entire process of wandering in cyclic existence is contained in true suffering and true cause. Clearly, the topics of the four noble truths and the twelve links are not mere theories meant simply for intellectual debate. Rather, they actually describe what we are experiencing right now, and thus are directly applicable to our lives.

True cessation

True cessation, or liberation, is the state of extinguishment in which disturbing attitudes, karma, and the suffering they produce have been extinguished. The four attributes of true cessation are cessation, peace, contentment, and definitively emerged. These can be logically established, and understanding them eliminates the four misconceptions about true cessation. The four attributes are:

1. Liberation is a cessation because the disturbing attitudes, karma, and the suffering produced from them have ceased.

2. It is peace because the disturbing attitudes and karma in a person's mindstream have been pacified, and therefore the troubles resulting from them have been pacified.

3. It is auspicious because when the disturbing attitudes, karma, and suffering are pacified in our mindstream, there is unfathomable happiness and pleasure.

4. Liberation has definitively emerged from suffering and its origin because these have been abandoned in such a way that they cannot reappear again. Once the disturbing attitudes, karma, and suffering are pacified, the resulting peace cannot deteriorate and will never return again.

These four attributes are the antidotes to the four misconceptions related to true cessation:

1. Thinking there is no cessation, i.e., that it is not possible to cease suffering and its origins

2. Holding certain contaminated states as liberation

3. Holding certain suffering states as liberation

4. Thinking there is liberation, but it does not last and one
   can once again experience suffering

Some people make the mistake of thinking that a state which is actually contaminated is liberation. They must be shown that it is not liberation. Liberation is the extinction of true sufferings and their causes. For example, the ancient Indian philosophical school of the Samkhyas believed that when a person realizes that all things he experiences are the emanation of something called the "general principal" or "cosmic force," the emanations dissolve back into it and the person attains liberation. They understand liberation incorrectly and think that something which is not liberation is liberation. They also think that a path which will not lead to liberation is the correct path, and they are therefore mistaken about the true cessations and true paths. This is a great tragedy, for if people mistakenly meditate diligently on something which is not the method for attaining liberation thinking it is the method, they will spend their life fruitlessly. They will not be able to attain the happiness and peace they wish because they are not creating the proper causes for it. Nor have they properly identified the causes of their problems, so they are unable to remove them. At the time of death, they will feel disillusioned and even angry, and these thoughts will have an adverse effect on their future rebirths.

The Buddha and his followers, Nagarjuna, Asanga, the great siddhas, and pandits pointed out these mistakes, but not out of jealousy or intolerance of others' views. Whenever they engaged in debate with other philosophical or religious traditions, the great masters did so with the motivation to help. They did not wish simply to prove the Buddhist viewpoint correct or to defeat their opponents. Rather, with compassion, in order to help people find a path that will bring the happiness they want, the Buddhist sages would point out that a certain path was mistaken or that a particular teacher was leading others on an ineffective path.

The cessation of the causes of our contaminated appropriated aggregates exists. Why? Because there is something which fatally harms their cause. All of our unsatisfactory conditions and experiences arise due to our own actions or karma. Our actions are motivated by our disturbing attitudes, and among these is self-grasping ignorance, which is the first of the twelve links. This ignorance is the very root of all the disturbing attitudes and therefore of cyclic existence in general. What harms this ignorance is the wisdom understanding selflessness. How? Ignorance apprehends self-existent phenomena while wisdom knows these phenomena lack self-existence. These two directly oppose each other, but ignorance hasn't got any valid foundation to stand on, whereas wisdom does. Therefore, when we meditate on that wisdom, it counteracts and eliminates ignorance. Due to removing this root cause, the other disturbing attitudes that arise from ignorance are damaged, and we no longer create karma under their influence. When these causes of suffering are stopped, the resultant suffering cannot arise. This is liberation. In this way, we can understand that liberation exists.

Tibetan Buddhism organizes Buddhist philosophy into four systems: Vaibhashika, Sautrantika, Chittamatra, and Madhyamika. The latter has two branches: Svatantrika and Prasangika. All of these talk of suffering, origin, liberation, and path in broadly the same way. However, what they assert to be the self-grasping ignorance that is the root of samsara varies in subtlety. For example, the Prasangika, which is the highest system, says that the root of samsara is the self-grasping ignorance that grasps inherently existent persons and phenomena. All the other systems say that this ignorance grasps a self-sufficient, substantially existent person. The lower systems say that to attain liberation we need only to realize the lack of such a self-sufficient substantially existent person, while the Prasangika says that that alone is not sufficient to eliminate the ignorance which is the root of cyclic existence. The Prasangika system states that we need to realize something much more subtle, the lack of inherent existence of both the person and all other phenomena.

Understanding the lower systems' presentations creates a basis for approaching the subtlest Buddhist assertion of selflessness, that of the Prasangika. As one goes from one system to the next progressively, one's view of selflessness becomes more and more subtle. In the lowest schools, one starts out by understanding the lack of a permanent, single, and independent self, and the lack of a self-sufficient, substantially existing self. The Chittamatrins assert a selflessness which is the lack of difference in substance between an object and the valid cognizer apprehending it. The Svatantrika assert a selflessness which is an emptiness of true existence, while still accepting that things exist by their own characteristics. The Prasangika assert the emptiness of a self existing by its own characteristics, i.e., inherently. This will be discussed further in the chapter on emptiness. It is helpful to know that great Buddhist sages of the past have explored this topic thoroughly and that their thoughts have been preserved so that we can learn from them.

According to each of the four schools of tenets, liberation is possible. All four agree that liberation is the state in which the cause of the contaminated appropriated aggregates—disturbing attitudes and karma—has been extinguished. In other terms, they say that liberation is the state in which we are never again obliged to take rebirth in cyclic existence under the force of disturbing attitudes and karma. The essential point for us to understand is that there is a state in which the contaminated appropriated aggregates which arise due to disturbing attitudes and karma have been extinguished. Knowing this gives us a tremendous sense of hope and inspiration.

Having thought of this, we need to examine what causes the contaminated appropriated aggregates, for if we can eliminate these causes, then their effects also are stopped, just as when a pot of oil finishes, the light fueled by it dies also. Through contemplating either the twelve links or true suffering and true origin, we see that the cause of these contaminated aggregates is ignorance. This ignorance is harmed by the wisdom of selflessness, which is contradictory to it. If we generate that wisdom and thereby destroy the cause, then the effect, all the suffering in cyclic existence, is destroyed. By practicing the path, the continuum of our mind will become purer and purer, life after life, until enlightenment is actualized.

The point is that we need to know the way of actualizing liberation. It cannot be attained with blind faith. We need to be clear about exactly what liberation is, what the path to liberation is, and how that liberation is attained by practicing that path. Through reasoning we establish that liberation can be attained because the cause of the contaminated appropriated aggregates can be harmed and ultimately eliminated by the wisdom realizing selflessness, which is opposite to it. Meditating on an antidote which is opposite to a disturbed state of mind causes that mind to weaken. For example, as the heat in a room increases, to that extent the cold there decreases. The more familiar we are with patience, the weaker our anger will be. Through familiarity with the wisdom realizing selflessness, over time our self-grasping will get weaker until it is extinguished. If we think about this, we will clearly see that liberation is possible, and that the true path to attain it is the wisdom realizing selflessness.

True path

The true path, wisdom realizing selflessness, has four attributes: path, suitable, establishing, and definitely emerging:

1. Wisdom realizing selflessness is a path because it is a valid path for attaining liberation, be it the liberation of the hearer, solitary realizer, or Bodhisattva.

2. Wisdom realizing selflessness is suitable as the path because it is the direct antidote to self-grasping ignorance, which is the root of all disturbing attitudes. It is a suitable antidote because it apprehends things in a way that is contradictory to self-grasping ignorance. Although both wisdom and ignorance have the same referent object—the person and phenomena—their way of apprehending these is in direct contradiction. The former apprehends phenomena as not self-existent and the latter apprehends them as self-existent. Therefore, wisdom realizing selflessness is suitable as the antidote to self-grasping ignorance.

3. Wisdom is establishing because it correctly establishes in a person's mindstream the actual way that things exist. It establishes or proves the way things exist because it realizes emptiness directly.

4. It definitely makes us emerge from cyclic existence because by generating this wisdom in our mindstream, self-grasping and the disturbing attitudes which it produces are destroyed so that they can never return. Thus, the root of cyclic existence is severed, and we definitely emerge from it.

The wisdom of selflessness is the higher training in wisdom. It cuts the disturbing attitudes at their root and is thus like a sharp ax used to cut down a tree. However, the sharp ax alone is not sufficient—we need a firm, strong arm that can hit the same spot with each stroke. The higher training of meditative stabilization is like this, because by overcoming mental excitement and dullness, it enables our mind to stay firmly on the object of meditation. For the stable, strong arm wielding the ax to cut the tree, a firm footing is also needed. The higher training in ethical discipline which abandons the ten destructive actions provides this foundation for our meditation on selflessness. Thus, although the wisdom realizing selflessness is what actually destroys the disturbing attitudes, all three higher trainings are necessary for it to be effective.

There are four wrong conceptions regarding the true path:

1. There is no path to liberation.
2. The wisdom realizing selflessness is not suitable as a path to liberation.
3. Something which in fact is not a path, such as certain meditative concentrations, is a complete path to liberation.
4. A path producing a state in which suffering and its causes have forever been extinguished does not exist, for inevitably they will arise again.

The four attributes of true suffering—impermanence, suffering, empty, and selfless—are realized in this order because the initial ones are easier to understand than the latter. However, the four attributes of true origin, true cessation, and true path have no set order in which they are realized. In each set of four, none is easier to realize than the others, and if we realize any of the four, we indirectly realize the other three at the same time.

The importance of the determination to be free

In the *Brief Lamrim*, also known as *Song of Experience*, Je Rinpoche states, "I looked at the faults of true suffering and generated a wish to be free. Later, I thought of the true origin, the way of cycling in samsara, understood the root of samsara and cut the root. Those who wish liberation should do likewise." By thinking continuously about the faults of true suffering and its causes, we will automatically develop a strong determination to be free from them and to attain liberation.

We have received the fruit of the practice of the middle level when we feel that any rebirth, from the blissful formless god realm to the hell realm, is undesirable. When we see that whatever marvels of cyclic existence we may experience, all are unsatisfactory and essenceless, and we do not wish for them even for a moment, then we have given birth to the determination to be free.

In *The Thirty-seven Practices*, there is just one verse on the practice of the middle-level person. It reminds us that the happiness of cyclic existence is unstable, like a dewdrop on the tip of a blade of grass, while the happiness of liberation is stable. Therefore it is worthwhile to develop the path leading to liberation. This explains the way we circle in samsara and how to attain liberation. Togme Sangpo, who has experience of this, could see the entire subject clearly, like a map set before him. This enabled him to explain the entire middle-level practice succinctly in one verse. We cannot understand the verse with just those few words. However, after we have heard an extensive explanation of the subject, we can see that all we have heard is contained in that one concise verse.

At the beginning our determination to be free is fabricated. That is, it does not arise spontaneously but needs to be cultivated through thinking of suffering and its causes. If we do not have at least a small, fabricated determination to be free, we cannot generate refuge. Without refuge, we cannot generate the various ordinations. Thus, in the ceremony to take refuge and precepts, the disadvantages of samsara are explained first.

The determination to be free is also one of the three principal aspects of the path, the other two being the altruistic intention and the wisdom realizing selflessness. If a positive action is not supported by the determination to be free, it is not a cause of liberation. Although we may meditate or do a kind action, if it is motivated by a wish for possessions, wealth, praise, or reputation it is not a cause of liberation. Even if we act constructively with the wish for a human birth, this also is not a cause of liberation; it is only a cause for birth in cyclic existence.

We might think that it is not necessary to generate the determination to be free if we meditate on the altruistic intention to attain enlightenment. That is not correct. We will be unable to experience the altruistic intention if we neglect to look deeply into the unsatisfactory conditions of our own existence. Why? First, we must recognize our own suffering and its causes and aspire to be free from them. Then we turn our focus to others and realize that they are in the same situation as we are. From that, compassion arises and then the altruistic intention to become a Buddha to be able to lead others from their suffering. The determination to be free is the basis of the path for the hearers, solitary realizers, and Bodhisattvas, that is, for anyone actually traveling the path to freedom. All the realizations of the three vehicles are based on the determination to be free. Also, since Vajrayana is a branch of the Bodhisattva practice, the determination to be free is essential to make progress in that practice as well.

When we consider that any good birth, any wonderful experience, or any fantastic possession in cyclic existence is without essence, our attachment will decrease and a sense of contentment will arise. Then, no matter what our situation is, we will have a sense of mental satisfaction and our mind will be free from the gross turbulence of discontent. Our disturbing attitudes will not arise as often or as strongly, and we will create less negative karma motivated by them. Consequently, we will experience less suffering. As our attachment to cyclic existence decreases, we will get closer to liberation. The more we dislike cyclic existence, the easier it will be to control our disturbing attitudes. All the Buddhas are of one voice on this point.

Once we have generated the determination to be free, things such as food, clothes, health, reputation, and praise, which are usually the causes of craving, become the means for eliminating it. Our possessions and our good image will become a teacher showing us impermanence, suffering, emptiness, and selflessness. We will see these things are transient, uncertain, uninteresting, and essenceless. We will cease our struggle to attain pleasure from them and will refocus our energy on worthwhile aims. We should not be concerned that we will have no purpose in life and no happiness if we stop our obsession with these things. Rather, a person free from such craving is free to develop compassion and wisdom, and be of service to others. He or she will have a truly meaningful and happy life.

People nowadays like tantra. They like to take initiations, practice visualizations, and recite mantras. We listen to a few teachings on the Gradual Path, and then immediately rush to take tantric initiations and do tantric retreats. Even if we lack the determination to be free, the altruistic intention, and the right view of reality, there is still some benefit, for we place powerful imprints on our mindstream. However, we will be unable to generate the tantric realizations without the experience of the three principal aspects of the path. The actual process is to meditate well on the Gradual Path first, and when that is firm, enter tantra.

We might wonder, "Doesn't the Chenrezig practice help develop compassion? After all, Chenrezig is the Buddha of compassion!" Yes, it does help; it is a condition for generating compassion. However, the cause of compassion is thinking of the suffering of sentient beings and wishing them to be free. Certainly meditating on Chenrezig, visualizing him, and reciting his mantra help us increase our compassion. Similarly, we can practice Manjushri to develop wisdom and Vajrapani to gain skillful means to overcome discordant conditions. Making requests to Lama Tsong Khapa is a condition for attaining all three simultaneously, since he embodies all three.

Strictly speaking, however, first we realize the three principal aspects of the path and then enter tantra. As Je Rinpoche says in *The Foundation of All Good Qualities*, "When, trained in the common path, I am a suitable vessel, let me enter with ease the great gateway of the fortunate ones, the Vajrayana, the highest of all vehicles—inspire me thus." However, life is short and the time that death will strike is not fixed. The times when tantra exists are rare, so if we do not get the imprint of tantra it is not good at all. Thinking in this way, it is reasonable to take tantric initiations without first having full realization or experience of the prior steps of the path. However, we should at least know and understand the three principal aspects of the path before taking initiations, even if we have not yet realized or experienced them.

The four noble truths as a summary of the path

Although the four noble truths are usually spoken of in terms of the middle-level practitioner, there is also a way of positing them according to the path of the initial-level practitioner. In this case, the meanings are not as subtle. True suffering refers to the three unfortunate rebirths. Their origin is the ten destructive actions and the motivations producing them. The cessation is the pacification of those three rebirths, that is, a good rebirth. The path is the ethical discipline of abandoning the ten destructive actions.

Similarly, we can posit the four aspects of the truth of suffering for the initial practitioner. In this case, impermanence refers to the gross impermanence of death. Suffering is being born in the three unfortunate realms which could occur after death. Empty refers to being empty of a permanent, partless, and independent self which is one or many, and selfless is the lack of a self that is permanent, partless, and independent. Here, permanent means not arising and disintegrating; partless means not depending on its parts; and independent refers to being autonomous and not relying on causes and conditions.

As an initial practitioner, we become mindful of death and the suffering of unfortunate rebirths that could occur after it. At this level, we take refuge and meditate on karma. Through this, we see that birth in the various realms is dictated by disturbing attitudes and karma, and in that way we see that at the moment we have no autonomy. This leads to understanding that there is no self which is permanent, partless, and independent. Meditating on the attributes empty and selfless is the antidote to grasping at the self. There are gross and subtle levels of selflessness, and the initial practitioner contemplates gross selflessness by seeing that there is no self which is permanent, partless, and independent.

As a middle-level practitioner, we meditate on subtle impermanence, the moment-by-moment disintegration of things. Then we contemplate the pervasive compounded unsatisfactoriness, which is subtler than the suffering contemplated at the initial level. We focus on the subtler selflessness, which is the lack of a self-sufficient, substantially existing self. According to this procedure, the initial and middle-level practitioners do not meditate separately on the attributes empty and selfless. For them, in the syllogism which establishes the lack of self, empty and selfless go together to oppose the wrong conception of self. However, the selflessness they meditate on differs in subtlety. The initial practitioner realizes there is no self which is permanent, partless, and independent, while the middle practitioner realizes there is no self-sufficient, substantially existing self. Here the grasping at a self-sufficient, substantially existing self is seen as the root of samsara. All the Buddhist philosophical schools except the Prasangika assert this.

Previously, empty was explained as the lack of a self-existing one and a self-existing many. In terms of the gross self, we say there is no permanent, single, and independent person that is one, nor is there a permanent, partless, and independent person that is many. In connection with a subtler self, we say there is no self-sufficient, substantially existent person because there is no person that is a self-sufficient, substantially existent one, nor is there a person that is a self-sufficient, substantially existent many. Therefore, the person is not self-sufficient and substantially existent. In terms of the subtlest self, as asserted by the Prasangika, there is no inherent or self-existent person because it is empty of being inherently one or many.

Lama Tsong Khapa counseled the initial practitioner, "First meditate on impermanence and death until it is so clear that you feel you could see it with your eyes." Why meditate on this first? We seldom have the opportunities that a precious human life affords. Nevertheless, even when we have them, it is difficult to make full use of them. We put off practicing the Dharma because we feel we will live a long time. If we meditate on death for even seven days, we will be inspired to do something and our laziness will be automatically and easily dispelled.

Once we take a birth that has arisen under the power of disturbing attitudes and karma, we are not beyond death. We have to die; we cannot prevent it. But by meditating on death, we can take steps towards liberation and enlightenment and stop the causes of unfortunate births. Thus the purpose of meditating on death is to energize us to prevent this suffering. If we understand impermanence through practicing mindfulness of death, suffering will become apparent to us, and we will want to put an end to it. This prompts us to look for a way to do so, and in this way, we come to meditate on selflessness, because understanding of selflessness destroys suffering definitively.

The advanced-level practitioner takes sentient beings as the object of meditation for developing love and compassion by recognizing that the four attributes of true suffering, as understood in the initial and middle levels, apply to all sentient beings. As a result, we think, "May all sentient beings be happy. May they be free of suffering." We then search for a way to free sentient beings from cyclic existence and see that only a Buddha can do that most effectively. Therefore we generate the altruistic intention and practice the six far-reaching attitudes in order to attain full enlightenment.

The Thirty-seven Practices is written from the meditative experience of its author, the Bodhisattva Togme Sangpo. His experience is based on having first studied and then thought about the meaning of the Buddha's teaching. The texts that *The Thirty-seven Practices* is based on are: *A Guide to the Bodhisattva's Way of Life*, *The Precious Garland*, and the texts of Maitreya and Asanga. Since Togme Sangpo had studied and understood the essence of these texts, he was able to convey it succinctly in these few verses. This commentary will help us to unpack the vast and profound meaning of these thirty-seven verses. Once we have studied the Dharma well, the meaning will spring from these verses and just a few words will reveal a vast subject. However, without study, these depths of meaning are not apparent to us.

For example, for someone who has studied the Prasangika texts, hearing "The meaning of dependent arising is emptiness, and the meaning of emptiness is dependent arising" will reveal great meaning. However, someone who has not studied will not recognize this meaning. Similarly, when a person who has studied well hears the word "empty," he or she will see the many differing ways of being empty—some subtle and some gross—of the four tenets' assertions on emptiness.

CHAPTER TEN

GENERATING THE ALTRUISTIC INTENTION

We have now covered the practices for the initial and middle-level practitioners. These are the basis for the practices of the advanced-level practitioner. Now, in speaking of the third level, we will learn how to generate bodhichitta, which can be translated as "altruistic intention" or "awakening mind," and then how to familiarize ourselves with it and apply it. Bodhichitta is the essence of the Universal Vehicle.

10   **When your mothers, who've loved you since time without beginning,**
      Are suffering, what use is your own happiness?
      Therefore to free limitless living beings
      Develop the altruistic intention—
      This is the practice of Bodhisattvas.

Since time without beginning, sentient beings, all of whom have been our mother in previous lives, have shown us great kindness and benefited us immeasurably. Since they experience suffering, what is the point of our being attached to just our own happiness? It is of no benefit. Therefore Bodhisattvas generate an altruistic intention to benefit all beings.

What is this altruistic intention or bodhichitta? Bodhichitta is a primary consciousness that has two aspirations: the aspiration intent on benefiting all sentient beings and the aspiration intent on enlightenment. First we aspire to benefit others. Then we become aware that although we are intent on this, we are not yet capable of doing it. Who has this capacity? A Buddha. If we attained Buddhahood and possessed the unending virtuous qualities of a Buddha's body, speech, mind, and activities, as well as a Buddha's compassion, wisdom, and skill, we would be able to help others in accord with their interests and dispositions. Once we realize this, we generate the heartfelt wish, "I definitely must attain enlightenment." The primary consciousness that comes together with that aspiration is bodhichitta. Thus we see that having a kind heart is a great quality, but it is not bodhichitta. Similarly, neither the aspiration to benefit others, nor the aspiration to become a Buddha is bodhichitta. The aspiration to benefit all beings is a cause of bodhichitta. It occurs prior to it, not at the same time. However, when, based on that aspiration to benefit others, we generate a primary consciousness with the aspiration to become a Buddha, then we have generated full-fledged bodhichitta. It is important to know exactly what bodhichitta is. Otherwise we will not be able to generate it properly and we will not be able to bring about the great benefits that come from it.

First we need a firm wish to benefit sentient beings. We can work for their welfare right now, but only minimally. To do it in the most complete and effective way requires that we transform ourselves into Buddhas. So we think, "I will become a Buddha." The primary mind that comes with that mental factor is the precious bodhichitta.

The great masters frequently advise us to "hold our virtuous activities with bodhichitta." This means that we should cultivate the wish, "I definitely want to work for the benefit of all beings. I can only do that fully when I become a Buddha, therefore I must attain the state free from all faults and with all good qualities fully developed. In order to attain that state, I will do this action." Then we do whatever the activity—prostrations, meditation, community service, going to work, caring for our family, and so forth. That action is held by bodhichitta and becomes very powerful. At our level, our bodhichitta may be fabricated, that is, developed by conscious effort, but after familiarizing ourselves with this over time, bodhichitta will arise spontaneously in us whenever we think of sentient beings. This is effortless or spontaneous bodhichitta.

Bodhichitta brings many benefits. It is a cause of happiness for ourselves and for others. It is also necessary for attaining enlightenment. Without it, this wonderful state remains beyond our reach. Bodhichitta is like a seed that will produce all a Buddha's qualities in us. We will not be poor in good qualities once we have this noble intention firmly planted in our hearts. Just like a wish-fulfilling jewel, it fulfills all wishes. In the past, it is said, one could find such jewels in the ocean. If one found such a jewel, washed and cared for it properly, then all one's wishes in this life would come true. Bodhichitta is actually better than this, for it fulfills the wishes of oneself and others, in this and future lives. It is like the best tool to cut down the tree of suffering. There is no negativity so great that it cannot be purified by bodhichitta, and nothing else can accumulate such great positive potential. If we make bodhichitta our motivation in the morning, all the virtuous acts we do that day—even feeding our pets—become very powerful and rich in goodness. Just like butter is the essence or richness of milk, bodhichitta is the essence and goodness of all the Buddha's teachings.

Bodhichitta is the door to the Bodhisattva vehicle, which includes both the vehicle of the far-reaching attitudes and the vehicle of tantra. Nowadays many people are interested in the tantric practices of visualizing deities. It is important to know that some level of bodhichitta is a prerequisite to those practices, and to actualize the beneficial results of tantra, we must have bodhichitta.

When we have generated bodhichitta, we become a "child" of the Buddha, in the sense that just as children grow up and carry on their parents' work, we will grow spiritually and be able to do the work of a Buddha. Just as a little piece of diamond eclipses other jewels, once we have generated bodhichitta, even if we are not that capable of training in the Bodhisattva practices, our good qualities will still outshine those of the hearers and solitary realizers, who attain liberation principally for their own benefit.

Atisha was a great practitioner of the altruistic intention. Due to this, Tara would appear to him face to face. They were just like two people speaking together! He always received visions of Tara and she continually advised him. Similarly, Lama Tsong Khapa saw Manjushri, and all the Indian pandits and siddhas appeared to him and blessed him because of his dedication to the welfare of others. All the great Buddhist sages were able to benefit a vast number of sentient beings because of their altruistic intention.

We should contemplate all these examples of the benefits of bodhichitta. As we become familiar with them, our mind will become very happy and enthusiastic and we'll feel, "I definitely must generate bodhichitta! It is so important! There is nothing else I would rather do." In this way, we have a joy whose source is internal. In other words, we ourselves will be able to make our own happiness. "It is amazing that I have this precious human life with all the freedoms and advantages to practice the Dharma. The fact that I can practice bodhichitta is even more marvelous. To generate it in my heart would be wonderful, but even if I can't do it in this life, I shall familiarize myself with it and work hard at it because it is marvelous beyond words." In this way, we will experience a sense of deep joy.

If someone is hungry, it is definitely better to give him food rather than to simply wish he had some. It is good to help in a practical way whenever we can. Yet in the long run, is it more beneficial to give food, medicine, material goods, and so on to those who are in need or to develop bodhichitta and then be able to offer extensive help? When we help others with material things, their suffering is eliminated, but only temporarily. They will get hungry again, fall ill again, or experience various other problems. By the force of the altruistic intention, we will dedicate ourselves to help others remove the root cause of all their sufferings in cyclic existence, the self-grasping ignorance. By cultivating bodhichitta, we will make ourselves capable of helping others in a very vast way over a long period of time without getting discouraged.

Of course this does not mean we content ourselves with meditating on compassion and ignore the suffering going on around us. For example, if we are untrained in medicine, is it better for us to treat people now as best as we can, or to leave that aside to go to medical school, and later be able to treat others properly and more extensively? Similarly, we benefit others however we can now, but put most of our effort into Dharma practice so that we can continuously increase our ability to be of service. If we ignore developing our internal qualities and strengths, our ability to help will remain limited and we will be more likely to suffer from "compassion fatigue" later on and give up helping others.

There are two methods to generate and then stabilize the altruistic intention: the seven cause and effect instructions, and exchanging self and others. The former will be explained in connection with this verse, the latter with the next verse. The seven cause and effect instructions are:

1. Recognizing that all living beings have been our mother
2. Recollecting their kindness
3. Wishing to repay this kindness

4. Heart-warming love
5. Compassion
6. Great resolve
7. Bodhichitta, the mind wishing to become enlightened
    in order to benefit sentient beings

The first six are referred to as causes, and the seventh, bodhichitta, is their effect.

Equanimity

Before proceeding with the seven cause and effect instructions, we need equanimity—a mind free from attachment to our dear ones, aversion towards people we find disagreeable, and apathy to strangers. Without equanimity, if we meditate on the love that wishes others to be happy, we will find it easy to love those we like, but very difficult to love those we perceive as harmful, threatening, or unpleasant. Developing equanimity is like leveling the ground before building a house. It enables us to have equal concern for all beings, instead of being subject to the emotional swings brought on by attachment and hatred.

To meditate on equanimity, we think of a person whom we dislike, one of whom we are very fond, and a person towards whom we are neutral. For convenience, we will use the term "enemy" to describe the disagreeable person, although this does not imply that we are fighting a war against him or her. Consider that our relationship with the disagreeable person hasn't always been what it is now. Earlier in this life perhaps he helped us, and definitely in previous lives he was our friend and helped us many times. Similarly, the person who we are presently so attached to was once a stranger, and in previous lives gave us many problems and harmed us. The stranger also has been both friend and enemy in past lives. If someone gives us money today and hits us tomorrow, and another person strikes us today and gives us money tomorrow, which is the real friend and which is the real enemy? We can see that holding rigidly on to our conceptions of people is unreasonable, and our emotional reactions of anger, attachment, and apathy to them are exaggerated. We should take our time thinking about this. As we become familiar with it, our clinging and unhealthy dependence on the person who has helped us a little recently will weaken, as will our wish to retaliate against those who have harmed us recently. If we continue, we will start to think there is not much difference between these three people and we will begin to have the same feeling of openness to all of them. If we can see these three people as equal in terms of the help and harm they have given us over long periods of time, we can extend that to all sentient beings so that we have an equal feeling towards all, and our relationships with others will automatically improve and be more stable. With this basis firm in our minds, we can begin the first of the seven meditations. This equanimity which precedes the seven cause and effect instructions is shared with the Individual Vehicle, and is called "limitless equanimity" because it extends to each of the limitless sentient beings.

Recognizing that all living beings have been our mother

Many people throughout the world have a special affinity to their mother because she was so kind and close to them when they were small. We have had countless lives in cyclic existence, and in many of these we have had mothers. Thinking of the vastness of this, we realize that each sentient being at some time or another has been our mother, not only once but countless times.

Recollecting the kindness of our mother

Here we reflect on the kindness of our mother or whoever took care of us when we were young. We can supplement this by looking around at the kindness we see mothers in general showing their children, because we won't be able to remember all that our mother did. They nourish and care for their children and often undergo hardships for their sake. As young children, we were incapable of caring for ourselves. Without the kindness of those who cared for us when we were little, we would not have survived. Mothers teach their children to speak, encourage them to get an education and develop social skills, being kind to their children not only when the children are young, but for many years. Only when a mother is under great pressure, is mentally or physically ill, or is forced by economic or other exceptional conditions does she not show this kindness. But all of us have experienced kindness from those who took care of us when we were young and it is important to remember that feeling. Having seen how kind our mother has been in this life, we can understand how kind all sentient beings have been to us when they were our mothers countless times in the past.

Repaying the kindness

If a sick old woman is tottering at the top of some stairs, her children should help her. If they don't, most people would consider it shameful and uncaring. Similarly, seeing the kindness all beings have shown us in the past when they have been our mother, it is only right that we feel an urge to help them in return.

Now, we have the fortune to have a precious human life and to know a little about the Dharma. If we practice Dharma well, we are repaying the kindness of sentient beings more than if we give a little food, clothing, or medicine. Although helping others by giving food and so forth is very important and worthwhile, it removes others' suffering only temporarily. Because they are in cyclic existence, their problems will resurface. However, if we are able to show others the Dharma, it enables them to practice the path which will free them from all suffering and bring them all happiness. This is an excellent way to repay their kindness. Most beings are ignorant of karma and therefore do not know how to create the causes of happiness and avoid the causes of suffering. Some know this, but do not have the opportunity to practice. We have met with a method that can lead us to full enlightenment, a state in which we will have the greatest capability to help others. Therefore we should put energy into learning, thinking, meditating, and practicing in order to progress on the path to enlightenment. All such efforts are ultimately the finest way to repay the kindness of others.

If we think well on these first three points of the seven, we will make a firm base for the altruistic intention wishing to work for the welfare of others. The actual mind that wishes to work for others starts with heart-warming love.

Heart-warming love

As a result of familiarizing ourselves with equanimity and the first three points, we will see all beings as very pleasant and pleasing. None of them will appear bad or suspicious to us. In this way, heart-warming love will arise naturally. At this point, seeing any sentient being is a pleasure, and we become like an affectionate mother seeing her only child: everyone appears lovable to us.

Heart-warming love is not the same as love. The former sees all sentient beings as kind and regards them fondly—thus it is called "heart-warming"—and it also wants them to have happiness and its causes. Love, in general, wishes another to have happiness and its causes, and it is not explicitly listed in the seven points. Heart-warming love precedes and is a cause of compassion, which wishes all beings to be free from suffering. However, in general, love and compassion have no fixed order in which they arise. If we observe sentient beings and first want them to be free from suffering, compassion will arise first. If we observe them and first want them to have happiness, then love will come first.

Compassion

Compassion is the wish for others to be free of suffering and its causes. The deeper our meditation on the four previous points, the more spontaneously our compassion will arise. To meditate on compassion, we focus on sentient beings and consider all the different unsatisfactory conditions they experience as described earlier when we talked about the truth of suffering and its causes. Our meditation on compassion has been successful when we feel for all beings in cyclic existence the way a mother feels for her only child when that child is sick. Whatever she is doing—eating, walking, and so on—she has her child in mind, feels his or her suffering is unbearable, and wishes her child to be free from it. This is only an analogy and is not similar to a Bodhisattva's compassion in all respects. Many mothers would experience a sense of personal distress at their child's suffering which could make them worried or depressed or immobilize them from helping. This sense of personal distress or helplessness is not present in the Bodhisattva's compassion, which we are trying to develop.

Sentient beings, whose minds are agitated by the three poisonous attitudes, do many destructive actions. As a result of these actions they experience unfortunate rebirths in places of suffering. Bodhisattvas think, "May they not have to be born there. May I be born there instead." Their compassion is so great that they are willing to be born in even the hell realms if it benefits sentient beings, and do not wish to be born in a pure realm if it is not useful for sentient beings.

Great resolve

This is the intention to take personal responsibility to free others from suffering and bring about their happiness. Rather than just think how wonderful it would be or leaving it to someone else to do something, we make the determination, "I myself will free sentient beings from suffering; I myself will give happiness to sentient beings." The former is the great resolve which is compassion, and the latter is the great resolve which is love. It is called "great" or "superior" because it is superior to the love and compassion of the hearers and solitary realizers. They want sentient beings to be happy and free of suffering, but they have not made the powerful decision to take personal responsibility to bring this about. In the prayer of the four immeasurables, the verse on immeasurable compassion says, "How wonderful it would be if all sentient beings were free of suffering. May they be free. I shall free them." The first two phrases are compassion, the last is the great resolve which is compassion.

The great resolve has no referent and aspect separate from those of love and compassion. Either it has the referent and the aspect of love or those of compassion. In the case of love, the referent is sentient beings and the aspect is wanting them to be happy. The great resolve which is love is not satisfied with wanting others to be happy; it adds the decision, "I shall bring about their happiness." It is similar with the great resolve which is compassion.

Altruistic intention or bodhichitta

In summary, to generate bodhichitta in our mind, we need, as a cause, the mind wishing to benefit others and work for their welfare. The first three of the seven points—recognizing sentient beings as our mothers, recalling their kindness, and wishing to repay it—are the basis for generating the aspiration to benefit others. Love, wishing them happiness, and compassion, wishing them freedom from suffering, are the actual attitudes wishing to benefit them. Thinking "I myself will free them" is the great resolve that is compassion, and thinking "I myself will give them happiness" is the great resolve that is love. These two great resolves are the actual thoughts deciding to work for others. Love, compassion, and the great resolve are the causal aspirations of bodhichitta.

The seventh point begins when we see that at the moment we are not able to free even ourselves from suffering and conjoin ourselves with happiness, let alone do this for countless sentient beings. The only person who has the ability to do so is a fully enlightened being, a Buddha. Such a person can work for all beings according to their interests and dispositions. It is only by becoming a Buddha ourselves that we will be able to actualize this deepest wish. Therefore, we make the decision that for the sake of all sentient beings we will attain the state of enlightenment. When that aspiration has become firm, we have generated the precious bodhichitta in our mindstream. This altruistic aspiration for enlightenment is a primary mind that possesses two aspirations. The first aspiration is intent on the welfare of others and is the causal aspiration for bodhichitta, and the second is the resultant aspiration, the aspiration for enlightenment. If we take our time and think about these points continuously over an extended period, our attitude towards others will be profoundly affected. At the beginning these attitudes will be fabricated with effort, but after a while they will arise naturally and effortlessly because our mind has been transformed.

We must not think merely superficially about the altruistic intention and allow it to become banal. If we think, "I've heard about bodhichitta so much. It's nothing special," its power will vanish in our mind. Bodhichitta is the indispensable seed of enlightenment, and if we remember this, our mind will find the very idea of bodhichitta moving. We will then be happy to hear about it and will think, "Even if I can't generate bodhichitta at present, I respect and admire this amazing attitude. As much as possible, I want to train my mind in this thought, which is the source of happiness for the world."

CHAPTER ELEVEN

COURAGEOUS COMPASSION

As persons aspiring to be Bodhisattvas, we must not only generate bodhichitta but also become familiar with it and apply it in all aspects of our lives. Although bodhichitta generally refers to the altruistic intention, or conventional bodhichitta, it can also refer to ultimate bodhichitta, or the wisdom realizing emptiness. In this text, practicing the conventional bodhichitta—the altruistic intention—entails meditating on equalizing and exchanging ourselves with others during meditative equipoise and transforming unfavorable circumstances into the path to enlightenment in the post-meditation times.

HOW TO MEDITATE ON EQUALIZING AND EXCHANGING SELF AND OTHERS DURING EQUIPOISE

11   All suffering comes from the wish for your own happiness.
      Perfect Buddhas are born from the thought to help others.
      Therefore exchange your own happiness
      For the suffering of others—
      This is the practice of Bodhisattvas.

As mentioned above, there is a second way to generate bodhichitta which the Buddha taught for those whose mental faculties are sharper than the practitioners for whom he taught the seven cause and effect instructions. This second method is called equalizing and exchanging self and others. The seven cause and effect instructions come to us from the Buddha via Maitreya and Asanga. The principal lineage for

equalizing and exchanging self and others is from the Buddha via Manjushri and Nagarjuna. Shantideva explains this method clearly in the eighth chapter of *A Guide to the Bodhisattva's Way of Life.*

There is a meditation on equanimity taught specially in the context of equalizing and exchanging self and others. It is not an equanimity that merely evens out attachment, anger, and apathy as does the equanimity preceding the seven cause and effect instructions. It is more than that. Usually we feel close to some beings and distant from others, and offer or withhold help and happiness accordingly. The equanimity that outshines this is equanimity in the context of equalizing and exchanging self and others, and it brings about the intention to benefit and give happiness to all sentient beings without such bias. Whereas equanimity explained in the context of the seven instructions is common to the Theravada tradition, equanimity explained in equalizing and exchanging self and others is a practice unique to the Mahayana. The nine points of this meditation enable us to develop the inner experience of this type of equanimity. The first six points approach the topic on the conventional level, and the last three on the ultimate level. Of the former, the first three look at matters from our own point of view, and the other three from the point of view of others.

Looking from our own viewpoint on the conventional level:

1. All sentient beings have equally helped us immeasurably, undergone many hardships, and faced many problems for our benefit. When we take into account our beginningless lifetimes, this is certainly the case. The kindness of others is certainly clear to us if we consider this life, since we have experienced it directly. But the same holds true in other lifetimes and in other realms. There we also received much kindness. Kindness does not have to be intentional. Here, kindness simply means that because others have done various things, we have received benefit. Without their efforts—no matter what their motivation was—we would be lacking many benefits. For example, thanks to other beings we have a house to live in, clothes to wear, and so on. Our having these depends on the efforts of other sentient beings. We may think, "But I paid for this!" The money also is due to their kindness. "But I worked for it!" The work also is given to us by others. When we were born, we did not have a penny, nor even a rag to cover ourselves. Everything we have owned, eaten, worn, and so on has come to us through the kindness of others. It is all thanks to them.

2. We may think, in response, that they also harm us sometimes. But the help is thousands of times greater. For example, if we check just

our present situation, we see some help us directly and some indirectly. So many people are involved in growing, transporting, packing, and preparing the food we eat. Many people worked together to construct the place we live, to make the clothes we wear, the roads we drive on and the vehicles we drive in. Everything we use depends on others. This is related to our experience so we can recognize it easily.

3. Even in the few cases when others have harmed us, seeking revenge is self-defeating. Since death is definite and the time is indefinite, wanting to harm others makes no sense. It is like the squabbling of prisoners condemned to death.

Looking from the viewpoint of others on the conventional level:

1. Sentient beings are equal in wanting happiness and not wanting suffering. They are equal in having a right to happiness and freedom from suffering. Every way we look at it, they are equal. We can't say that anyone—ourselves, friends, enemies, or strangers—is more important in wanting and having a right to happiness and freedom from suffering.

2. Given their equal wish and right to happiness, it would be inappropriate if we helped some beings with a partial mind. For example, if ten beggars come to our door, hungry and thirsty, all hoping that we will give them something to eat and drink, it would not be at all right if we were to be attached to some and averse to others. They are equal in their hunger and thirst, equal in wanting food and drink, and equal in hoping that we will help. Therefore, attachment and aversion are totally inappropriate. On a practical level, it is not possible to help everyone equally. There are those we can help directly: some through our actions, others through our speech. Those that we cannot help directly we can help with our thoughts and prayers. However, on an internal level, we can cultivate the attitude that regards all of them equally and would like to be able to help them all equally.

3. Suppose that we are a doctor and ten very ill people come to us in the hope of receiving medicine and treatment. Since they are equal in their hope and in not wanting to be sick, it would not be right for us to be biased in our treatment of them. This reason, like the preceding one, is to amplify the meaning of the first point in this set. It is talking about our internal attitude, not our practical ability to alleviate suffering.

The first point is the main one. The second and third are examples amplifying it.

Looking from ultimate level:

1. We develop attachment to those who help us a little and see them as good people. Those who harm us a little we loathe and see as bad people. We regard them as being good and bad from their own side. This state of mind is not realistic. If it were, the Buddha would see things that way, but this is not the case. If one person on one side of the Buddha anoints him with fragrant oil, and another person on the other side hacks at him with a knife, the Buddha does not regard one as good and the other as bad, becoming attached to one and disliking the other. If there were a real difference between the two people, the Buddha with his clear-sighted wisdom would see it. However, he does not see one person as inherently good and the other as inherently bad.

2. People appear nice and horrible to us from their own side, but that is not how they actually exist. The appearance of someone as good or bad is a dependent arising, an event that comes about in dependence upon the gathering together of particular causes and conditions, such as a little help or harm. It is thus something changeable by nature. It is not fixed because friend and enemy are not friend and enemy from their own side. We can see in our lives that as conditions change, people easily change roles in relationship to us. Thus, they are not permanently our friend, enemy, or stranger.

3. Similarly, we think, "This person is my enemy, and this is my friend," as if they were always, permanently, and irrevocably that way. In fact, friend and enemy are relative, like saying "this mountain" and "that mountain." We call the mountain we stand on now "this" mountain and the one on the other side "that" mountain. But if we crossed over to "that" mountain, it would become "this" mountain, and "this" mountain would become "that" mountain. Thus, "this mountain" and "that mountain" do not exist from their own side. They are relative. It is similar with those whom we call friend and enemy. These terms are relative and changeable. No one is inherently a friend and worthy of attachment; no one is inherently disagreeable and worthy of aversion.

In brief, the last three reasons show that friend and enemy do not inherently exist. First, they do not exist that way from their own side because if they did, the Buddha would see it like this, but the Buddha doesn't. Second, they are not permanent because they change. Third, they are not absolute categories because the designations "friend" and "enemy" are relative.

The meaning of equalizing and exchanging self and others

In general, self and others are equal in being transient, empty of independent existence, and selfless. But this is not the equality of self and others discussed here. Rather, we are equal in wishing for happiness and freedom from suffering and in having the right to be happy and free from suffering. For this reason, self and others are equally to be cherished.

Our body has many parts—a nose, legs, arms, chest, and so on. We cherish them because we feel we need them, that they are of benefit to us. Similarly, we must cherish all beings, because we need them all and they are all helpful and so kind to us at the times of the basis, path, and result, i.e., before we have entered a spiritual path, while we are practicing on the path, and when we have attained the final result of our path.

What does exchanging self and others mean? It does not mean I become you and you become me. Rather it means decreasing the feeling that we are extremely important and increasingly thinking of others as very important. At present, we neglect others and cherish ourselves. This is to be turned around. We should forget about ourselves and cherish others. The object of our cherishing should change from self to others. There is a very good reason to do this: others are limitless in number, whereas we are only one. Therefore it is appropriate to care for the limitless others and pay less attention to oneself. When we cherish self and neglect others, only bad comes. We can easily confirm this by our life experiences. If we do not care for others or their possessions, we engage in all sorts of negative actions, and the only result that can follow such actions is misery. If we care for others and their possessions, being considerate and holding them as important, we can visibly see that the results are excellent: others are happy and they are kind to us in return.

We need to understand that there is a reason to exchange self and others, that we are able to exchange self and others, and that it is very important to do so. The reason is that it is very profitable to ex-change self and others, and we all like profit. The reason we are able to exchange self and others is that if we keep thinking about the faults of self-centeredness and the benefits of cherishing others, our mind will become familiar with these ideas and exchanging self and others will be easy. It is important to exchange self and others and it is worthwhile to go through the hardships of doing so because it will enable us to generate bodhichitta, practice the six far-reaching attitudes and attain the final result of Buddhahood. By understanding this, we will be very enthusiastic and eager to do the practice.

The nine points to develop equanimity are a preliminary practice to equalizing and exchanging self and others. After meditating on them, we practice the five decisions:

1. Not only is there no reason to discriminate among different sentient beings, as the nine points illustrate, there is also no reason to differentiate between myself and others. Whatever they do, however they might harm me, I will not retaliate, I will not be biased, feeling attachment to some and hatred for others, but rather I will help them all. There is no other way: I must practice the thought wishing to benefit all others equally. "There is no difference between myself and others. None of us wishes even the slightest suffering, nor is ever content with the happiness we have. Realizing this, I seek your inspiration to enhance the bliss and joy of others." This verse and the verses quoted in the following four points are from the *Guru Puja*. In this verse we request inspiration from the merit field to help us transform our minds.

2. We must see our self-preoccupation as the real enemy, the one that harms us terribly, and decide to give it up. "This chronic disease of self-centeredness is the cause of all our unwanted suffering. Perceiving this, I seek your inspiration to blame, begrudge, and destroy the monstrous demon of selfishness."

3. Seeing the attitude of cherishing others as being rich in qualities, we decide to develop it in ourselves. "The attitude that cherishes all mother sentient beings and would secure them in bliss is the source from which arise boundless virtuous qualities. Seeing this, I seek your inspiration to cherish these beings more than my life, even should they all rise up as my enemies."

4. Having thought about the faults of self-centeredness and of the benefits of cherishing others, we decide to exchange self and others. "In brief, infantile beings labor only for their own ends, while Buddhas work solely for the welfare of others. Discerning the disadvantages of the one and the advantages of the other, I seek your inspiration to be able to equalize and exchange self and others."

5. When we have meditated over and over on the disadvantages of self-preoccupation and the advantages of cherishing others, we decide we must devote ourselves one-pointedly to the practice of exchanging self and others, seeing it as the most essential practice. "Since cherishing ourselves is the doorway to all torment, while cherishing our mothers is the foundation of all that is good, inspire me to make my core practice the yoga of exchanging self for others."

In summary, first we meditate on the nine reasons for developing equanimity which come before equalizing and exchanging self and others. After that, we contemplate the five decisions according to the request verses from the *Guru Puja*. The five decisions are related to equalizing and exchanging self and others, but the latter is more vast. In the five decisions, we request the inspiration of our spiritual mentors and the Three Jewels, while in equalizing and exchanging self and others we meditate to actually equalize and exchange ourselves and others.

To generate the attitude intent on benefiting others, we first have to see others in a positive light. If we see them as troublesome, we will not have the thought of working for their benefit. Thus we need to cultivate heart-warming love which sees others as pleasing. There are two methods to do this. One was described in the previous chapter: meditating on equanimity, recognizing others as having been our mothers, recalling their kindness, and wishing to repay it. The other method will now be described. It is seeing the faults of self-centeredness and the advantages of cherishing others. This method comes to us from the Buddha via the great Indian sage Shantideva. By contemplating again and again the faults of the self-centered attitude, we will come to see it as our enemy and will not follow it. By reflecting on the benefits of cherishing others, we will see it as wonderful and will be eager to practice it. When practicing the seven cause and effect instructions, training the mind in the intent to benefit others is done by meditating on compassion, love, and the great resolve. When practicing equalizing and exchanging self and others, it is done when we meditate on taking and giving.

The disadvantages of self-centeredness

A person who is in the habit of thinking of him- or herself alone, and whose words and deeds are totally self-centered will not be liked by others in the community in which he or she lives. Conversely, a person who is accustomed to thinking of the welfare of the group and who says and does things useful for others is well liked by all. Even the sight of such a person makes us happy.

Self-centeredness and self-grasping ignorance are related but not the same. Self-centeredness or self-preoccupation is an attitude which wants to protect ourselves and considers ourselves to be the most important of all. Self-grasping—which is also called the conception of true existence, ignorance, and so on—is an attitude whose object appears to be truly existent and which apprehends it as truly existent just as it appears. It is the opposite of the wisdom realizing emptiness, while self-centeredness is the opposite of the mind cherishing others. They are the opposite of wisdom and method respectively. Self-grasping ignorance is the root of cyclic existence and it produces self-centeredness. It is behind self-centeredness. Due to our self-preoccupation we are attached to "our side," want to protect our body, our possessions, our friends and relatives, and we have hatred for the "other side" and anger towards anyone who interferes with our happiness. In this way, all the various types of disturbing attitudes arise, we accumulate karma, and experience suffering.

We often feel that someone "out there" is responsible for things happening to us that we do not like and for our not being able to do what we want, but in fact other people are only the condition for those difficulties. They are not the main cause. The main cause is self-grasping. Our difficulties and suffering have causes that are concordant with those experiences. They cannot be produced by discordant causes—that is, causes that are unable to produce them. For example, a daisy will grow only from a daisy seed, its concordant cause. It cannot arise from a dandelion seed, which is a discordant cause for it. Similarly, if we think about it, we see that all undesirable experiences come from concordant karma. That is, they happen because we have previously created the causes for them. This karma is accumulated under the influence of disturbing attitudes, whose basis is self-centeredness. That, in turn, comes from conceiving the I as truly existent. Thus, right at the bottom of all these problems is self-grasping ignorance. What use is this self-grasping to us? None.

Although they have eliminated self-grasping and all the deluded obscurations, the hearer and solitary realizer arhats still have some self-preoccupation because they place their own liberation from cyclic existence above the liberation of other sentient beings. Therefore, self-centeredness is not a deluded obscuration but an obscuration to omniscience, for even those who have eliminated the former may still have the latter. Self-grasping is a discordant factor for all three vehicles in that it prevents the culmination of the path of each vehicle. However, self-centeredness is only a discordant factor for the Mahayana.

If there is someone who always harms us, and we discover that this person lives in our own house, we think, "This is too much!" Once we figure out that he is causing all our hardships, we kick him out; we do not see it as a laughing matter at all. Here, it is worse: we have been wandering in the six realms of cyclic existence since beginningless time, undergoing great pain and confusion. What is the main cause of all this? Self-centeredness and its basis, self-grasping ignorance. These two are right inside us, in our own mindstream. How can we continue to tolerate that? It is just too much! We definitely must evict these sources of harm. When we know the antidotes to them, we will use them, just as we would go to any length to evict a troublemaker from our home. With strong determination, we will find out what harms self-centeredness and self-grasping and then go ahead and destroy them.

The purpose of looking at the faults of self-centeredness is to make ourselves thoroughly dislike it and want to be free from it. It is important to remember while recalling all the shortcomings of the selfish attitude that it is not our inherent nature. It is an attitude that afflicts us. In criticizing self-centeredness, we are not criticizing ourselves. In fact, we are wishing ourselves happiness by identifying the source of our troubles as the self-centered attitude and then determining to free ourselves from it.

Then we can tell self-centeredness and self-grasping off and say we want nothing more to do with them. "Self-centeredness, you are a slaughterer." Slaughterers destroy the life of animals. Similarly, self-centeredness and self-grasping sever the existence of good rebirths, liberation, and enlightenment because they bring forth wrong views which consider virtue to be useless and negative actions not to be harmful at all. For example, we think there is no benefit in taking refuge and no harm in dismissing the Three Jewels as non-existent. With such cynical attitudes, we do what we please with total disregard for cause and effect. As a result, fortunate rebirths, liberation, and enlightenment recede far away while suffering looms closer.

"Self-centeredness, you are a robber." A robber deprives us of our possessions. Similarly, by making us say and do unkind things to others, self-centeredness steals away our happiness and its causes. "Self-centeredness, you are a trouble-maker." Together with self-grasping, it makes negative karmic imprints accumulate in our mindstream, and thereby we are harmed by humans and non-humans. "Self-centeredness, you are a farmer of evil." Farmers sow seeds in their fields, water and fertilize them, and in this way grow various crops. Similarly, under the influence of self-centeredness and self-grasping, negative karmic imprints are planted in the consciousness. At the time of death, these are nourished by craving and grasping, and many suffering births are taken in the six realms.

Now we insult self-centeredness, stating its faults clearly. "Lazy self-centered attitude!" Enlightened beings such as Buddha Shakyamuni used to be in cyclic existence together with us. Now, through cherishing others they have become Buddhas. Meanwhile we remain in cyclic existence. This is due to our self-centeredness. We have the mind wishing to benefit others in our mindstream, but we do not make this a habit because self-centeredness makes us lazy, complacent and bored. If we habituate ourselves to the wish to benefit others again and again, it will continue to get stronger, and right away, in this life we will experience happiness. In addition, with time we will experience the boundless happiness of enlightenment. Then, by simply seeing, hearing, or thinking about us, others too, will be happy.

"Covetous self-centered attitude!" The Buddha and all the highly realized masters tell us that wherever we are born in cyclic existence—from the top to the bottom—is a place of suffering. Whoever our companions may be, they are "companions in suffering." Whatever possessions and enjoyments we have, they are "possessions of suffering." In spite of their repeated warnings, we still strive for samsaric bodies, friends, possessions, food, abodes, and so on. We covet all the beautiful things of cyclic existence, like bees gathering nectar from flowers. This is the fault of self-centeredness. Our inability or reluctance to see the faults of the enticing features of samsara and thus to let go of them is due to self-centeredness.

"Hopeful and suspicious self-centered attitude!" Sometimes we strive for things which we cannot be sure will be of any use to us. With great hopes we put a lot of time and energy into things which we think will be wonderful but in the end are a waste. Other times we strive to avoid harm from someone or something that we aren't at all sure is harmful. Yet, with suspicion and fear we line up many avenues of escape and create a big fuss. Our becoming involved in such hopes and fears is the fault of self-centeredness.

"Self-centered attitude with no integrity or consideration for others!" When something goes wrong, we shirk responsibility and with no sense of integrity or consideration for others, blame our parents, friends, relatives, or spiritual guides. When some profit is made by our work, we take the credit even though the project was done with many other people. These faults are due to self-centeredness.

"Uncontrollable self-centered attitude!" Jealous of those who are better than us, competitive with our peers, arrogant towards those who are inferior in some way, puffed up by a little praise, irritated when we hear something that does not completely suit us—these are all produced by self-centeredness.

"Self-defeating self-centered attitude!" The Buddha and great masters taught that happiness comes from positive actions and suffering from destructive actions. This is unmistaken and incontrovertible. We have heard this many times and understand it, yet we are still not able to act constructively and create the cause for happiness even though we desire it. Again and again, automatically and effortlessly, we act destructively, creating the cause of suffering even though we do not want it. This pitiful situation is brought about by self-centeredness.

"Utterly blind self-centered attitude!" Our disturbing attitudes have been harming us from beginningless time until the present. They continuously create problems and destroy our happiness and all that is helpful to us. Although this is the case, we are like blind people because we are able neither to see the disturbing attitudes as faulty nor to abandon them. This, too, is created by self-centeredness.

Being irritable, lashing out at others, and even being predisposed to violence towards others is due to our long familiarity with the self-centered attitude over countless past lives. Experiencing fear, being worried about our reputation, craving praise, and fearing blame are also due to self-preoccupation. There are times when we worry about our relationships, feeling uncertain and insecure about whether others will like us and if our friendships will last. Other times, we become close to people quickly and then our dissatisfied, fickle mind terminates the relationship without warning. All this comes from self-centeredness.

Self-preoccupation creates all suffering and all causes of suffering. If we allow our actions, words, thoughts, and feelings to be under its sway, it will harm us in many ways and bring us much misfortune. As Shantideva said, "Now I have understood that it is you, self-centered attitude, who has destroyed me in lives without beginning up until now. Now I will apply the antidote and destroy you. You have nowhere to go. You cannot resist. You will not destroy me again like you have in the past!" In this way Shantideva personifies self-preoccupation and talks to it like an actual person. In brief, if we keep thinking of the many faults of the self-centered attitude, our disgust with it will grow. As that happens, we will naturally be less willing to let it run our lives, and we will begin to oppose it. If we continuously reflect on the harm self-centeredness has brought us, we will certainly make progress in this meditation and our mind will change.

We must use our body, speech, and mind to destroy self-preoccupation. When using a mortar and pestle, one Kadampa geshe would imagine he was pounding the head of self-centeredness and self-grasping. We need to use that kind of creativity. Kadampa Geshe Ben Gunggyel kept up his mindfulness at all times and said, "When he is alert, I shall be alert; when he relaxes, I will relax." This means that when the disturbing attitudes aren't arising, he will take it easy. But when they show signs of activity, his mindfulness will immediately move into action and he will apply the antidotes.

The benefits of cherishing others

There is no one who does not have the mind wanting to benefit others and bring them happiness. All sentient beings have it, although they differ in how extensive that mind is. A small intention is the seed for cultivating the attitude to benefit others extensively. No one lacks this seed; it is in everyone's mindstream. When it is said that all sentient beings have the potential to become a Buddha, this is what is referred to. This seed is extremely important, and we should take great care of it, cherish it highly, and cultivate it so it will grow.

We accuse self-centeredness of so many wrongs, identifying it as the culprit who is responsible for everything that goes wrong in all our lives. At the same time, we encourage ourselves to allow only the mind cherishing others to arise. When we think about the disadvantages of being preoccupied with ourselves and the advantages of cherishing others, our mind will become very peaceful and happy. If we do not think in this way, even if we receive a thousand initiations, hear a lifetime of teachings, offer many mandalas, make thousands of prostrations, and so on, they will not be that beneficial. Although they will still be of some use, they will not bring great benefit. If we train our mind in seeing the faults of self-preoccupation, we will become extraordinarily wise. We will stop fighting the world in a futile attempt to have everything and everyone conform to our ego's desires. When we go through difficult situations—problems with finances, relationships, or health—our mind will not be disturbed.

The Eight Verses of Thought Transformation advises that we "accept defeat and give the victory to others." For example, when we work together with someone on a project and the time comes for someone to get the credit for it, we should try to make sure that the other person receives it. When we divide something up and the portions are of unequal size, we give the larger one away and take the smaller for ourselves. If we are sharing things and one of them is defective or slightly worn out while the others are new, we take the old one. This is what is meant by "accepting defeat and giving the victory to others." These are examples of how to act when we see sentient beings as important. If we do not understand that self-centeredness causes all our suffering, this method does not make sense and it seems that we are being masochistic and sacrificing our own happiness unnecessarily. But if we have a deep understanding of the reasons behind this, we want to act in this way and feel joy when others have good things.

Why should we view other sentient beings as important? Because everything good and excellent, both temporarily and ultimately, comes in dependence upon sentient beings. For example, our development of spiritual attainments comes through sentient beings because in dependence on them we develop great compassion. In his *Supplement to the Middle Way* Chandrakirti praises great compassion as important in the beginning, middle, and end of our practice. Take the growth of a plant, for example: a good seed is important at the beginning, water and fertilizer in the middle, and good fruit at the end. In the growth of spiritual realizations, great compassion is likewise important in the beginning, middle, and end. At the beginning, it is the foundation for generating the great resolve and bodhichitta. In the middle, great compassion gives us the courage and stamina to continuously improve the Bodhisattva practices of the six far-reaching attitudes. Without familiarity with great compassion, we may become discouraged when we think that we have to train in the Bodhisattva practices so extensively and for such a long time. At the end of the path great compassion is the force motivating us to work for the benefit of others. It enables us to perform the peaceful, increasing, powerful, and fierce activities, and to engage in innumerable activities in accordance with the dispositions, thoughts, and interests of sentient beings. The Buddha's qualities of realization and abandonment, his physical, verbal, and mental qualities, and all the inconceivable attributes of an enlightened being are all rooted in great compassion.

Great compassion is developed by depending on sentient beings, because they are the referent, i.e., the object compassion refers to, observes, focuses on, or thinks about. Thus, just as great compassion is necessary at the beginning, middle, and end of the path, so too are sentient beings valuable and important at these times, because great compassion cannot be generated without them. As we think more about this, we will conclude that sentient beings are extremely important. In fact, without depending on each and every sentient being—from the smallest insect to the magnificent beings of the god realm—it is impossible for us to attain enlightenment.

Not only is our practice of bodhichitta dependent upon sentient beings but so is our practice of the six far-reaching attitudes and the four means of gathering. For example, practicing generosity is done by being generous to sentient beings. Ethics entails not harming sentient beings by avoiding the ten destructive actions. Patience is cultivated for the sentient beings who threaten or harm us. Joyous effort is enthusiastically practicing generosity, ethical discipline, and patience, and concentration entails practicing them one-pointedly. Knowing the advantages of cultivating the first five far-reaching attitudes involves wisdom. Similarly the four means of gathering rely on sentient beings—(1) being generous to sentient beings, (2) talking to them of things which interest them, (3) giving them Dharma advice and teachings, and (4) acting according to what we teach. In brief, the entire collection of causes for enlightenment depends on sentient beings. They cannot be developed in isolation from them. In addition, all of a Buddha's enlightened activities, which are inexhaustible, unending, extensive, and limitless, are done in relation to sentient beings.

The root of all qualities of the Bodhisattva vehicle is caring for sentient beings. We admire and respect the Buddha because he has reached the state free of all faults and possessing all good qualities, knows the method to reach that state, and teaches it to us. If we do as the Buddha did, by meditating on love and compassion for all sentient beings, not harming or getting angry with them, we too can become a Buddha.

Our enlightenment depends on the Buddhas and on sentient beings, and from this point of view, they are equally important to us. Thus when we look at any sentient being, we should recognize that she is indispensable to our attainment of enlightenment. Our enlightenment comes from cherishing sentient beings; it does not come from cherishing only ourselves. Understanding this, whenever we encounter people in our lives, it becomes easy to feel, "May this person be happy and free from suffering."

Caring for sentient beings means freeing them from the suffering of unfortunate rebirths and of cyclic existence in general, teaching the Dharma to those who want to hear it, providing the means for them to eliminate the causes which bring suffering temporarily and ultimately, not harming them, not lying to them, not creating discord among them, not speaking harshly to them, and so on. Through caring about them now, excellent results will follow, for us and for them.

By cherishing sentient beings and working to bring about their happiness, we accumulate great positive potential and as a result will enjoy fortunate rebirths. On the basis of such births, we can attain liberation and enlightenment, which is also called non-abiding nirvana. On the other hand, if we do not cherish sentient beings, regard them as unimportant, and consequently neglect or harm them, many troubles and hardships will befall us in this and future lives.

Hearer and solitary realizer arhats have abandoned the disturbing attitudes in their own mindstreams, but have not abandoned all the imprints of the disturbing attitudes or the mistaken dualistic appearance (i.e., true appearance). That is, they have abandoned the deluded obscurations which prevent liberation but not the obscurations to omniscience which prevent Buddhahood. Thus, hearers and solitary realizers attain the lower levels of enlightenment but not the great enlightenment of a Buddha, who is free of all faults and possesses all excellent qualities. This is because they have not habituated themselves extensively to the mind cherishing others. They have love and compassion and feel, "May all sentient beings be free of their suffering, and may they have happiness." However, they do not familiarize themselves again and again with the thoughts, "I alone will make them happy, and I alone will free them from suffering," which are the love and compassion of the great resolve. Bodhisattvas, on the other hand, attain the highest enlightenment because they have the intention to benefit others and habituate themselves to it continuously. We also should give up like poison our attitude of neglecting others.

It is helpful for us to investigate, "What harm comes from self-centeredness? What benefit comes from cherishing others?" In this way, we will see clearly from our own experience that we should not give in to self-preoccupation for a moment. Through thinking about this continuously, our mind will naturally change and we will think that trying to achieve just our own aims is foolish and that working to achieve the welfare of others is desirable. That will be our clear experience when we consider the faults of self-centeredness and the benefits of cherishing others.

Developing patience

When trying to develop a positive attitude which sees sentient beings as lovable and cherishes them, we are met with the question, "Yes, but what about the times others have harmed me and caused me great pain? Isn't it justifiable to be angry?" The practice of patience is essential here. When a person harms us physically or emotionally with a negative motivation, the disturbing attitudes in his mindstream act as the perpetuating cause for his motivation. That is, his previous disturbing attitudes cause his later disturbing attitudes, and these motivate his actions. The cooperative condition for his actions is the harm we have given in past lives. If we had not accumulated this karma in the past, the cooperative condition for his present actions would be missing, and because all the causes would not be complete, he would not have done the action which we find so unpleasant. Therefore there is a connection between the harm done to us and the karma that we accumulated in past lives from harming others. The harm done to us now is the result of our negative actions in past lives. Therefore, it is useless to be angry at the other person when we ourselves participated in creating the cause for the harm we received. In addition, by harming us with a negative motivation, the other person is creating the cause for his own future suffering. Thinking in this way will induce our compassion.

We can also reflect that in past lives this person has been our mother innumerable times. We have been born as her child innumerable times and been cared for by her. Think of the way in which mothers of all species protect and look after their young. Although this person is harming us now, her kindness has been far greater. How can we be angry? Other times, when she was not our mother, she was also kind and at times even sacrificed her life for us. Sometimes she may have been an animal and we ate her flesh and wore her skin. It is not right to focus on only the present harm the person is inflicting; if we see the larger picture which includes her great kindness towards us in other lifetimes, then our anger will dissolve and compassion for her will arise.

When a person harms us, we should try to bear it without getting angry or retaliating. If we resent him and return the harm, what would the result be? Our negative attitudes and actions would leave more negative karmic imprints in our mindstream which will ripen in our meeting yet again more harm and horrible conditions. What is the use of retaliating? Who does it really harm? Only ourselves.

When we practice patience, the practices of the six far-reaching attitudes will come automatically. With an attitude of love and compassion, we give to others. When giving, we have to be ethical and not harm others in the process. We also have to be able to bear their ingratitude or even their misunderstanding when we help them, and for this patience is essential. Thus the far-reaching attitudes of generosity and ethics are the preliminaries to patience. With patience, we are then able have joyous effort for Dharma practice and can generate concentration and wisdom without being distracted by anger. Thus, joyous effort, concentration, and wisdom come after the practice of patience. In this way, practicing patience strengthens our practice of the other far-reaching attitudes.

Thinking in this way, we will come to see that the person who harms us is in fact very helpful. It is as if she is handing us our enlightenment on a plate. If we are able to think like this, then wherever we live, and however many people we are living in the midst of, whether we are in an isolated place or in a place full of hustle and bustle, it will not make a great deal of difference. We will be able to live peacefully and happily no matter what situation we encounter. The more we are able to reduce our attachment and anger, and remain free from angry thoughts of "This person is harming me!" and free from clinging thoughts of "This person helped me. She is so wonderful and I want to be with her," the more we will be happy in any situation we encounter. Everyone will equally appear as the cause of our attaining enlightenment and we will cherish them.

We regard our Dharma teachers as kind because they teach us, give us precepts, and lead us on the path to liberation and omniscience. Like our Dharma teacher, the person who harms us encourages our practice of patience, which enhances our practice of the other far-reaching attitudes, and therefore they are very kind in helping us on the path. In fact, their kindness is equal to our teacher's, and without either we would not be able to attain full enlightenment.

If we found a treasure chest full of all sorts of precious gems in our house and we didn't have to exert the slightest effort to acquire it, we would naturally be delighted. Similarly, when we are harmed by someone, we should think we just received an aid to achieving enlightenment and feel overjoyed. If we get angry and retaliate, our virtuous roots will be destroyed and we will create more negative karma. Therefore, because we care about our own happiness, we should try to avoid anger.

When someone disparages or criticizes us, speaks badly about us to others, or spreads rumors or lies about us, we should try not to get angry or retaliate, but to think, "This is helping me to get enlightened." In fact, if we practice patience, the person is helping us to get enlightened.

Sometimes we help someone and hope that in return we can call on them for help if we experience hardships. But if we do, and that person not only refuses to help us but also harms us, we should see the disadvantages of being upset with him and meditate on compassion.

Training our mind means knowing how to apply the antidotes to our disturbing attitudes. The more we are able to this, the more we will be able to practice the Dharma and to be content in every situation we encounter. Thought transformation—another name for mind training—is a ticket to happiness. It is like going to a treasure island covered with gems. Through mind training, everything and everyone becomes an opportunity to practice. Nothing can be found that cannot be used for training the mind.

There is a Tibetan phrase, "One practice for one person." It means that if we cherish others and habituate ourselves to this way of thinking, we will accomplish what we wish. If we understand the way of thinking explained above, whatever practice we do will develop our bodhichitta. There is no need to practice many different things, going from one practice to another in an attempt to find the best one to do. Cherishing others is useful for everything: having good relationships and getting along well with people now, having fortunate rebirths, attaining liberation and gaining all the inconceivable qualities of the body, speech, and mind of a Buddha. Cherishing others is the method to attain all the virtuous things we desire.

Having thought of the faults of self-centeredness and the advantages of cherishing others, we should exchange self and others. That does not mean thinking self is other and other is self. Rather, we should cherish others the way we cherish ourselves now and neglect ourselves like we neglect others now. We should care for and protect others just like we now care for and protect our own body, speech, and mind, which we hold as "mine."

If we have strength of mind and a strong wish to attain enlightenment, the thought, "I definitely must exchange self and others," will arise after we think about the faults of self-preoccupation and the advantages of cherishing others. Even if we are not able to exchange self and others right away, our selfishness will get weaker, and even when it does arise we will easily recall the points of this meditation and it will diminish. When suddenly anger or jealousy arise towards someone, we will notice it and think, "This attitude is not right." This will start to happen automatically the more familiar we are with this way of thinking. But of course, we should not expect this to happen immediately.

Meditating on equalizing and exchanging self and others is another method to train the mind in the aspiration which is intent on benefiting others. In this method, the practice of taking and giving helps us to develop compassion and love. It also trains us in the actual aspiration intent on benefiting others.

To review, when we equalize self and others we think that self and others are equal in wanting happiness and not wanting suffering. We decide to aim our thoughts and actions at accomplishing the happiness of sentient beings and all that is useful to them, without differentiating between them, holding some close and others at a distance. After thinking strongly and from many points of view about the disadvantages of self-preoccupation and the benefits of cherishing others, we generate heart-warming love in which all sentient beings appear pleasing and lovable to us. This heart-warming love is more extensive and profound than that generated in the seven instructions. That is because this method of generating bodhichitta is for those of higher capability. To cherish others and neglect ourselves involves completely turning around our usual way of looking at things. It is a very direct and incisive method. A person of meager strength of mind and intelligence would find it extremely difficult. For this person, it is more productive to meditate on the seven instructions; it is a more gradual and gentle approach where our deep-rooted concepts are not immediately challenged.

Thus the two methods of developing the altruistic intention arose in view of the difference in capabilities of the practitioners. Those who generate it by equalizing and exchanging self and others are very courageous and their minds are sharper. Other practitioners' minds are not so brave; they cannot directly destroy self-centeredness. For them it is better to go gradually by way of the seven instructions. There is also a way of combining the two methods in an eleven-point meditation which will be explained at the conclusion of this chapter.

Because it is so challenging to our usual way of looking at things, equalizing and exchanging self and others was not taught publicly in ancient times. It was kept more or less secret, and was taught only to a few fortunate disciples. Atisha gave it to Drom Tonpa, who taught it to the three Kadampa brothers, who also taught it to only a few select disciples. Geshe Chekawa saw that if this custom was continued, there was a danger that the stream of the instruction would be discontinued, and therefore he taught it to many students.

In general all Bodhisattvas are equal in having love and compassion, but the strength of their love, compassion, and bodhichitta can differ greatly. The strength of their practice of the six far-reaching attitudes is correspondingly different, as is the time taken to attain enlightenment. For example, Bodhisattvas on the path of accumulation are equal in being Bodhisattvas, but some of them will have stronger bodhichitta than others. Thus, some will have a stronger practice of the six far-reaching attitudes and will attain enlightenment quicker. When we look strongly at the faults of self-cherishing and the advantages of cherishing others, in the way described above, the love and compassion which come afterwards are much stronger. As a consequence, the bodhichitta which is generated will be very powerful.

For example, in a life when Buddha Shakyamuni was still a Bodhisattva, he was born as a Mahabrahmin. One day he was walking through a forest with his companion, the Bodhisattva Mapampa. They came across a tiger who had just given birth but had no milk to give her newborn cubs, nor had she any means of obtaining food since she was so worn out. They saw that either the mother would eat the cubs, or all of them, cubs and mother alike, would die of starvation. The two Bodhisattvas were equal in having compassion, but there was a difference in the strength of their compassion. Mapampa, not having reflected strongly on the faults of self-centeredness and the benefits of cherishing others, went elsewhere in search of fresh meat for the cubs and their mother. When he had gone, the Mahabrahmin, who was well trained in equalizing and exchanging self and others, immediately gave his own body.

Mapampa was aware of the shortcomings of self-preoccupation and the advantages of cherishing others, but his insight into this was not so deep. A mind of self-protection reared up and he was unable to give his own body. The Mahabrahmin, on the other hand, thought to himself, "Selfishness is my greatest enemy; I will not allow it to develop!" Seeing that those sentient beings were about to die, he decided to help them and threw himself from a nearby precipice so that they could eat his body. He was able to do this happily and without fear because his understanding of the faults of self-centeredness and the advantages of cherishing others was so deep.

The benefits of love and compassion

Before meditating on taking and giving, it is helpful to contemplate the benefits of love and compassion. This will make our mind happy and joyful, and we will spontaneously want to meditate on them. *The King of Concentration Sutra* explains that if a person completely filled many tens of millions of enlightened beings' pure lands, each the size of our world, with many different kinds of beautiful offerings, constantly offered this to the Buddhas, the positive potential would be immeasurable and inexpressible. But if we meditate for just a short while on love, feeling "If only each and every sentient being could be happy," the positive potential would be millions of times greater.

In *The Land of Manjushri Sutra*, the Buddha said that to the northeast of our world, there is a world called "The World of the Great Sovereign," which contains thousands of Buddha lands. When the monastics in that world enter the meditative absorption of cessation, they experience great pleasure and peace because the gross disturbing attitudes are prevented from manifesting. If we were able to make many sentient beings possess peace and pleasure like those monastics have for tens of millions of years, the positive potential would be very great. But the positive potential of meditating on love generated equally for all sentient beings even for the duration of a finger-snap would be far greater. If the benefit of meditating on love for such a short time is so great, what need is there to mention the benefit of meditating on it for hours, days, months, or years? Why is there such benefit from meditating on love and compassion? When we reflect on them, we create the unique causes of bodhichitta, and bodhichitta is the basis of the Bodhisattva practices of the six far-reaching attitudes.

The Precious Garland of the Middle Way says that if we were to give many types of delicious food to all the beggars three times each day, great positive potential would be created. Yet there would be even more positive potential in meditating on love and compassion because in the long term having these attitudes will enable us to benefit a far greater number of beings in more ways. In addition, we will naturally stop harming them and thus will be spared the negative experiences that result from our negative actions.

Simply meditating on the equanimity that precedes the seven instructions brings great benefit. As we develop equanimity, the gross conceptions of attachment, hatred, and partiality towards sentient beings diminishes. Consequently, the many negative actions motivated by those gross conceptions decrease, and thus we are spared the negative experiences that result from those negative actions.

If we practice love and compassion well, others will have a good opinion of us. They will look upon us with kindness, be friendly to us, and happily help us when we are in need. We will receive less harm from others, and even if we are harmed, we will not be distressed. In addition, our mind will be happy and well, and we will be able to accomplish what we want without a lot of effort. Even if we are unable to gain liberation from cyclic existence in this life, by practicing love and compassion, we will take a good birth in our next life.

When the Buddha was about to attain enlightenment, he was attacked by many demons who were trying to hinder and harm him. In response, he meditated on love and his kind thoughts automatically pacified them. For us too, meditating on love or compassion towards people who maltreat us is by far the best way of calming conflict and averting harm. It is much more effective than the wrathful rituals for averting harm. Maitreya Buddha said in the *Ornament of the Mahayana Sutras*, that when many illnesses, harm from evil spirits, and so on befall us, meditating on love, compassion, and the mind wishing to benefit others is extremely efficacious.

The Buddha said that if we practice compassion well, it will progressively bring all the qualities of a Buddha into the palm of our hand. By gradually familiarizing ourselves with great compassion over a long period of time, our mind will be transformed automatically and all the qualities of a Buddha will follow without great effort.

Taking and giving

The taking and giving meditation profoundly challenges our usual views for in it we imagine taking on the suffering and problems of others and giving them our body, possessions, and positive potential so that they are satiated with happiness. The Buddha taught this meditation in the sutras, and it was elaborated on by Nagarjuna and Shantideva, as well as the Kadampa masters of Tibet. In the *Flower*

Ornament Sutra, Buddha taught taking on the sufferings of sentient beings and giving them our own happiness and virtue. Similarly, Nagarjuna said in *The Precious Garland,* "May all their evils ripen on me, and may my happiness and virtue ripen on them." Shantideva in *A Guide to the Bodhisattva's Way of Life* explained that if we do not exchange self and others, taking the suffering of others and giving them our happiness, we will not become enlightened and if we do not become a Buddha, we will remain in samsara where there is no happiness at all. Knowing the source of this teaching on taking and giving helps us to develop certainty and conviction in its efficacy.

However efficacious this meditation may be, it does not suit everyone. If this is the case, we do not have to force ourselves to do it. Some people feel afraid of taking others' suffering and it is difficult for them. They feel that they already have plenty of problems and do not need to take the hardships of others on top of that. There is no need for these people to practice taking.

In doing this practice, we spread our compassion and love equally to all sentient beings, so there is no sentient being we can point out and say, "I do not wish for this one to be free of suffering," or "I do not want this sentient being to have happiness." With our love and compassion embracing all beings without differentiation, we wish that all their negativities, various non-virtuous actions, ripening results, results similar to the cause, and so on ripen on us because we want them to be free of suffering.

We practice taking from two sources: from sentient beings and from the environment they inhabit. First we take three things from sentient beings: suffering; the causes which produce it, disturbing attitudes and karma, which are the deluded obscurations; and the imprints left by the disturbing attitudes, which are the obscurations to omniscience. Masters often recommend, "Start taking from yourself," which is a helpful way to become accustomed to taking. In the morning, we take upon ourselves any suffering we might experience later in the day. We think of voluntarily accepting it and experiencing it now. When we are accustomed to this, we take the suffering we will experience tomorrow, then the suffering of the day after, the next month, next year, and gradually our future lives as well. We are taking upon ourselves the suffering which is going to be experienced by people in the same continuum as ourselves. When we are somewhat trained in this meditation, we start to take the suffering of those who are close to us: our parents, siblings, partner, and friends. Finally, we imagine taking the suffering of all sentient beings in the six realms. All the time, we should think, "Their suffering and negative karma has ripened on me and they are free from suffering and negativities."

When taking the suffering, causes, and imprints, don't think that they land somewhere around us, but that they pour onto the self-centeredness in our heart. This is the case whether we take from the people in the same continuum as us, our parents and dear ones, or all sentient beings. By their landing on our self-centeredness, it is destroyed and becomes non-existent.

In general, we take suffering, its causes, and imprints. Specifically, each group of sentient beings in the six realms has its own particular suffering. The beings in the hell realms suffer from intense heat and cold, the hungry ghosts from hunger and thirst, the animals from stupidity and confusion, the demigods from jealousy and frustration, the gods from wasting away and separating from all they are attached to at the time of death, and the humans from birth, aging, sickness, and death.

We imagine all sentient beings in front of us, each experiencing his or her various problems. Having generated compassion which takes responsibility for their welfare, we imagine that their suffering separates from them in the form of black light that comes out from their right nostrils. This enters our left nostril and descends to our heart where it destroys our self-centeredness, which we imagine there like a heap of black dust. The light strikes it forcefully and destroys it like water gushing from a water cannon and washing away a pile of dust. We imagine taking others' suffering and using it to destroy the cause of our own suffering—our self-centeredness.

By pouring the worst things on top of our self-preoccupation and self-grasping, we harm them as much as we can, and they will have to leave. It is like the cat at our monastery who stays only because we are friendly, treat her well, and feed her. If we were nasty, she would leave. Similarly, when contemplating the faults of self-centeredness, we insult it, calling it a butcher, say it is lazy and stupid. To heap more abuse on it, we pour everything horrible that afflicts sentient beings onto it.

Up until now we have taken from ordinary sentient beings who have not entered the path. What do we take from those who have already entered a path? From the hearers and solitary realizers on any of their five paths we take the inner and outer adverse conditions preventing them from entering the Bodhisattva path. We also take the deluded obscurations which they have not yet abandoned as well as their obscurations to omniscience. These are their problems. From the

Bodhisattvas—those on the first path, the path of accumulation, all the way up to those on the tenth ground—we take all the inner and outer adverse conditions obstructing them from attaining the next ground up. In addition, we take on their deluded obscurations and obscurations to omniscience.

Secondly, we practice taking from sentient beings' environments, impure places which arose due to the karma of sentient beings. When taking the faults and pollution from the environment, we imagine as described above—they strike the self-centeredness and self-grasping at our heart and make them vanish. By taking the faults of these environments they become pure lands.

Extensive giving

In the sutras, the Buddha taught the practice of giving away our body, possessions, and root of virtue to all sentient beings. Shantideva said in his *A Guide to the Bodhisattva's Way of Life*, "I must give away my body, possessions, and virtue generated in the three times, without any sense of loss, for the sake of all sentient beings." Asanga said in *Stages of the Bodhisattva* that Bodhisattvas should stay in an isolated place, collect their minds and prevent them from wandering to external objects. They should think of the great kindness of sentient beings, and the fact that they have neither great happiness nor great virtue. They should reflect that sentient beings are tormented by all the various types of unsatisfactory experiences and their causes, and lack knowledge of the cessation of suffering and the path which leads to it. Then they should think deeply of the different ways to give to sentient beings. This practice of generosity does not take much effort and is very powerful. By practicing in this way, when we later meet situations in which we can give to or help others, there will be no obstacles or reservations in our minds about doing so; we will accumulate vast positive potential.

We need to train ourselves to give without miserliness or regret in order to attain Buddhahood for the sake of all sentient beings. First we train in imagining giving our body. Usually we consider our body, which is currently connected to our consciousness, as much more important than the leaves and branches of a tree. However, when giving our body, we should give it as if it were the leaves, flowers, and branches of a tree. That is, we give it without regarding it highly.

When we give our body, we do not think of it in its usual aspect of flesh and blood. In general, giving it in its ordinary aspect is not suitable for most people. However, there is a way of giving our body in the aspect of blood and flesh to those unruly, aggressive spirits who mainly want that and who crave the life of human beings. That will be explained further on.

How do we give our body? In the *Array of Tree Trunks Sutra*, the Buddha taught that we should imagine our body as a wish-fulfilling jewel. When such a jewel is properly cleaned and prepared, it can bestow all temporal wishes that people pray to it to grant. We think that whatever each sentient being wants arises from this body. Or, we can imagine our body actually transforming into a six-faceted or eight-faceted wish-fulfilling jewel from which all sentient beings get whatever they want. But the shape and aspect of our body does not have to be that of a gem. The main idea is that everything sentient beings like arises from our body, as from a wish-fulfilling jewel. What they need and want comes to them, and because they receive it, they are satisfied, and happy.

Different sentient beings want, need, and hope for different things, and when giving our body, we imagine giving all these things. For example, during a time of drought and famine, sentient beings receive food and drink. Those who are without a refuge and protector receive one. Those who have to cross a great expanse of water and need a boat or bridge receive those. Those who are at sea and seek dry land find it. Those wanting light receive that. Those wanting a place to stay or clothes receive them. Those who need a friend, an employee, a helper, or a companion receive one.

Different mind training texts explain diverse ways to imagine giving our body. Some say that from our one body comes the vast variety of things sentient beings wish for. Some say that our one body emanates as many bodies as there are sentient beings. An emanation appears in front of each sentient being, and from that body each sentient being gets all that he or she wants. Either visualization is fine.

The four great elements—earth, water, fire, and air—are the main supports of our life. When this very universe formed, the four elements acted as the cause for all the phenomena which arose, and the four elements allow them to abide and develop. Whether we speak of the bodies of sentient beings or the things in the environment such as crops, visible forms, sounds, smells, tastes, and tangible objects, the water element holds them together, the fire element causes them to mature or makes them edible, the air element makes them increase and develop, and the earth element makes them firm and hard. The four elements perform many functions and are very useful. When giving our body, we can imagine it dissolving back into the four great elements and being used by sentient beings as the basis and support of their life. The wet portions of our body, such as the blood and lymph, dissolve into the water element. The hard parts of the body dissolve into the earth element. The warmth dissolves into the fire element. The air which travels through the channels dissolves into the air element. Similarly the empty space in our body dissolves into space. Sentient beings can only survive by depending on the elements and on space; they cannot live without water, earth, fire, or air. We imagine our body dissolving into the four elements and becoming the basis and support of the lives of sentient beings and thereby benefiting them greatly.

Similarly, we should think, "I have become the cause and basis for all sentient beings that pervade the extent of space to receive all forms of happiness, not only temporary but ultimate, including the happiness of non-abiding nirvana." Having imagined giving all sentient beings our body, we should think that sentient beings now possess happiness and its causes. This brings great joy to our mind and accumulates great positive potential, which we then dedicate for the happiness of sentient beings. This practice is for a courageous person with a strong mind, wisdom, and the ability to think well. If a person lacks these qualities at present, this practice is not suitable for his mind.

Just as in taking, we now give to sentient beings and to the environment they inhabit. When giving to sentient beings, we give to both ordinary beings who have not entered the path and to those who already entered the path. When giving to ordinary beings, we start with the beings in the hell realms. The ground of the hell realms is iron, ugly and black. By giving our body to the beings there, we visualize the ground becoming golden. Similarly, all ugly colors and fearful or threatening appearances are transformed, and the beings themselves come to have an excellent and attractive body, wonderful possessions, dwellings, food, drink, friends, companions, assistance, family, country, and so on, whatever they want or need. The suffering that they are undergoing is pacified, and they attain a precious human life. But all these things are not enough to practice the Dharma, which is the path bringing them ultimate happiness. Now we imagine giving them all conducive conditions and necessities for Dharma practice: external conditions, such as spiritual teachers, teachings, books, supportive friends who encourage their practice, and so on; and internal conditions such as the seven arya jewels (faith, ethical discipline, hearing the Dharma, generosity, wisdom, integrity, and consideration for others), the three trainings (higher ethics, concentration, and wisdom), and the five powers (faith, wisdom, mindfulness, concentration, and joyous effort) at a mature level of development.

Since they now have excellent conditions for practice, love, compassion, and bodhichitta develop in their mindstreams. They practice the six far-reaching attitudes, and finally become Buddhas. Similarly, think that the hungry ghosts and the animals receive all they need. Their bodies transform into excellent ones, and they receive excellent possessions, friends, and so forth. They have all the outer and inner conditions for practicing Dharma, generate all the realizations of the path from the beginning up to full enlightenment. We can go slowly through this, imagining in depth and feeling how happy they are to have all their temporal and ultimate needs fulfilled. As we give, we can think that masses of white light rays leave from our right nostril and go to all beings, entering them through their left nostril. This light gives them all they want and makes them experience pure happiness.

After that, think of the human beings who lack the opportunity to practice the Dharma. Not everyone who has a human body has this chance: some have wrong views, some are born in places where no Buddha has come, some lack religious freedom. Think that you give your body to them, they receive all the conducive conditions to practice, and attain the bliss of the truth body, just as before. To those people who enjoy conditions conducive to Dharma practice, we can give our body so that their inner and outer conditions improve and they attain enlightenment quicker.

After that, we give to the six types of desire realm gods, the demigods, the gods of the seventeen abodes of the form realm, and the gods of the four levels of the formless realm. Also we give to the beings in the intermediate state. The way of thinking is as before.

There is a particular way of meditating with respect to those beings who are full of hatred towards us and who harm us. Here we think specifically of all the violent, vindictive beings in all worlds of the ten directions, who have malicious and hateful minds. They may be unruly spirits and interfering forces, those to whom we are in debt from distant past lives and who are awaiting repayment, those who we harmed in the past, or those who lust for this life's body and life-force. We emanate wonderful things in great quantities to give them—splendid houses, food, drinks, and all the outer and inner necessities. After meditating on love and compassion towards them, and with the motivation of bodhichitta, we hook them in front of us to the place where we have emanated all those marvelous things. Then we speak the truth to them, "In the beginningless past you have been my mother countless times. Each time you helped me and gave me happiness to the best of your ability and you protected me from harm and suffering." These words are really true; when we think about it, they have in fact been extremely kind. We can definitely come to sincerely feel this when we understand this situation and continuously reflect on it. We should develop the sense of their kindness very strongly.

These beings were also kind to us when they were not our mother. For example, we may have eaten their flesh when they were born as cows or chickens. We may have worn their skin when they were born as sheep or foxes. And as human beings, of course, they helped us in many ways in previous lives. We continue, "Today I am going to repay your great kindness. Those of you who like meat, eat meat. Those of you who like drinking blood, drink blood. Those who like gnawing bones, gnaw them. Those who like skin, take skin." Here we imagine giving our body as meat, blood, and bones. To those who are vegetarians we imagine giving the three sweets (honey, sugar, and molasses) and the three whites (milk, yogurt, and butter). We think that they receive anything they want from our body; their desires are sated, their minds become happy, and they are free of the hardships of hunger, thirst, and poverty. Those beings who are our vicious enemies, who obstruct and hinder us, are now transformed. Their harmful, violent minds become peaceful, and they generate love and all the realizations of the path until they attain the truth body (*dharmakaya*) of a Buddha.

Then we teach them, "The result of helping is happiness; that of harming is suffering. Take your own body as an example: if it is harmed even a little, you suffer. Consider this, and do not harm others." Due to our uttering these words, their malicious thoughts and cruel actions are completely pacified. They generate love, compassion, and bodhichitta and attain the four Buddha bodies.

That is how we give to the sentient beings who have not attained a path. It may seem that thinking like this will not facilitate our achieving our ultimate goal. We might think this kind of meditation is pointless and a waste of time. In fact it is highly worthwhile and is a practice for people with great wisdom! When we meditate on compassion, we think, "If only all sentient beings could be free of suffering," and when we meditate on love, we think, "If only all sentient beings could have happiness!" However, that compassion and love do not have a means to do something concrete to accomplish this. But here in the taking and giving meditation, we are not just thinking. We are also, as much as we can, blending it with a method for bringing sentient beings happiness and freeing them from suffering. That is why it is so worthwhile. We give our body, possessions, and the virtue we have accumulated all for the sake of sentient beings. Thinking in this way is very useful and extensive, and it prepares us to have the courage, love, and compassion to give whenever the opportunity arises in our daily lives. In addition, the positive potential from this meditation brings us closer to the Bodhisattva stages and enlightenment, our ultimate goal, when we will be able to help sentient beings extensively. Taking and giving is, in fact, an indispensable means for Bodhisattvas to attain their ultimate goal.

We also give to those who have attained a path, both those who have attained a path of the hearer or solitary realizer, from the path of accumulation to arhatship, and to those who have attained a path of the Bodhisattva vehicle. To the former we give all the outer and inner conditions needed to practice love, compassion, and bodhichitta and to ascend the paths of the Bodhisattva vehicle and become Buddhas.

To those on one of the Bodhisattva paths, from the Bodhisattva path of accumulation up to the tenth ground, we offer our body, from which they receive all the inner and outer conditions to attain the higher paths. Attaining a higher path necessitates purifying the stains of the previous path. For example, on the path of seeing, certain obscurations are to be purified, and the first ground has its portion of stains to be purified. Each path and ground has its object to abandon and each has its antidote to develop. We offer all that the Bodhisattvas need to accomplish the ground and paths, and to finally attain the truth body.

Normally, we train our minds in pure appearance regarding our glorious, holy, root and lineage spiritual mentors and the countless Buddhas abiding in limitless worlds in the ten directions, and try to see them as free from all faults and possessing all qualities. It may seem that there is nothing for us to give them because they already have all inner and outer conducive conditions, but we make offerings to them by imagining that we emanate countless bodies. Each body has countless heads, and each head has countless mouths. With all these bodies, we then physically prostrate, verbally praise them, and mentally generate faith. From our body, which is like a wish-fulfilling gem, we also emanate infinite, inconceivable, and beautiful offerings that completely fill all the Buddhas' pure lands. We offer beautiful sights, sounds, smells, tastes, and tangible objects. They accept these offerings and generate the exalted wisdom of great bliss and emptiness. Then pray, "May all sentient beings again and again make offerings to all the Buddhas in this way, and may they thereby constantly experience the uncontaminated happiness of the Buddhas. May whatever aspiration the Bodhisattvas have to achieve the welfare of others come about exactly as they wish. May sentient beings receive whatever the Buddhas wish them to have. May the practitioners of the hearer and solitary realizer vehicles gradually progress and develop the qualities of the Bodhisattva vehicle and finally attain the bliss of the truth body."

Next, we give our body to each world's environment. Due to giving our body, all faults of the environment that are caused by disturbing attitudes are purified, and all environments become the appearance of the exalted wisdom itself, like Buddhas' pure lands. Previously, we gave our body to the inhabiting sentient beings and due to that they became Buddhas. Now, we give our body, and the places they inhabit become pure lands. Pure lands do not arise from disturbing attitudes and karma. They are special places arising due to prayers and the roots of virtue which are free from all defilement. The plains and mountains in the pure lands are made of precious substances, the air is fresh, and the water sweet. There are birds, fields of fragrant flowers, springs, waterfalls, and the like, all of which automatically fill the mind with joy on sight. Thinking in this way is like preparing our own pure land, for when we become a high Bodhisattva, we will need a place where we attain enlightenment, and an impure place will not do for that. Meditating in this way helps to collect the causes for such a pure land, where the environment is inconceivably beautiful and pleasing to the mind.

A Guide to the Bodhisattva's Way of Life says, "Everywhere may the ground be pure, free from the roughness of stones and the like. May it be the nature of lapis lazuli and be as smooth as the palm of our hand." "Free from the roughness of stones" means free of any faults. The ground in a Buddha's pure land is even, expansive, and soft to touch. It is smooth by nature, like lapis lazuli. Buddha lands are characterized by many marvelous qualities. In a pure land, the trees make the sound of Dharma when the wind blows through them: this sound indicates the four noble truths and the four seals. Meditating like this brings great joy to our mind, purifies our deluded appearance which arises due to our negative attitudes, and creates the cause for us to eventually actualize a pure land of our own where we will be enlightened.

We have now finished the explanation of how to practice giving our body to the inhabiting sentient beings and the inhabited environment. Giving our possessions and our roots of virtue are not explained in detail here. We meditate in the same way as we do when giving our body. The recipients of our gifts are the same—the beings of the six realms, the beings who have attained a path, our spiritual mentors, and the Buddhas—and the way to meditate is the same. But the gift is different. Here we offer all our belongings by transforming them into wish-fulfilling possessions. Like wish-fulfilling gems, our belongings bestow whatever is wanted or desired. Having received our gifts of worldly and supermundane possessions, sentient beings receive the collection of causes needed for attaining enlightenment, and they attain the happiness of the truth body.

The third gift is our virtue and positive potential. While we can give only our present and future bodies and possessions, we can give our virtues of the three times—the past, present, and future. The virtues of the past can be given because they remain as imprints on our mindstream.

Where is giving away virtues taught? Shantideva, in *A Guide to the Bodhisattva's Way of Life*, describes the practice of giving away our virtues accumulated in the three times without any sense of loss. Nagarjuna says, "Due to this virtue, may all beings accumulate the two collections of positive potential and exalted wisdom, and attain the two holy bodies which arise from them." This passage encourages us to dedicate and give away our virtue as causes for all sentient beings to attain the form body and the truth body of a Buddha.

We give all our virtue, from the smallest—such as that created by giving an animal a little food—up to the very powerful virtues of meditating on bodhichitta. The way of giving is the same as explained above. By giving our virtue, sentient beings receive every cause and condition needed to attain enlightenment in this very life. They complete the two collections and finally attain the bliss of the truth body.

General advice on taking and giving

We can practice a concise taking and giving meditation in conjunction with the verse in the *Guru Puja*, "Thus, venerable compassionate spiritual mentors, inspire us so that all negativities, obscurations, and sufferings of mother sentient beings without exception ripen upon me right now, and that I give my happiness and virtue to others and thereby invest all beings in bliss." The first time we recite it, we take the suffering of mother sentient beings and give our body. The second time we take their causes of suffering—disturbing attitudes and karma—and give them our possessions. The third time we take their obscurations to omniscience—the imprints of the disturbing attitudes—and give them our roots of virtue accumulated in the past, present, and future.

We should take our time doing the taking and giving meditation, first cultivating the wish to do what is of use to others, and then commencing the actual practice. We can spend as long as we wish taking or giving. There's no need to rush.

When we become accustomed to the practice after a long period of time, the thought transformation texts recommend that we "Mount the two on the breath," which means that when we inhale, we take on sentient beings' suffering and hardships, their causes, and the subtle imprints on their mindstreams. We take these in the aspect of black light which enters though our left nostril and hits our self-centeredness and our false concept of a self, imagined as a lump at our heart chakra. Think that now sentient beings are free from all their problems and attain the happiness of the truth body. At the same time, our self-grasping ignorance and self-preoccupation lose their strength. They become weaker and weaker until they totally vanish. When we exhale, we give our body, possessions, and virtues accumulated in the three times, imagining they benefit sentient beings extensively, eliminating their hardships, so that finally they all attain the happiness of the truth body. Gradually, with training, this practice will come naturally as we breathe in and out. At that point, just breathing becomes very potent and virtuous.

We might think there is not much point in improving our generosity in this way. Quite the reverse: many great sages have encouraged us to meditate in this way, saying that the results are by no means small. By meditating on taking, we cultivate powerful compassion and by meditating on giving, we develop great love. The problem is not that this meditation is difficult to understand; it is a question of whether we want to meditate. When we understand its importance, the wish to do it will grow. Buddha praised love and compassion highly, stating on many occasions the great benefits of meditating on them. All those benefits also result from meditating on taking and giving, so this is certainly worthwhile.

At present, even if we want to give a small thing to someone, our miserliness often prevents us. This is because we are not familiar with the mind of giving. We have not accustomed ourselves to that attitude or gained experience in it. By meditating on taking and giving and thereby gaining experience in it, later when there is a need, we will be able to give our possessions and even our life without any sense of loss. The Buddha said in the *King of Concentration Sutra* that if we habituate ourselves to the mind of giving, our intention to give will automatically induce the ability to actually give. When our generosity becomes highly evolved, we will not only be extremely happy to actually give our body and life, but the happiness we will derive merely from hearing someone ask for something will be far greater than the bliss of the peace that hearer and solitary realizer arhats experience in nirvana.

The Buddha said that thinking again and again, "If only I could make all sentient beings happy and free of suffering," will act as a condition for us to be able to help others automatically. If we do not think in this way, this wish will never come about. Although we are not able to benefit others immediately in the way we wish, thinking in this way is an excellent method for coming to the point where we actually can benefit them. Therefore, it is said we should think about this repeatedly. When we train our minds in this way we must reflect that it is very important and worthwhile, recognizing that this is the very path along which the Buddhas and Bodhisattvas have passed.

The Kadampa masters say that meditating on taking and giving is a very difficult practice which destroys something very difficult to destroy. Self-centeredness is difficult to eliminate, and yet that difficult practice eliminates it.

"May anyone who merely sees, hears, remembers, touches, or talks to me be freed in that very instant from suffering and receive all the help and happiness they need." If we think and pray in this way, when we later become enlightened this will actually happen. At this time, we will be able to benefit easily and extensively those we come into contact with.

We aspire, "May all the suffering and negativities of all sentient beings ripen on me. May my virtue free all migrators from suffering and its causes and give them happiness and peace. May this happen not just in this life, but in all my future lives. May I benefit sentient beings in whatever way they desire by means of my body, speech, and mind."

By imagining that all sentient beings receive all that they need in the short term and long term through giving them our body, possessions, and virtues, we accumulate vast positive potential. This is so because the positive potential is proportionate to the number of sentient beings we help, and the number of sentient beings is immeasurable. Thus, Nagarjuna said if the virtue from meditating on taking and giving were transformed into form, there would not be enough space to hold it.

It would be very useful to do retreat on this. People who have studied the seven cause and effect instructions and equalizing and exchanging self and others have a lot to meditate on, and if they base their retreat on these topics it is very beneficial.

Can we use the things we have given?

After we have sincerely dedicated and given everything we possess to others, what will happen if we use those things? If we use them with craving and attachment and forget about using them for the benefit of others, that is a fault. If we use them with little or no craving and attachment, but nevertheless forget the welfare of others, that is still a fault, although it is not as bad. The point is that having dedicated our body, possessions, and positive potential for the benefit of all beings, we should continue to use them with that thought in mind.

The Vinaya explains that there are many parasites living in our body and if we are alive, they will remain alive, and if we die, so will they. When we eat, we should think that we are doing so to keep them alive and think, "Now I will nourish them with food. In the future may I satisfy them with the Dharma." This is one way to think while eating.

In our meditation we have also offered all that we have to our spiritual mentors, the Buddhas, and the Bodhisattvas. We might therefore think that we have no right to use those things. However, since the holy beings' aim is to accomplish the welfare of sentient beings, if we use the things we have offered to them for that purpose, there is no fault. This is similar to getting our food from our employer's kitchen when we work for him. Since we are working for him and accomplishing his wishes, it is fine to use the things required to do so.

In tantra, we think of ourselves as the deity, consecrate the food before eating, and then offer it to the deity. In this way we accumulate great positive potential. If we do not have any of the above motivations to benefit others, and simply eat, drink, and enjoy our possessions for our own pleasure, there is the danger of accumulating a lot of negative karma, while if we use these objects for the sake of sentient beings, there is no fault and there is even great merit.

Usually while offering a mandala we recite words such as, "I offer the body, speech, and mind of myself and others, our possessions and virtues accumulated in the three times to the spiritual mentors, Buddhas, Bodhisattvas, and deities." When we practice giving and taking we give away our body, possessions, and roots of virtue. Some people might think that after we have given all those away, it is not good for us to use them because they do not belong to us any more. This is not correct. If we use them with the proper motivation for the sake of others, there is no fault.

Practice in daily life

Training in conventional bodhichitta has two parts: the practice during the actual meditation session, and the practice after the session. The practice in the actual session is meditating on taking and giving. Now we will discuss how to practice developing the intent to benefit others when we are going about our daily life after the meditation session.

Objects of the senses can appear pleasing, displeasing, or neutral. When the object is pleasing, attachment arises in us; when it is displeasing, anger arises, and when it is neutral, a neutral state of mind arises. Whenever attachment, hatred or anger, or apathetic ignorance arise in our minds, we should pray, "May these three poisonous attitudes never be generated in the mindstreams of any sentient being. May they arise in my mind instead." Whenever things do not go right for us, we should pray, "May I bear this problem instead of sentient beings' having to endure theirs. May they never have difficulties and always be happy." We can think in this way no matter where we are or what we do, and thus keep love and compassion alive and growing in our hearts.

While we think in this way, we can recite, "May sentient beings' negativities ripen on me and my virtue ripen on them. May I experience their suffering, and may they all be happy through my virtue. May the all suffering of migrators, whatever it is, ripen on me. By the virtues of all the Bodhisattvas may migrators enjoy happiness." When we recite this, we should try to experience its meaning deeply in our hearts. If we do, our self-centeredness will vanish, and we will be free from the harm and pain we suffer under its influence.

We need to be decisive. If we dither, wondering whether there is benefit in training the mind in this, or worrying if we will be successful in doing it, we will waste a precious opportunity. Rather, we should dispel these useless doubts and train from our heart. We know through all the quotations that this practice is supported by the Buddha and the great practitioners throughout the centuries. We know through our own experience that this practice benefits ourselves and others. We should make up our mind to train in this practice and then do it, without doubting ourselves. If we do that, eventually we will be able to perfect this practice.

The two ways to generate bodhichitta

To compare the two systems of generating bodhichitta: in the seven cause and effect instructions we meditate on an equanimity which evens out our attachment, aversion, and apathy for beings we consider friends, enemies, and strangers. Prior to meditating on equalizing self and others, however, we meditate on an equanimity which feels, "Sentient beings are equal in terms of wanting happiness and not wanting suffering. Therefore I must be without any partiality in my beneficial intentions and actions towards them." When we meditate on equalizing and exchanging self and others, we reflect on the faults of self-centeredness and the advantages of cherishing others. Reflecting on those is equivalent to recognizing all sentient beings as having been our mother, thinking of their kindness, and repaying their kindness in the seven instructions. Thinking of the faults of self-preoccupation and the advantages of cherishing others induces heartwarming love, the fourth of the seven instructions. The compassion, which is the fifth, and love come when practicing taking and giving. The sixth is the great resolve, which also comes when meditating on taking and giving, because during the course of that meditation we decide that we alone will do what is required to free sentient beings from suffering and to bring them happiness. The result of both these systems is bodhichitta.

There are two stages in developing bodhichitta. The first is aspiring or wishing bodhichitta, which is simply wishing, "How wonderful it would be if I were to become a Buddha. I must do that for the benefit of others." After that, when we think, "I will never give this mind up or allow it to degenerate until I attain enlightenment," it is called aspiring bodhichitta with a promise. Engaging bodhichitta occurs when, in addition, we are committed to practicing the six far-reaching attitudes. The difference between the aspiring and engaging minds is like the difference between wanting to go somewhere and actually setting out to go there.

Combining the seven instructions and equalizing and exchanging self and others

When generating bodhichitta, we need first to have heart-warming love. The way of creating this is different in the seven-fold instruction and equalizing and exchanging, but from that point onwards the two methods are the same in the sense that both are aimed at producing love, compassion, the great resolve, and finally, bodhichitta. If we wish, we can combine the two methods, equalizing and exchanging self and others and the seven cause and effect instructions, into an eleven-point meditation:

1. Equanimity. This is the same equanimity as in the four immeasurables and in the seven cause and effect instructions. Here we free ourselves from attachment to friends, aversion to people we find disagreeable, and apathy to strangers, and develop an equal attitude of openness to all.

2. Recognizing all beings as having been our mother

3. Recalling the kindness of others. This has two parts. The first is recollecting the kindness of sentient beings when they have been our mother, as in the seven instructions. The second is the special recollection of kindness, which involves recollecting the kindness of others in general. Here we recognize that all the things we use and enjoy—food, clothing, and so forth—come from the efforts of sentient beings. In addition, to develop love and compassion in our minds, we need sentient beings. The Buddha turned the three wheels of Dharma and performed all the enlightened deeds of a Buddha to benefit sentient beings. It was for their sake that the Buddha appeared on this earth. Sentient beings are kind while we are in samsara, while we train on the path, and when we become enlightened

4. Repaying the kindness

5. Equalizing self and others. Here we think that self and others are completely equal in not wanting even the least suffering and wanting happiness. Therefore, it is not correct to see oneself as more important than others.

6. Thinking of the faults of self-centeredness

7. Thinking of the benefit of cherishing others

8. Exchanging self and others

9. Taking and giving

10. Great resolve

11. Altruistic intention or bodhichitta

These eleven come to two points: training in the aspiration to benefit others, which includes the first ten points; and training in the aspiration to enlightenment, which is the eleventh point.

CHAPTER TWELVE

Transforming Unfavorable Circumstances into the Path

During meditation on conventional bodhicitta, we focus on equalizing and exchanging self and others. After our meditation sessions end and we go about our daily activities, it is essential that we integrate the altruistic intention into all that we do and encounter. Effective Dharma practice touches upon and transforms every aspect of our being and our life.

While we are still in cyclic existence, we will definitely encounter adverse circumstances, for that is the very nature of samsara and is to be expected. If we buckle under the pressure of stressful situations, it will be difficult to maintain, let alone advance our Dharma practice. Therefore, we must transform these unfavorable circumstances into the path to enlightenment. Togme Sangpo now tells us how to transform distressing events, difficulties, wealth and ruin, and the hated and the desired into the path.

The first part, transforming distressing events into the path, deals with how to handle loss, suffering, blame, and criticism.

Transforming loss into the path

12   Even if someone out of strong desire
       Steals all your wealth or has it stolen,
       Dedicate to him your body, possessions,
       And your virtue, past, present, and future—
       This is the practice of Bodhisattvas.

If someone robs us of our wealth and possessions or instructs others to, it is the Bodhisattvas' practice not to retaliate. Not only do they not return the harm, but also they give their bodies, any possessions they have left, and their virtues of the three times, with the wish that all of the thief's desires be totally satisfied.

When our things are stolen or ruined by others, it is helpful to remember that wealth and possessions chain us to samsara, so by stealing them, this person has broken some of those chains. When we have money and possessions, we continuously suffer from dissatisfaction, always wanting more and better. We also worry about our possessions being stolen and have to protect them vigilantly. Through having money and possessions and clinging onto them with attachment, we create much karma which will result in suffering. Thinking in this way, we will feel that the thief has taken away the basis for our creating negative karma. He has released us from our chains and has opened the door to liberation for us.

In addition, in past lives we accumulated so much karma to suffer, and this is stored in our mindstream like money in a secure bank. By stealing our things, this thief has made some of that karma ripen so that now we are free of it. How kind he is to have robbed us of some of our bad karma! We should not see this person as an enemy, but as a good friend who helps to free us from suffering. Thus we want to give him our virtue, body, and anything else he did not already take. In this way, we practice patience and develop compassion.

Transforming suffering into the path

13 Even if someone tries to cut off your head
  When you haven't done the slightest thing wrong,
  Out of compassion take all his misdeeds
  Upon yourself—
  This is the practice of Bodhisattvas.

Although we have done nothing to deserve it, someone may attack us, beat us, or perpetrate other forms of violence on us. Certainly it is tempting to get angry in such a situation, but our anger will do no good. In fact, this person is creating the cause for his own unfortunate rebirth by attacking us, and the karma he creates is even heavier if we hold any of the three sets of vows: pratimoksha, Bodhisattva, or tantric. Thus, we cultivate compassion, and wish to take the person's karma and resultant suffering on ourselves. For example, if a crazy person attacks a person who is sane, the latter will not only not fight back but try to help, by giving him medicine and wanting him to get well. The sane person sees that the crazy person does not know what he is doing. He is out of control. Similarly, when someone harms us, we should recognize that he too is out of control and is being lead by his three poisonous attitudes. Similarly, we can remember that we are experiencing the ripening result of harmful actions we did in past lives, so why blame the other person? In addition, that person is causing our negative karma to be exhausted now, rather than later when the result could be much more difficult to bear. In this way, we will not be angry or retaliate, but will pray for and try to help the other. In *The Eight Verses of Thought Transformation*, it says, "Whenever I meet a person of bad nature who is overwhelmed by negative energy and intense suffering, I will hold such a rare one dear, as if I had found a precious treasure." People like this suffer greatly because they think only of themselves, not of others, and thus they are worthy of compassion, the wish that they be free from suffering and its causes.

Being patient when harmed by others does not mean that we take no action to prevent harm from occurring. Rather, patience frees our mind from the fog of anger and gives us the clarity and kindness to respond to a situation in a helpful way. Free of anger, we look for ways to resolve conflict other than seeking revenge.

Transforming blame into the path

14   **Even if someone broadcasts all kinds of unpleasant remarks**
      About you throughout the three thousand worlds,
      In return, with a loving mind,
      Speak of his good qualities—
      This is the practice of Bodhisattvas.

When others criticize us to our face or behind our back, and fill the whole universe with malicious gossip ruining our good name, we should not respond with anger and say all sorts of unpleasant things about them in return. If we retaliate, they will be unhappy, the conflict will escalate, and they will continue to say many bad things about us. We should remember that the other person's mind is under the control of disturbing attitudes which force him to act in this way. We should also recognize that our experience is the "wheel of sharp weapons" returning to us from the harsh words we have said to others. If we are honest, we recognize that we have criticized, blamed, insulted, and said many harsh words to others in the past. Now we are experiencing the karmic result of those actions. There is no reason to be angry at the other person since we are the ones who created the principal cause of this situation. In addition, should we get angry and try to ruin the other person's reputation and relationships in return, we will only create more cause to experience such painful situations again in the future. Therefore, instead of retaliating with more criticism and slander, we can cultivate compassion towards them. There is no sentient being who is devoid of good qualities. We can look for those good qualities and speak of them with a loving attitude that wants this person to have happiness and its causes.

Many other sages give similar advice. *The Precious Garland of the Middle Way* states, "Because we said unpleasant things to others in past lives, so we hear the same now." The great Atisha said, "When we hear unpleasant things said about us, think it is not true in the way it is heard, like an echo." In *The Eight Verses*, it says, "When others, out of jealousy, mistreat me with abuse, slander, and so on, I will practice accepting defeat and offering the victory to them." This means that when people are jealous of us and say all sorts of unpleasant things, criticizing us in many ways, we should give them the victory by agreeing with them and accept the defeat ourselves, by concurring that we are at fault. This does not mean that we blame ourselves in a psychologically unhealthy way whenever something goes wrong. Rather, it means that we give up having to be right, having to have the last word, and having to prove ourselves.

Thus, the Bodhisattva Togme Sangpo explains how to practice, and the quotes above corroborate his advice, acting as reasons to support his interpretation. Each quote shows a slightly different way of thinking, but they say basically the same thing: that unpleasant words are to be taken into the path.

Transforming criticism into the path

15   Though someone may deride and speak bad words
      About you in a public gathering,
      Looking on him as a spiritual teacher,
      Bow to him with respect—
      This is the practice of Bodhisattvas.

Suppose someone in a big gathering of people criticizes us to our face, saying we have certain faults and made certain mistakes, or even criticizes our Dharma practice, saying we are hypocritical. In this case, we should not only not be angry, but also respect that person as a spiritual mentor who is pointing out our faults. We should consider his or her actions as beneficial to us. Sometimes we do not recognize our faults and may even think we are wonderful because of them. In this case, if someone points out our faults in front of a large group of people, it may be unpleasant to hear, but in the long term it is very helpful to us.

The Kadam lamas say that the best spiritual guide is the one who points out the heap of faults we possess, because only by seeing them can we correct them, and only by correcting them can we progress on the path. We know others' faults so clearly, but to know our own we have to look in the mirror of the Dharma teachings, like looking in a mirror to check if there is dirt on our face. As Atisha remarked, "The supreme instruction is to damage the faults in our own minds." That is, the best advice is that which helps us to see our faults. We cannot see our faults by ourselves; we need help.

To avoid becoming angry when we are criticized or blamed, we can also think that not everyone on the planet criticizes us. There are people who have nice things to say about us. We don't need to get angry and be offended by what this person says. Similarly, when others praise us, instead of getting puffed up, we should think that not everyone says nice things about us. Some people say awful things; so there is no reason to be proud. This can help us remain more emotionally balanced, without reacting so much to either praise or criticism.

These are conventional ways to cut our anger and pride. On the ultimate level, we should think that the words are mere designations and do not exist from their own side at all.

The second part, transforming difficulties into the path, concerns dealing with ingratitude and derision.

Transforming ingratitude into the path

16   **Even if a person for whom you've cared**
          Like your own child regards you as an enemy,
          Cherish him specially, like a mother
          Does her child who is stricken by sickness—
          This is the practice of Bodhisattvas.

In the case of someone who, instead of repaying our kindness with kindness, responds by considering us an enemy, we should practice forgiving this person and not holding a grudge against him. We may have helped someone in a worldly or a Dharma way, cared for and cherished him with affection, and he may turn around and hurt us by rejecting us, damaging our body or possessions, spreading evil stories about us, and so forth. Here we are advised not to get angry, but to act like a mother does when her beloved child, who is afflicted by harmful spirits, hits her. Knowing that he acts in this way due to these spirits, she reacts with compassion and wishes him to be free of this harm. Similarly, the mind of a person who betrays our trust or who returns our kindness with harm is under the control of his disturbing attitudes and cannot help what he does.

A scriptural source which authenticates this idea is the *Ornament of the Mahayana Sutras* by Maitreya: "Some people act under the control of evil and harm others. Wise people, in reply, do not let their minds go in that direction, but instead transform the situation into a condition for increasing compassion and love." We understand that this person is without self-control and is controlled by her disturbing attitudes. If we, in turn, retaliate because of our own disturbing attitudes, we are being very foolish. This is certainly not a sign of wisdom or of having studied Dharma.

Therefore Geshe Chekawa said, "If others respond to our kindness with harm, retaliate with a meditation on compassion." *The Eight Verses* says, "When someone I have benefited and in whom I have placed great trust hurts me very badly, I will practice seeing that person as my supreme teacher." Such a person gives us an incredible opportunity to grow and to practice patience; therefore he or she is like our spiritual guide.

Transforming derision into the path

17   If an equal or inferior person
      Disparages you out of pride,
      Place him, as you would your spiritual teacher,
      With respect on the crown of your head—
      This is the practice of Bodhisattvas.

In a situation in which someone who is at our level or lower in their education, financial status, age, job status, physical attractiveness, or athletic ability belittles and derides us out of pride, we should not only not be angry, but respect her as we would our spiritual mentor. If we act in this way, it is a very high practice.

The person who harms us is in a weakened state of mind; she is under the oppressive control of her disturbing attitudes. This is clearly the case, since if she had a strong positive mind she would not act in this way. If we retaliate with angry aggression to someone who is in this mental state, this will not only inflame her emotions and increase the conflict, but also make our practice of virtue deteriorate. Therefore, Mahayana practitioners are given four points of advice:

1. If someone scolds us, we should not scold or speak harshly in return.

2. If someone criticizes us, pointing out real or imagined faults, or making small faults into big ones, we should not criticize that person in return.

3. If someone hits us, we should not strike back.

4. If someone gets angry with us, we should not get angry in return.

When we do not act in this way, we are not practicing patience. We cannot practice with people who are nice to us, only with those who harm us. Therefore, the person harming us is being very kind by providing the circumstance for us to practice patience. Nagarjuna advised, "The cause of attaining enlightenment is sentient beings. Therefore, those wanting the state of peerless enlightenment should see them as equal in importance to the Buddhas and gurus." When thinking of the kindness of others, we should not think that we too are special because we have been kind to others! That is for others to think.

In addition, having taken refuge in the Dharma, we are advised to abandon all violence—physical, verbal, mental, and emotional. Why? Because it harms others and results in our having an unfortunate rebirth and much suffering in the future. No good comes from harming others.

Some people think that cheating in business results in wealth; they witness others stealing in this way and their families having carefree comfortable lives. What they do not see is that the one who cheats will have to face the result in the future. The comfort and wealth he has now is due to his generosity in past lives. His present conniving is only the condition—not the cause—for receiving wealth.

If someone hurts us, we may get a little angry and say something in return. This may not be the best response, but if we pretend to be patient, yet keep the anger smoldering inside of us, thinking, "I will not forget what happened. I will never help her. I will get back at her for that," then we commit the great Bodhisattva downfall of abandoning sentient beings. This is also the tantric root downfall of abandoning love for sentient beings. This anger, which seems like it is protecting us, is completely self-defeating and brings us only harm. There is no use in it. We must remind ourselves of this over and over again so that it sinks in.

These two last verses are called "transforming difficulties into the path." Because these practices are very difficult, it is helpful to remember what it says in *A Guide to the Bodhisattva's Way of Life*: "There is nothing that does not become easier with familiarity." We will definitely get used to this way of thinking and be able to transform our emotions if we persist.

The third section, transforming wealth and ruin into the path, shows ways to handle situations of ruin and wealth.

Transforming ruin into the path

18   Though you lack what you need and are constantly
          disparaged,
      Afflicted by dangerous sickness and spirits,
      Without discouragement take on the misdeeds
      And the pain of all living beings—
      This is the practice of Bodhisattvas.

When our financial situation is pitiful and we lack the things we need, when we are looked down upon or belittled by others, when we are beleaguered by illness, in short when every thing that could go wrong for us has gone wrong, there is no point in becoming discouraged. We need to be brave. Instead of focusing on our own problems, we can think of others and how awful it would be if this were to happen to them. In this way, we develop compassion. Then we can practice taking others' suffering and its causes, while praying, "May all sentient beings' suffering and its causes ripen on me." The authenticity of this practice is confirmed in the *Precious Garland*, "Though one is reduced to a state seeming as pitiful as a hungry spirit, do not be discouraged but practice taking the suffering of others."

In Tibet, when merchants were traveling a long distance over rough terrain, a heavy snowfall could be disastrous for their business. But if they saw the good side of the situation and regarded the snow as an opportunity for them and their animals to rest, they would enjoy the experience rather than be despondent. If we think like this when facing difficulties, after a while when suffering arises it brings happiness. Suffering does not harm a Dharma practitioner. It does not become a hindrance because the practitioner can see that the suffering is using up negative karma and that later things will get better and better. If we think this way, then even if we cannot be happy, at least we will not feel miserable.

Obstacles urge us to practice. When we are in a good situation, it is difficult for us to think of suffering; we cannot generate the determination to be free from cyclic existence, and therefore our Dharma practice becomes rather automatic and lacks sincerity—if we do it at all. On the other hand, experiencing problems diminishes our complacency. Past masters said they were not so happy when they had lots of possessions, were well respected, and everything was going smoothly, because in those conditions, their mind became so busy with all the good things that the three poisonous attitudes would blaze out of control. When things go badly, the mind turns to Dharma, and that is very good, for in this way our disturbing attitudes and karma start to vanish. Suffering is our spiritual master, pointing out the faults of cyclic existence to us and inspiring us to develop love and compassion for others who are in a similar plight. From suffering, real Dharma practice comes. Thus suffering becomes a condition for much goodness. This does not mean that we should inflict suffering upon ourselves or deliberately put ourselves in bad situations. Rather, when problems and difficulties arise, as they naturally will because we are in cyclic existence, we should transform them into the path by thinking in this way. If we do not have a way to handle the problems that naturally come our way, our Dharma practice will not be stable and we will be forever on the verge of giving up.

We may be tempted to think, as many do, "When I was not involved in Dharma, my business went well, my health was good, my relationships were fine, everything was all right. Now it is completely opposite!" If we think like this, we have missed the point. Our troubles are not because of our Dharma practice. When bad things happen, it is due to our disturbing attitudes and negative karma. It is a mistake to blame the Dharma for our problems.

In brief, the practice of transforming difficulties into the spiritual path is summed up in a verse from the *Guru Puja,* "Should the environment and the beings therein be filled with the fruits of their negativity and unwished-for sufferings pour down like rain, inspire me to take these miserable conditions into the path by seeing them as causes to exhaust the results of my negative karma." When there is war and pollution in the environment, and people's minds are filled with clinging attachment, anger, and jealousy so that negative actions abound, at that time a Dharma practitioner becomes susceptible to harm. If one has no method to use at such times, he or she will not be able to practice.

Therefore, it is essential to train the mind so that hindrances can be transformed into a help for practice. If this is not possible, at least, these factors should not be allowed to harm the mind.

Taking misfortune into the path is an instruction that is admired by all the past holy beings. Therefore, if we really wish from our heart to practice, we should train in this method. At this point the author of the commentary we are following begs us with hands pressed together in supplication to engage in this holy instruction.

Transforming wealth into the path

19   **Though you become famous and many bow to you,**
      And you gain riches to equal Vaishravana's,
      See that worldly fortune is without essence,
      And be unconceited—
      This is the practice of Bodhisattvas.

When we own a lot, we develop great attachment and our mind bubbles over with thoughts about our possessions. At that time, we may let our Dharma practice slide. When we have great wealth, an attractive appearance, knowledge and good education, and are respected and appreciated in our work, we should not become inflated by these things, but regard all these marvels as essenceless. Under whatever pretext—worldly or Dharma—if we feel pride towards those inferior to us, compete with people equal to us, or are jealous of those who are better than us, our disturbing attitudes have taken over. To stop them, we should see that they are as ephemeral as a water bubble, lightning, and a dewdrop on the tip of a blade of grass. Because they are without essence and they are not a source of security, we should not be proud.

Atisha recommended, "Do not be proud, haughty, and arrogant because of having many possessions and so on. Rather, be subdued, don't make a big deal out of yourself, be respectful and compassionate." Drom Tonpa advised, "The more I have that others do not, the more I should be polite and offer respect and service to them. The water of good qualities cannot flow up the mountain of pride." This is true. When we think we are knowledgeable and important, our minds are not open to learning and our good qualities get exhausted.

Nagarjuna cautioned us against feeling smug and proud due to our wealth or even due to the Dharma practice we have done. We may think we are special because of having done retreat, taken certain initiations, or knowing some excellent teachers. In our arrogance, we tend to put others down and become reckless. Having become careless, we do many negative actions, which will bring suffering in future lives. We will have a lower position in society and be subjected to scorn. Therefore, whatever marvels we may come to possess, we should not feel superior, but think, "May all sentient beings have happiness like this," and respect those who currently lack these things.

This way of taking happiness and suffering, good and bad, into the path is a Bodhisattva practice. If we practice it as best we can, it will become easier. If we think it is too difficult and do not try, then we will never become familiar with it.

The fourth section, transforming the desired and the hated into the path, shows us how to deal with our anger and the objects which generate our attachment.

Transforming anger into the path

20   While the enemy of your own anger is unsubdued,
      Though you conquer external foes, they will only increase.
      Therefore with the militia of love and compassion
      Subdue your own mind—
      This is the practice of Bodhisattvas.

Our worst enemy is the disturbing attitudes, and of these, the worst is hatred. We cannot destroy all of our external enemies. If we destroy or harm one, the problem will increase. But the inner enemy of anger can be destroyed and this is the same as overcoming all of our enemies. If we tame our mind, external enemies cannot harm us. The Buddha vanquished the hordes of beings who came to harm him, not with bombs and guns, but with the enormous power of his love and compassion. Therefore, we should pacify the enemy of anger with the armies of love and compassion. By meditating on love and compassion, we come to see Avalokiteshvara and Maitreya directly, just like Metriyogi and Asanga did. To the extent that we can generate impartial love and compassion for all beings in this lifetime, we make our lives meaningful.

Transforming the desired into the path

21   Sensual pleasures are like salt water:
      The more you indulge, the more thirst increases.
      Abandon at once those things which breed
      Clinging attachment—
      This is the practice of Bodhisattvas.

Most of our attachment is to the five objects of desire: visual form (shapes and colors), sound, smell, taste, and tangible objects. Our world is part of what is called the desire realm because of this. Our desires gravitate towards beautiful appearances, pleasant sounds, fragrant smells, delicious tastes, and objects pleasant to touch. Being attached to them, we crave them and pursue them in many ways.

There are three types of attachment according to time. Our attachment towards our favorite music, clothes, and food is called "craving for the present." When we feel, "May I always have these things. I never want to be separated from these pleasures," this is called "craving that aspires for the future." Recollecting past enjoyments with fond memories, we yearn for them again. That is called "craving for the past." We can see from our own life's experience that the more attachment we have, the more dissatisfied we are and the more fearful we are of losing the things we enjoy. Although we may have many good things and wonderful experiences, we are not content. This is the fault of attachment. Experiencing good things with attachment is like drinking salt water: the more we drink, the thirstier we become. Similarly, the more we have these objects, the more we want them.

Attachment manifests in many ways. Before we go to visit a friend, especially around the holiday season, we many speculate, "Will he give me a present? What will it be?" Or a teacher who is in a position to receive various offerings from his or her students may wonder what the students will give. Attachment of this kind is a great fault.

It is important to point out that the problem is not the objects per se, but is our clinging attitudes towards them. We can give up the object but still crave it. Therefore, the real thing to relinquish is our attachment. If we have few desires, we will be satisfied. Whatever we have will be good enough and we will enjoy it. Contentment is a good quality to cultivate.

On many occasions, the Buddha praised simplicity and contentment as the greatest possessions. Simplicity means having few desires, that is, not wanting lots of things. Contentment is being satisfied, considering what we have to be good enough. The best treasures to own are the seven arya treasures: faith, ethical discipline, hearing the Dharma, generosity, wisdom, integrity, and consideration for others. The more we cultivate these, the richer we become.

Many people nowadays are very attached to alcohol and recreational drugs. These cloud our mind, obscure our good judgment, and make spiritual practice difficult. The Buddha counseled that monastics and lay people alike avoid these substances. Why? First we have one drink, then another, and gradually, without recognizing it, we become psychologically, if not physiologically, addicted to these substances. It is especially harmful if parents indulge in these. They use the family's savings to get intoxicated. When they come home, they argue with their spouse, beat their children, and in general get into all sorts of trouble. Substance abuse is frowned upon by society in general. From a Buddhist perspective, serving intoxicants as well as taking them is to be abandoned for they both cause suffering.

The Buddha advised against taking alcohol even equal to the size of a dewdrop. This is clear in the texts on ethical discipline, the Vinaya. The Buddha did not even allow sick monks to drink a liquid containing one percent alcohol. He only sanctioned the use of alcohol for old monks ailing from disorders of the wind energy. They could smell it or rub it on their chest. However, those with the five lay precepts of the *upasaka* (Tib. *genyen*) ordination, as well as monastics, are never to drink alcohol, not even a drop mixed with something else.

Someone might think, "What you are saying applies to sutra, but not to tantra." This is not correct. Alcohol is forbidden in the *Tantra Purifying the Lower Realms* and the *Vajra Smithereens Tantra*. Some say, "But we are instructed to drink alcohol at the anuttarayoga tantric offering circle. In the Kalachakra, it is said that alcohol is a pledge-substance for offering to the vajra speech." These statements are true, but it is never said that because we call ourselves tantric practitioners we are entitled to drink as much as we like. If we think like this, we should ask ourselves, "The main pledge substances are the five meats and five liquids. I say I am a tantric practitioner, but can I eat those substances? If I can't, I lack the realizations that qualify me to bless and drink alcohol." If one is actually able to transform alcohol, it is fine. But drinking alcohol and calling it nectar while retaining our ordinary concept of body, speech, and mind is never acceptable. Pretending to be a great practitioner of tantra and behaving in a reckless manner is totally inappropriate.

The Tibetan word for nectar is *dutsi*. *Du* has the connotation of destroying the demons of the five disturbing attitudes of ignorance, anger, attachment, pride, and jealousy. *Tsi* refers to the wisdom of great bliss. Thus, drinking nectar destroys the five disturbing attitudes by means of the wisdom of great bliss. If we can transform alcohol into nectar, it is acceptable for us to drink it. If we can cut off the appearance of ordinary body, speech, and mind, and see all appearances as deities through having developed the wisdom of great bliss and emptiness, the time has come when we may drink alcohol, and enjoy meat and sex freely. If we are not at this point yet, restraint is certainly called for. Even if we are, we may still demonstrate restraint out of compassion for others and to set a good example for them.

Should we recklessly enjoy alcohol, meat, and sex before we have stable realizations, our qualities of hearing, thinking, and meditation will deteriorate, and we will create the cause for further wandering in cyclic existence. Meat, alcohol, and sex are not negative. However, when we are attached to these things, or to anything else, we should be honest with ourselves and recognize it as attachment, and not justify it by thinking we are a high practitioner when we are not.

As Jetsun Milarepa said, "From alcohol comes craving, and in the end it severs the vital artery of liberation." Padmasambhava said, "Drinking alcohol is a cause of birth in the unfortunate realms, so do not drink it. Give it up." He said this because drinking alcohol is an obstacle to single-pointed concentration and induces sleep and dullness. In addition, when under the influence of intoxicants, we lose all sense of integrity and consideration for others, due to which we act in many regrettable ways. However, Padmasambhava himself was able to drink as much as he liked. For him it was no problem; in fact, it was a condition for him to increase his wisdom of bliss and emptiness. But it is another issue altogether for those of us who are not on the spiritual level of Padmasambhava.

Killing sentient beings for sport or for a living are great faults. Similarly, ordering meat so that the butcher kills an animal is also wrong. According to the Vinaya, it is permissible to eat the flesh of a dead animal as long as it was not killed especially for us and we did not ask another to kill it. In fact, it is said that one may not eat the meat of an animal that one has seen, heard, or suspected was killed for oneself to eat.

Those who practice Mahayana should not eat meat. Although many do, it is not good. If it is for health purposes, there is a reason, but usually it is out of craving. Just eating a plate of meat does not directly kill the animal, for it is already dead. But we cannot deny that indirectly we are causing the death of a sentient being. After all, shop owners know the amount of meat they must order to satisfy their customers. Those with Bodhisattva vows should avoid harming sentient beings even indirectly. Of course, eating a plate of vegetables indirectly involves the death of many beings, but it is not the same as killing an animal to eat its flesh. Reciting the dharani-mantras of the Buddhas and Bodhisattvas and blowing on the meat reduces the negative energy, but it is still not good. Also, it is incorrect to think that because the animal gave its life for a meritorious cause—our Dharma practice—it will automatically have a good rebirth.

Thus, it is essential to be honest with ourselves, and for our own happiness we should try to abandon attachment to objects of desire as much as possible. This is a gradual process, and we cannot force ourselves to do it with a critical, judgmental attitude. Rather, by deeply understanding how attachment causes us misery, we will apply the antidotes to attachment and, in the meantime, keep our distance from things that cause our attachment to run wild.

CHAPTER THIRTEEN

MEDITATION ON EMPTINESS

We speak of two bodhichittas: conventional and ultimate. There is no fixed order in which they should be explained. Some people first listen to and reflect upon emptiness (ultimate bodhichitta) and later train in conventional bodhichitta. Others first train in the altruistic intention (conventional bodhichitta) and then meditate on emptiness.

Ultimate bodhichitta refers to the wisdom realizing emptiness. Emptiness is regarded as the "ultimate" object, but not because it is some sort of absolute truth that is independent of everything else. Rather, empty of inherent existence is the ultimate or deepest way in which all phenomena exist. Developing the wisdom realizing emptiness involves looking beyond superficial and deceptive conventional appearances. This is explained in two sections:

1. How to meditate on space-like emptiness during meditative equipoise
2. Between meditation sessions, how to overcome the belief that the desired and the hated are real

How to Meditate on Space-like Emptiness During Equipoise

22 Whatever appears is your own mind.
   Your mind from the start was free from fabricated extremes.
   Understanding this, do not take to mind
   [Inherent] signs of subject and object—
   This is the practice of Bodhisattvas.

Here, Togme Sangpo speaks of how to realize emptiness during the meditation session, the time of meditative equipoise focused single-pointedly on emptiness. How to apply our understanding of emptiness after the meditation session, that is, while we engage in daily activities, is described in the next two verses.

In exploring the emptiness of inherent existence of phenomena, we are focusing on the ultimate truth, the deepest mode of existence of persons and phenomena. The persons and phenomena themselves are conventional truths, dependently existing things that appear with their own characteristics and perform various functions in the world. These two truths are related in that conventional truths are what appear to our mind on a day-to-day basis, while ultimate truths are their deeper mode of existence.

Nothing can ever be found that is self-existent or that exists by itself independently of other phenomena. Whatever appears to the mind, both inner objects related to sentient beings' minds and outer objects in the environment, is merely labeled by mind. If we analyze the final mode of existence of the subject—the mind which labels—we find that it too is free from elaborations of the two extremes of true existence and total non-existence. Thus the final way of existing of both object and subject is that they do not exist from their own side. They are like space, which in this context is defined as a mere lack of tangibility and obstruction. Wherever we look in space, we never find anything tangible or any impediment. Similarly, if we look for existence from its own side in any phenomenon, we never find it. We simply find freedom from the elaborations of the two extremes.

The teachings on emptiness are extensive and we will touch only upon the major points here. The concepts and some of the terms used to convey them may be new to us, but with some patience and enthusiasm, their meaning will become clear. It is helpful to learn them, first because it makes us examine things more acutely and clearly, and second because it enables us to understand the great texts written by the previous masters on the subject.

Who is suitable to receive teachings on emptiness?

Teachings on emptiness are primarily given to a trainee who is an appropriate vessel. This does not mean that others should not listen or be taught. But the trainee who is an appropriate vessel should definitely be taught, because such a person will quickly develop many qualities as a result of that explanation. Someone who is not at all a suitable vessel should not be taught for the time being because it could be harmful to his or her spiritual development.

A teacher knows who is an appropriate vessel by examining certain outer signs. We can infer inner states of mind from a person's outer conduct. For example, when a person has strong compassion, there are certain external manifestations of his internal attitude. When he sees sentient beings with suffering and hardships, he may cry, tremble, and his hair stand on end, while he thinks, "How terrible! What can I do to help?" Whether that is actual great compassion or compassion developed with effort, still it is a sign that the person has some kind of strong compassion inside. We can see this from his behavior. Similarly, when people repeatedly exert themselves in making offerings and prostrations to the Three Jewels, we can infer that they have a positive attitude, just as when people are unhappy about something, we know it by the way they speak and from their facial expression.

In the same way, we can know who is an appropriate vessel for hearing about emptiness from outer signs. For example, a person who becomes very happy and feels strong faith in the teachings when she hears about emptiness has deep imprints in her mind from having had teachings on emptiness in the past. Due to this, she may cry, tremble, or the hair on her body stand on end due to feeling so happy. These are all signs. If a person has this reaction again and again, he or she is a trainee who is an appropriate vessel to learn emptiness. Such a person has imprints to realize emptiness due to having familiarized him or herself with emptiness in past lives. Of course, everyone has the seed for realizing emptiness, because everyone has the potential to become a Buddha, but this is a special potential which makes the person an appropriate vessel at this moment. This seed, which was planted in her mindstream due to having studied and familiarized herself with emptiness in the past, will enable her to realize emptiness quickly if it is taught to her now.

"All phenomena are empty" means there is a lack of, or non-existence of, a certain quality in relation to those phenomena. They lack an existence which does not depend on other factors such as causes, conditions, parts, and the consciousness which conceives and labels them. All things are established through reliance on various factors. Because they depend on and are related to something else, they are empty of existing independently; they are empty of not being established through reliance. Nevertheless, they still exist. Karma and its results are empty of independent existence, but they still exist. Some people, however, misunderstand the meaning of emptiness. They think that because karma and its results are empty they do not exist at all, and that therefore whatever we do, whether virtuous or negative, no results of happiness or suffering follow. People holding such beliefs should not be taught emptiness. They have fallen to the extreme of nihilism, and therefore are not appropriate vessels to learn emptiness. In fact, teaching emptiness to such people will harm them, for they could mistakenly use emptiness to justify unethical behavior. People who misunderstand the meaning of emptiness, who are unappreciative of it, or who are frightened by it should not be taught emptiness because it would not benefit them.

Most of us lie somewhere between being an appropriate vessel and an inappropriate vessel. We see that karma and its results are established through relying on causes and conditions, and that they are empty of independent existence. We do not take emptiness to mean that karma and its results do not exist, that there is no point in practicing virtue, or that it makes no difference if we do negative actions. Therefore, although we are not the best trainees who are appropriate vessels, neither are we trainees who should not listen to teachings on emptiness. We know clearly that our actions bring results in terms of our happiness and suffering.

"Emptiness is difficult to realize, but is worthwhile realizing." Meditation on emptiness is like a sword that cuts through the root of the disturbing attitudes and eliminates them completely. If we actually realize emptiness, there are many benefits, but even if we briefly mull over the meaning of emptiness, it is extremely useful and diminishes the power of our conception of true existence. It would be hardly possible for a person who has not accumulated a great store of merit to even wonder about the emptiness asserted in the Prasangika Madhyamika system, which is the most subtle emptiness asserted by any of the Buddhist philosophical systems. If we make an effort to learn about and contemplate emptiness now, we will plant the seeds in our mindstreams to become an excellent vessel to receive teachings on emptiness in future times.

If emptiness is taught to suitable trainees, many good results will follow. For example, they will appreciate the functioning of cause and effect and will practice the six far-reaching attitudes. They will practice ethical discipline well because they see that if they do not, the results of practicing generosity will ripen in the lower realms. If they do not practice generosity, in future lives they will lack resources, and that will mean they will lack one of the conducive conditions needed for generating the higher paths. Similarly, if they do not practice patience and get angry instead, the virtue they have accumulated in the past will be destroyed. Seeing that, they will engage in the practice of patience. Also, they will exert themselves with delight in the practices of generosity, ethics, and patience, thereby practicing joyous effort. Their minds will abide one-pointedly on the focal object of meditation held by mindfulness and introspection, and they will be conscientious with their three doors of body, speech, and mind. In this way, their understanding of emptiness enhances the rest of their practice.

How meditating on emptiness destroys our suffering

When we understand the evolution of our unsatisfactory experiences in cyclic existence, we will see that meditating on emptiness is their antidote. All knowable things—people and phenomena—appear to our minds to be inherently existent. We then grasp at them as existing inherently. Our inappropriate attention focuses on them, and that gives rise to the various disturbing attitudes of anger, attachment, and so on. These disturbing attitudes motivate our actions, which in turn leave karmic imprints on our mindstreams. When these imprints ripen, we meet with suffering. Let's look at this process in more depth and see how meditating on emptiness stops this process.

When an object appears to us, it appears as if it existed from its own side. Since our perspective is that of the Prasangika Madhyamika philosophical view, the following terms have the same meaning: existing from its own side, inherently existing, truly existing, independently existing, and self-existing. They all mean that something exists without depending on causes, conditions, parts, or the consciousness which conceives and labels them. If we think about it, we will very likely say that, of course, things do not exist from their own side because we know they are not established or existent without relying on causes, conditions, or other factors. However, when a table, for example, appears to our visual consciousness, it appears as if it existed from its own side. The mind to which the table appears to exist from its own side—in this case, the visual consciousness that apprehends the table—is not the conception of true existence. When objects appear to our five sense consciousnesses—the visual, auditory, olfactory, gustatory and tactile consciousnesses—and our mental consciousness, they appear as if they existed from their own side. After they appear in this way, another mind comes along which conceives of them being exactly like that: existing from their own side, without depending on causes and conditions, or anything else. That mind is the inborn conception of true existence. It is a mental consciousness, not a sense consciousness. This is the unknowing ignorance to which objects appear to exist from their own side, and which then conceives of them as actually existing in that way. Ignorance itself is the conception of true existence. It does not see an object's actual way of being and conceives its objects to exist from their own side. After that, the various other disturbing attitudes, such as attachment, hatred, jealousy, and pride arise. These attitudes do not conceive the object to exist from its own side, but they arise based on the ignorance which does. The disturbing attitudes do not all arise at the same time, of course. Sometimes ignorance will be followed by attachment, sometimes by anger.

Whether an object appears attractive or ugly to us, ignorance, a mind which conceives of it as existing from its own side, will arise in us. After that, but before either anger or aversion arise towards the object, there will be a conceptual consciousness called "inappropriate attention." If a pleasing object is slightly beautiful, inappropriate attention exaggerates, makes it much more beautiful, and thinks, "This is really good!" This inappropriate attention induces attachment, a mind of desire that thinks, "If only I could have that." If anger is going to be produced, first there is inappropriate attention which exaggerates the unpleasant aspect of the object, making it more negative. As a result, we then get angry and want to destroy or run away from what we think is harming us.

Attachment, anger, and the other disturbing attitudes motivate us to say and do various things, and thus we accumulate negative karma. As a result we experience their results, feelings of suffering. Ignorance is also behind our experiences of happiness in cyclic existence. For example, ignorance grasping at a truly existent I arises, and we think, "I want to create good karma so I'll be happy in the future!" This thought is a form of attachment, which clings to just our own happiness within cyclic existence, and is also a disturbing attitude. With such a motivation, we create positive karma which leaves the imprints in our mindstreams that will ripen into our future experiences of happiness. Although this is a good motivation compared to the previous ones, it nevertheless does not free us from cyclic existence because it still thinks all phenomena exist inherently.

The present explanation accords with the Prasangika system, which understands ignorance to be the conception of true existence. According to lower philosophical systems, ignorance means merely not knowing, while the conception of true existence is a mind which apprehends its object wrongly. However, the Prasangika system does not make this distinction. It says that ignorance itself is the conception of true existence, and is a mind which apprehends its object as existing from its own side. Since its object does not exist in this way, but ignorance thinks it does, it apprehends its object incorrectly.

According to the Prasangika system the root of all the disturbing attitudes is ignorance. The root is also said to be the view of the transitory collection (Tib. *jigta*). Chandrakirti in his *Supplement to the Middle Way* says, "All disturbing attitudes without exception are (based) on the view of the transitory collection." Also, the root of all disturbing attitudes is the conception of true existence. It is correct to think of any of these three as the root of all disturbing attitudes. Each contains all the characteristics of the others.

The view of the transitory collection is more specific than the conception of true existence. The observed object of the former is the "I" and "mine" in one's own continuum. In other words, while ignorance and the conception of true existence incorrectly grasp all phenomena, the view of the transitory collection incorrectly grasps only the "I" and "mine" in one's own continuum. Of these two kinds of view of the transitory collection, the first one observes and grasps the I as inherently existent. After this, we observe "mine," that is, "*my* aggregates and possessions," and the grasping at them as inherently existent arises. The view of the transitory collection, ignorance, self-grasping, and the conception of true existence all have the same way of grasping: they all grasp at something existing from its own side, independently of any other phenomena. Therefore, they are all wrong consciousnesses, that is, minds which engage their objects incorrectly. They are similar to an eye consciousness which sees a snow mountain as blue when in fact the snow is white. Nothing exists in the way self-grasping apprehends it to exist, for in fact things do not exist from their own side, but exist in dependence on other factors: causes, conditions, parts, and a consciousness which conceives and labels them.

Does meditating on love, compassion, and bodhichitta act as the direct antidote to ignorance? Does it help us to realize emptiness? It does help, because by means of such meditations we accumulate a vast store of positive potential, which is necessary for understanding emptiness correctly. But these meditations are not the direct antidote that realizes the non-existence of the referent object of ignorance. The object of ignorance refers to the truly existent object which appears and which ignorance then grasps or conceives to truly exist. In the case of the person, this is the I that appears when we experience strong attachment or anger, for example. However, such a truly existent object does not, in fact, exist. To contradict this incorrect referent object we need a mind that apprehends it in a way that contradicts, or is opposite to, the way ignorance apprehends it. That is, since ignorance apprehends its object as existing from its own side, to eliminate that misapprehension we need a mind which apprehends its object as not existing from its own side. We need a mind that knows, "This does not exist from its own side. Not even the smallest atom of it exists from its own side," and which thus apprehends its object in a way that is contradictory to that ignorance. The conception of true existence in our continuum holds its object as existing from its own side. We must search to see if there is in fact an object existing from its own side. When we fail to find that object, the strength of the conception of true existence in our continuum can be destroyed. Thus, to contemplate emptiness, we need to know how the conception of true existence apprehends its object, that the object does not exist in the way that ignorance apprehends it, and that ignorance is an incorrect, false mind.

If we were to compare the strength and validity of a mind which apprehends the object as existing from its own side without depending on causes, conditions, and so forth, and the mind which apprehends its object as not existing from its own side, but as related and depending on other factors, the latter would be stronger because it is a correct mind. The mistaken mind cannot be more powerful because it can be disproved by other valid minds. However, a valid mind realizing emptiness, or a mind realizing the dependent nature of all phenomena can never be contradicted by any other valid consciousness.

"Empty" means empty of true existence or empty of existing from its own side, that is, empty of existing without depending on causes, conditions, or anything else. There is nothing which exists without depending on causes, conditions, or other factors. We can never find anything which exists in that way.

To truly understand emptiness we have to meditate and to understand its import in our lives The path to realizing emptiness fully is gradual. First we need to hear teachings on the meaning of emptiness. The teachings in the Middle Way, or Madhyamika, texts use many examples and reasons to establish that nothing exists inherently. Because of our study, we will start to wonder, "Maybe things are not truly existent." This mind is not certain one way or the other, and is therefore called doubt inclined towards the correct conclusion. By contemplating emptiness more, we will generate a correct belief in the meaning of emptiness. "Correct belief" refers to an understanding that is not firm. It is not the realization of emptiness, but as we continue to reason and meditate again and again, that belief will become firm. It will turn into a valid mind of inference, which realizes emptiness unshakably. By continued familiarity, the inference will transform into a direct, non-conceptual realization of emptiness, and with this wisdom, which directly sees that the referent object of ignorance is nonexistent, we will be able to cut the root of cyclic existence.

According to the Prasangika system, the terms *emptiness* and *selflessness* are synonymous. In tantric practices or sadhanas, we come across the Sanskrit mantra, *Om svabhava shuddah sarva dharmah svabhava shuddho ham* ("*Om* by essential nature all phenomena are pure; by essential nature, I am pure"). At this point, we should not simply think, without contemplating the meaning, that all phenomena are empty. Rather, we should think that they are empty of self-existence, empty of existing without depending on causes, conditions, or any other dependent arisings. We should reflect that all phenomena are dependent and related, and therefore that nothing exists from its own side. In this way, we will familiarize ourselves with emptiness. Before we generate ourselves as the deity in a tantric sadhana, it is essential to first meditate on emptiness. Otherwise, our practice will be quite shallow and will not bring the desired results.

The advantages of understanding emptiness

Knowing the purpose of meditating on emptiness helps us feel joyful, confident, courageous, and firm in our meditation. When we meditate on emptiness, the ten negative actions will be purified quickly. For example, the sutra *Dispelling the Guilt of Mageda* describes a king who committed the boundless negative action of killing his father. To eliminate his great sense of guilt, Buddha told him that even if a person had committed all five of the boundless negative actions, thereby creating immense negative karma, if he meditated on emptiness, it would be fully purified. If even actions as negative as this would be purified, what need is there to mention that lesser negative actions would also be purified.

Similarly, if we familiarize ourselves with emptiness and reflect on its meaning, negativities and obscurations built up over eons and eons will become less and less powerful. When we realize emptiness directly, even negativities accumulated over billions of eons will all be eliminated. For example, even if a cave had remained in darkness for billions of years, if we introduce the light of a lamp into it, the darkness is dispelled in an instant. Similarly, the light of the wisdom of emptiness is able to dispel the darkness of ignorance. Therefore meditating on emptiness is very worthwhile.

Through meditating on dependent arising or the four essential points (which are explained below and are both methods for meditating on emptiness), we create the unique close cause for attaining enlightenment and liberation. The seed for liberation and enlightenment is planted in our mindstream. This is so even if we haven't yet realized emptiness but simply have a strong belief or correct assumption regarding it. The reason for this is we recognize that the object held by self-grasping does not exist and that ignorance is a wrong consciousness. This directly challenges the attitude which is the root cause of our cyclic existence. Even having doubt thinking that maybe things are empty tears the fabric of cyclic existence to tatters. As we progress from doubt to correct belief to inference to direct non-conceptual realization, we become closer to enlightenment.

Without the wisdom realizing that all phenomena are not truly existent, we have no method for calming our disturbing attitudes even though we may strongly wish to do so. If we do not calm them, then under their influence we will accumulate various karmas, and as a result, even though we do not want to, we will take birth in unfortunate circumstances and wander without end in cyclic existence. Therefore, the Buddha, out of his great compassion, explained emptiness for those who wish to be free from cyclic existence and attain liberation.

Just by reading one book or listening to one teaching we will gain some understanding, but only a person of exceptionally sharp intellect and great merit will thereby immediately have a correct understanding. We need to read, listen to teachings, and contemplate emptiness again and again. As a result, more and more imprints will be left on our mind. Eventually, these imprints will be activated and we will gain a deeper understanding of emptiness. The more we are able to reflect and meditate on emptiness, the closer we get to liberation, and thus gradually leave samsara behind.

In the *Heart Sutra*, it says, "All the Buddhas abiding in the three times awakened to peerless, perfect, and complete awakening by depending on the far-reaching attitude of wisdom." The Buddhas first listened to explanations of emptiness, then reflected upon them. Once it had become clear to their minds, they placed their minds on it and became familiar with emptiness. Through this process they became Buddhas.

In the *Vajra Cutter Sutra*, the question is asked, "If a man or woman were to completely fill with precious gems as many sets of the "three thousand" (i.e., a thousand to the third power) worlds as there are atoms of water in as many Ganges rivers as there are atoms of water in the River Ganges (that is, the number of atoms of water in the River Ganges to the second power times one thousand million worlds, each filled with precious gems) and offer them each day to the Buddha, how much virtue would there be?" The reply is, "The virtue would be limitless." This is because, for all practical considerations, the atoms of water would be countless. It then says, "There is hundreds and thousands of times more benefit in explaining the meaning of emptiness with a good motivation, even if it is only one line indicating the meaning of emptiness, or in listening to an explanation of the meaning of emptiness, without fault in motivation." Thus, thinking over the meaning of emptiness is clearly of great benefit. If we understand the benefit, happiness and enthusiasm will automatically arise.

The importance of gaining a correct understanding

The method side of the path—training the mind in love, compassion, and bodhichitta—was taught by many masters in the past. There is very little difference in their presentations of these topics. However, there are great differences in the subtlety of the presentation of the wisdom side of the path, the meaning of selflessness. When Lama Tsong Khapa was seeking the meaning of emptiness, he went to many great masters, received teachings from them, thought over what they had said, but still he did not discover the meaning of emptiness. Later on, he received a direct vision of Manjushri, the Buddha of Wisdom, and found the meaning of emptiness by depending on his instructions. When he found it he said, "Depending on the instructions of Manjushri, I have clearly and correctly understood that which many experts have not understood clearly, and I will explain it to trainees with a compassionate intention." Of course, he did not mean that none of the masters he had previously studied with understood emptiness!

He merely meant that what many experts did not understand, he had understood, because emptiness is not easy to understand.

When we contemplate emptiness, there is a danger of misunderstanding it. If we do so, all the efforts we make on the basis of that mistake will be wasted. So we should make effort to gain an unmistaken view of emptiness. There is a danger of certain passages being explained erroneously. For example, if the passage "beyond thought, beyond expression" (unthinkable and inexpressible) is taken literally it means that emptiness cannot be expressed verbally, nor thought about mentally. That may seem correct, but it is not, because emptiness can be understood by depending on an explanation and instructions on how to meditate on it. On the first path, the path of accumulation, one hears many explanations of emptiness. On the second path, the path of preparation, one realizes emptiness conceptually, by way of a mental image. Only on the third path, the path of seeing, does one realize it directly. On the path of meditation one continues to meditate on that which has already been realized. Therefore that literal explanation of the passage does not work. Many Tibetans have written texts in which they take the above passage literally. Therefore, the same mistaken interpretation may have appeared English translations as well. If we meditate with the assumption that emptiness cannot be thought about mentally, nor expressed verbally, our wisdom will not grow.

"Beyond thought, beyond expression" means that ordinary people cannot express emptiness nor conceive of it in exactly the same way that it is known by the exalted wisdom of the aryas when they directly realize emptiness in meditative equipoise. That is, the way in which emptiness is known and experienced by an arya's mind during meditative equipoise cannot be expressed or thought about by ordinary people. Words and concepts cannot take emptiness as an object in the same way that direct experience does. If you study well, you will be able to distinguish what is correct and what is not. If you do not study well you may easily be misled.

Because emptiness is so important, Buddha instructed Ananda to prevent the Prajnaparamita from degenerating by committing each and every word of it to memory. He was emphatic about this. This is because the Perfection of Wisdom sutras explicitly indicate the meaning of emptiness, and so if the words which express it degenerate or are mistaken, the subject expressed will be faulty.

The Perfection of Wisdom is the best and most superb of all Buddha's teachings, because its subject is so extraordinary. These sutras explicitly teach emptiness, and implicitly teach the stages of clear realizations which are to be produced in the mindstreams of the trainees. The essence of all the teachings of the Buddha is the meaning of emptiness, because hearing about and reflecting on this is the method for attaining the enlightenment of the hearer, solitary realizer, and universal vehicles.

The Buddha taught in order to benefit people. He did not teach everyone the ultimate, or final, view and demand that they practice it. That would be like trying to make everyone wear the same size hats irrespective of differences in head size. Rather, the Buddha taught in accordance with the various natures, thoughts, and interests of the various trainees. If he had given the ultimate explanation to all, it would not have suited some people. Therefore, sometimes Buddha taught true existence, sometimes non-true existence, sometimes the existence of external objects, sometimes the non-existence of external objects, and so on. All these explanations can fit into the stages of a single person's path to enlightenment. To a person who is not suited for an explanation of the ultimate view, a teaching is given which suits his mind. By studying that, his mind will change, and gradually he will be more receptive to the higher views. Thus, many Tibetans study four systems of philosophical tenets, all of them taught by the Buddha: Vaibhashika, Sautrantika, Chittamatra, and Madhyamika. The latter has two divisions: Svatantrika and Prasangika. These different tenet systems reflect the differences in nature, thoughts, and interests of the trainees. Only the Prasangika system contains the ultimate explanation. The other three are methods for guiding the mind until it is prepared for the Prasangika system. Knowing the assertions of the lower systems is the best way to clearly understand the meaning of the upper systems.

Thus we talk about the definitive teachings and those requiring interpretation. For example, when the Buddha taught that there was true existence, this was not definitive. It is a teaching requiring interpretation, which was taught as a method to gradually lead certain trainees to the ultimate meaning of emptiness. Depending on the distinctions made by the two great charioteers, Nagarjuna and Asanga, we are able to know which sutras are definitive and which require interpretation. The Buddha predicted how long after he had died Nagarjuna and Asanga would come, and said that they would indicate the distinctions between these two types of sutras. He said that we could reach certainty regarding the view of emptiness by following these two great masters.

According to the great Indian sage Atisha, we can find the ultimate view of the Chittamatras by relying on Asanga, and the ultimate view of the Prasangikas by relying on Nagarjuna. Aryadeva clarified Nagarjuna's teachings, and Chandrakirti and Buddhapalita explained Nagarjuna's view further. The Tibetan sage Lama Tsong Khapa, clarified this even more. These sages demonstrated that no logic can harm the position that all phenomena are empty of true existence, and many reasons can be found to establish it validly. However, many arguments harm the position of true existence and make it difficult to hold by showing its inner inconsistencies. Thus we come to know that true existence is not the ultimate view.

Lama Tsong Khapa, an emanation of Manjushri, composed texts that provide us with extensive explanations of the ultimate view. He explained all the difficult points in the treatises, giving many logical reasons to support his interpretations and many reasons to refute other interpretations. He supported his ideas by quoting Chandrakirti's *Supplement to the Middle Way,* Aryadeva's *Four Hundred Stanzas,* and Nagarjuna's works. Nagarjuna relied on definitive sutras from the Buddha such as the *Akshayamati Sutra,* the *King of Concentration Sutra,* and so on. Lama Tsong Khapa's explanations go right back to the source, the Buddha. Thus, by studying his works, it is possible for an intelligent person to reach unmistaken conclusions and to know that these conclusions are free of error. We are not obliged to remain in doubt. Once a person has clearly seen the unmistaken view, even if a thousand people were to line up against her and tell her that she was wrong, she would not believe them.

Identifying ignorance

The great masters stress that at the beginning it is very important to identify ignorance. Once we work out what it is, we will be able to understand what to do to eliminate it. If we dismiss this step, our understanding will remain superficial. When we want to realize selflessness, we have to know clearly what the object of negation is. Often we think we already understand what ignorance is and what the object of negation in the emptiness meditation is. Having only looked superficially, we consider it easy and go ahead. Of course, nothing good comes of this. Seeing this danger, the past masters emphasized the importance of identifying ignorance and the object of negation. If we have clearly identified these, we will not have difficulty in realizing emptiness. Having difficulty in understanding emptiness is due to not identifying the object of negation properly.

Ignorance believes the object of negation actually exists. If we want to attain liberation, we need to abandon samsara, and to do that we have to abandon its root. Therefore, we have to identify that root, which is ignorance. What is this ignorance? How does it apprehend its object? Thinking like this is the best of meditations. This is what people who want to reach liberation or enlightenment need to think about.

Ignorance is included in the discordant class of knowing. The terms, "discordant class" and "concordant class" are explained in the Collected Topics. There are three types of discordant classes:

1. The discordant class because of being non-existent. For example, the horn of a rabbit is the "non-existent discordant class" of impermanent phenomena because it is not impermanent and it does not exist.

2. The discordant class which is other. These are things which aren't the concordant class but are not contradictory with it. For example, object of knowledge (i.e., existent object) is the "other discordant class" of impermanent phenomena because it is not impermanent although there are things which are both an object of knowledge and impermanent.

3. The discordant class which is contradictory. For example, permanent is the "contradictory discordant class" of impermanent because it is not impermanent and it is the opposite of impermanent, i.e., nothing can be both permanent and impermanent.

Ignorance is the discordant class which is contradictory to the wisdom realizing selflessness. This means that it is exactly the opposite of this wisdom. It is not just a lack of, or non-existence of this wisdom; nor is it just something other than that wisdom. In this context, this wisdom is the concordant class. Ignorance is not this wisdom, therefore it is in the discordant class. Moreover, ignorance is contradictory to the wisdom so it is the contradictory discordant class of that wisdom.

If ignorance is the exact opposite of the wisdom realizing selflessness, we need to know what that wisdom apprehends and what is contradictory to it. What that wisdom apprehends, that is, its object of the mode of apprehension, is selflessness. The object of the mode of apprehension (Tib. *dzin wang kyi yul*) is synonymous with the engaged object (Tib. *jug yul*) of that mind, that is, the main object with which that mind is concerned. For example, in the case of the wisdom realizing emptiness, the main object with which it is concerned is emptiness, non-true existence. The wisdom realizing emptiness apprehends a lack of existence from its own side. The contradictory discordant class, the opposite of this lack of existence from its own side, is true existence. Apprehending true existence means apprehending something as existing without depending on causes, conditions, or any other factors. The main object with which ignorance is concerned is a truly existent one, and this kind of object does not exist at all. Self-grasping ignorance is a mind that apprehends existence from its own side, so we can see that it is exactly contradictory to the wisdom realizing selflessness.

The word "self" has different meanings in different situations. In the terms "self-grasping ignorance" or "selflessness," it means inherent existence and can refer to the inherent existence of any object. When the word "self" is used to mean person or I, then it refers to the conventionally existent person. There are two forms of self-grasping ignorance (here "self" means inherent existence): the ignorance which is the self-grasping of persons and the ignorance which is self-grasping of phenomena. There are two forms of selflessness: the selflessness of persons and the selflessness of phenomena, and so there are two wisdoms realizing selflessness: one realizing the selflessness of persons and one realizing the selflessness of phenomena. Thus, there are two ignorances exactly contradictory to these: the ignorance which is the self-grasping of persons, and the ignorance which is the self-grasping of phenomena. Both of these ignorances are incorrect minds, because they superimpose true existence where there is none.

The self-grasping of persons and of phenomena are differentiated only in terms of their focal object (Tib. *mig yul*). They are the same in apprehending, or grasping, self-existence. They are also the same in subtlety. However, one grasps at the inherent existence of persons, the other at the inherent existence of phenomena other than persons, for example, the aggregates or things in the environment.

To realize emptiness, we have to realize the non-existence of the referent object (Tib. *zhen yul*) of the ignorance which is the root of cyclic existence. This is an inborn or innate self-grasping, not one which is intellectually acquired. Innate self-grasping ignorance thinks phenomena exist from their own side, and it is unmixed with reasons learned in philosophical study. It is an ignorance which emerges spontaneously, without our having to learn it or put effort into making it arise. Birds and other creatures have it in their continuums too. They also wander in cyclic existence, and this same ignorance grasping at self-existence arises in them spontaneously. Their thought of things existing truly obviously is not connected with any reasons. They are not able to think in that way. Intellectually acquired self-grasping also holds things to exist from their own side, but it has faulty reasons and proofs learned through studying a mistaken philosophy. Only the innate ignorance is the root of cyclic existence. When we first realize emptiness directly, we eradicate only intellectually acquired self-grasping. By familiarizing ourselves with emptiness, our realization increases in strength and gradually eradicates the innate ignorance. Thus, innate grasping at true existence can still occur in the mind of a person who has realized emptiness directly, although it is not very strong.

Avoiding the two extremes

When working out what selflessness is, we have to negate the object of negation, self-existence. In doing so, we must avoid two faults: negating too much and negating too little. Our degree of negation has to be exactly right. Negating too much means negating something which should not be negated along with that which should. This error leads us to the extreme of nihilism or total non-existence. If we have not negated all that should be negated, something remains and we fall to the extreme of eternalism or permanence. When meditating on selflessness we have to negate self-existence, no more and no less.

For example, when we are negating true existence, if we also negate the general, conventional existence of the object, we are negating too much. If we eliminate conventional existence as an object of mind, then we eliminate something that exists, and we will have no basis on which to speak of karma and its results and of what to practice and what to avoid. We will be unable to talk of the four truths, the twelve links, refuge, and so on because we will think that they do not exist. If we negate the existence of conventional objects, we will not be able to contemplate the path which combines method and wisdom, and in that case we will not be able to attain the union of the two bodies of a Buddha. In fact, we will not even be able to say, "I go to the store," because we will think that no person exists at all, that there is no store, and there is no action of going. Clearly, negating too much is a big mistake. This could happen if, when we meditate and conclude that there is no true existence, we negate too much and also think there is no existence of any kind whatsoever.

When we contemplate the emptiness of inherent existence, we should think that if something inherently existed, it would exist without depending on any causes, conditions, parts, designating concept or name. In that case, if we were to search for or investigate the basis of designation, we would have to be able to find something which we could point out as this independent thing. The basis of designation is the parts or attributes upon which something is labeled. For example, the basis of designation of the person is his or her aggregates of body and mind, and the designated object is the person. If the person existed from its own side, if it were truly existent, established without depending on causes, conditions, or anything, then if we were to search among the aggregates for such a person, we would have to find it. Yet such a person is not to be found.

The mind which thinks of non-true existence does not itself have to think that the person exists conventionally, that it is established by valid cognition, and so on. That is to say, the investigating mind, which is a mind analyzing the ultimate, does not have to think about how the conventional functioning of things works. A mind analyzing the ultimate focuses only on the non-existence of a truly existent person. It does not have to think that a conventional person exists. However, if a person who meditates on the ultimate nature, emptiness, emerges from her meditative equipoise into the subsequent attainment, and at that time is not able to posit cause and effect or dependent arising, that is the fault of negating too much. In the time of subsequent attainment, he or she should know how to posit the stages of the path of the vast, conventional side with valid cognition and to avoid negating its existence. A person is able to do this because she has valid cognizers in her continuum realizing conventional phenomena and these phenomena are established by conventional valid cognition.

To put it simply: phenomena do not exist ultimately, but do exist conventionally. Even though we negate ultimate existence, we need to know how to posit conventional existence. For example, the parts of a clock—the face, the battery, the back, the knobs, and so forth—are called the basis of designation of the clock. The clock is the object designated upon that basis. The clock, which is designated in dependence upon its basis, exists. However, if we search for a truly existent clock that exists from its own side independently of everything else, we cannot find it. However, when the clock appears to our mind, it appears as if it existed from its own side, independently of all else. Certainly, when we think about it we see that it exists through relying on causes,

conditions, and so on, because we know that it was made by someone. But when we see the clock, it appears to exist from its own side,
as does everything else around us. Just as it appears that way, so does
our mind automatically apprehend or grasp the object as existing from
its own side. The mind which apprehends it as existing from its own
side is called the innate true grasping, i.e., the innate conception of
true existence. If the clock did exist in the way that it appears, we
should be able to find it when we look in its basis of designation. But
if we search in the basis of designation—the parts—to see whether
there is an object existing from its own side or not, we don't find it.
That is negating its existence from its own side. But, if we also negate
the fact that it does exist in general, that is too extensive. The clock
does exist; if we do not analyze, we see it performs a function, specifically that of telling time. All phenomena have some unique function
that they can perform when we do not analyze and look for their ultimate existence. If we analyze the basis of designation and search for
what it is that performs the function, we cannot find it. For example,
when we think about the selflessness of the person, we have to refute
self-existence based on the person. But when we are refuting that, if
we negate the person itself, something which does the actions of being produced and ceasing, coming and going, and so on, our negation
is too extensive.

Levels of selflessness

Because the emptiness of inherent existence is hard to realize, the Buddha taught different levels of emptiness or selflessness, each with its
own object of negation. By progressively understanding these different levels of negation, we can eventually arrive at refuting inherent
existence. We start with a gross emptiness, which is the lack of a gross
object of negation, and then move onto more subtle emptinesses. The
first emptiness is the emptiness of a permanent, single, and independent self or person. "Permanent" means it is not subject to production
and destruction; it does not change. In fact, the person is impermanent, meaning it is produced and perishes moment by moment. Things
which are permanent do not change moment by moment. "Single"
means it does not rely on parts. But the person depends on its parts,
for example, the former and latter moments of the self. "Independent"
means not relying on causes and conditions. However, the person does
depend on causes and conditions to come into existence. If the person

were permanent, partless, and independent, it could never experience pleasure and pain, because it would never change and would be affected by conditions.

The Buddha explained that the person is empty of being permanent, single, and independent, because we do not understand it clearly. It is not the case that first the person was permanent, single, and independent, and then because the Buddha taught that the person is empty, the person stopped being permanent, single, and independent. The emptiness of the person being permanent, single, and independent is the gross selflessness of persons. Although the person is empty of being permanent, single, and independent, a mistaken mind apprehends it to be so, and this is called the gross self-grasping of the person. We should check by contemplating and meditating whether compounded phenomena—that is, all things which are produced and under the influence of causes and conditions—are empty of being permanent, single, and independent or not.

When we negate a person existing as a permanent, partless, and independent self, we have a good basis for being able to understand the more subtle emptinesses because we realize that the person exists in dependence on other factors. We are making progress, but the extent of the object of negation is still too small. We have not yet negated the subtle object of negation, true existence.

The next level of selflessness that is a bit more subtle, although it is not the subtlest one, is the emptiness of being self-sufficient and substantially existent. The person, for example, is empty of being self-sufficient and substantially existent. If it were not, it would have to exist without depending on the aggregates, whereas it does depend on them. All beings of the three realms have four or five aggregates which are their bases of designation. Formless realm beings do not have the form aggregate because they lack a gross body, while all other beings have five aggregates: form, feeling, discrimination, compositional factors, and consciousness. In reliance upon seeing the five aggregates, which means the aggregates appear to our mind, we are able to recognize a person, thinking, "This is this person, that is that person." Since this happens by the aggregates appearing to the mind, the five aggregates are called the basis of designation of the person. The persons of the form and desire realm rely and depend on five aggregates. The formless realm gods depend and rely on their four aggregates. Thus, no person is self-sufficient and substantially existent; persons are empty of being self-sufficient and substantially existent. This selflessness is more subtle than the previous selflessness because its object of negation is more subtle. But compared to the subtlest selflessness, it too is coarse.

It is necessary to be very clear about the selflessness of the person because it is the person—that means us—who circles in cyclic existence, and it is the person who abandons cyclic existence and attains nirvana. The person being empty of existing independently is the very subtle selflessness of the person. Only when this is negated has our negation stopped being too limited and become sufficient. The person appears to us to be self-existing, which means not dependent on causes, conditions, or other factors. The person relies and depends on its causes and conditions and on the aggregates which are its basis of designation. The person is not self-existing, a thing which is totally indepen-dent of everything. It exists in dependence on other factors.

A clock, for example, exists depending on the collection of its many parts. It depends on the people who made it, and on those who gave it the name "clock." It arose in dependence and in reliance on other things. It cannot exist through its own power, as an object that exists from its own side. Rather, it exists by depending on other factors. It is the same with the person. But when a person appears to us, she ap-pears to exist from her own side, not dependent on anything. When we analyze, we start to see that things do not exist from their own side, even if that is how they appear.

For example, if another person hurts us, we think "I!" very strongly. "He hurt *me*!" We grasp at an I as if it existed from its own side, with-out depending on the aggregates. Similarly, if someone helps us, we think, "She really helped *me*," and we grasp at an I as if it were truly existent. First, there is the appearance of the I as existing from its own side, and then we apprehend it as existing just like that. This is self-grasping of the person. Although there is the appearance of inherent existence to the self-grasping mind and that mind apprehends it as inherently existent, there is no object which exists in that way. It is a mistaken, wrong consciousness.

Both the self-grasping ignorance and the mind realizing the person as empty of true existence have the same focal object, the person. How-ever, these two consciousnesses apprehend the person in contradictory ways because one apprehends the person as inherently existent and the other apprehends the person as non-inherently existent. One is a wrong consciousness, the other is a valid one. One is to be cultivated and leads us to liberation, the other is to be abandoned because it leads us into cyclic existence.

If the I existed from its own side, when we search the aggregates, which are the basis of designation of the name "I," to find an I which exists from its own side, we should be able to find something. If the I existed as it appears to the self-grasping mind, we should be able to find it in its basis of designation, the aggregates of body and mind. However, when we search, we do not find it. If the person existed from its own side, when we eliminate all the aggregates there should be a person existing from its own side left over. But that is not found either. Thus the person is empty of true existence.

Merely designated by concept and name

The meaning of true existence is existing from its own side, without being merely designated by conception. In fact, all phenomena are merely designated by conception. Therefore they do not exist from their own side without being designated by conception. This is an important point to understand. Take a pen, for example. It is designated depending on the mere collection of its parts. The first person ever to use the name "pen" did so by having the motivating conception thinking, "It would be good to call this 'pen.'" There was that appearance to his conceptual mind, and through that the name was designated. Then, depending on the name having been designated, the pen was established, i.e., came into being.

The name "pen" did not definitely have to be designated to that object. Another name could have been used. The same principle can be understood with any object. For example, a person named Susan could have been called by another name. That person came to be Susan because the person who gave her that name thought, "It would be good to call her this," and once that appeared to his mind he designated her, saying, "Your name is Susan." How was she established as Susan? Through mere designation by name. If we can understand this in relation to one thing, we can apply the same principle to everything else, and it will be a great aid in understanding emptiness.

When we understand how things are established through being merely designated by conception, we will understand how they rely on conception to exist. That means that they cannot exist from their own side without relying on anything else. When it is said that things are established merely through designation by conception, it means they are established through relying on this designation and thus do not exist from their own side. It really gets deep down into the object of negation of emptiness.

For example, "outside" and "inside" do not exist inherently. They are established in relation to each other. Something does not become the inside of a room unless something else is established as the outside of the room. Thus they depend on each other. The front of a table is also relative. If we go to the other side, what used to be the back of the table becomes the front, and the front becomes the back. East and west, long and short, good and bad, high and low are all posited in relation to each other and therefore do not exist from their own side.

Our birth as a human being depended on karma. Some people experience a lot of suffering, others a lot of happiness. These experiences also depend on the person's previous actions and therefore do not exist inherently. External objects come into existence depending on the aggregation of many atoms. When the collection of atoms disintegrates, only atoms are left and they are dependent on the larger object they came from.

Our mind is also a dependent arising. For example, our sense consciousnesses arise in dependence on three conditions: an external object, the sense organ, and the immediately preceding moment of consciousness. The visual consciousness perceiving blue, for example, arises in dependence on the color blue, the eye organ, and the moment of consciousness that immediately preceded it.

The visual primary consciousness that is produced is a primary consciousness that knows the mere presence of the object, which in this case is blue. Together with it are produced the five ever-present mental factors: feeling, discrimination, intention, contact, and attention. These mental factors know specific attributes of the object. The visual consciousness perceiving blue depends on both the visual primary consciousness of blue and the mental factors which accompany it. Thus, this visual consciousness also arises depending on other factors and is not inherently existent. This can be understood in greater detail by studying texts on "Mind and Awareness."

The idea that all phenomena exist through reliance or dependence should be clear from this explanation. In reflecting on their dependent nature, sometimes we consider that they exist through relying on causes and conditions; other times we reflect that they depend on parts, or on the mind which conceives and labels them. In fact, most things exist in dependence on many different causes, conditions, and other dependent arisings. Without depending on these factors, they cannot come into existence. In particular, phenomena depend on being merely designated by conception. Thus everything which exists relies on and depends on other things.

Being dependent and related means being empty. Being empty means being dependent and related. We can understand that because an object arises through depending on and in relation to something else, it is empty of existing from its own side. And we can understand that because an object is empty of existing from its own side, it arises through depending on and in relation to something else. Even if we cannot understand this clearly right now, the two do in fact support each other if we think about it.

It is easy to see how functioning things and compounded phenomena—that is, phenomena which are produced by causes and conditions—rely on something else, since they rely on causes and conditions. To see that phenomena which are not functioning things, such as space or true cessations, are dependent takes more thought. For example, space relies on a lack of obstruction and contact. If there is obstruction and contact somewhere, there is no empty space there. A true cessation occurs when a disturbing attitude in one's mindstream is extinguished through meditating on the paths which realize emptiness directly. The state of a disturbing attitude having been extinguished is a true cessation. It relies on the uninterrupted path—a consciousness realizing emptiness directly that has the power to eliminate a portion of the disturbing attitudes—having extinguished whichever of the disturbing attitudes it has to extinguish. A true cessation cannot come about without those disturbing attitudes having been extinguished. There are many types of true cessation because each level of the path forever abandons certain disturbing attitudes. Each true cessation relies on its corresponding disturbing attitudes having been eliminated by an uninterrupted path. It also depends on the mind realizing emptiness directly. Therefore, true cessations are empty of inherent existence and exist dependently.

Emptiness also exists dependently and is empty of inherent existence. "Emptiness" is a general term, but when we look closer, there is the emptiness of the cup, the emptiness of the daisy, the emptiness of the person, and so on. Each of these emptinesses depends on the basis of which it is the emptiness. That is, emptiness exists in general, but each emptiness has to be the emptiness of some particular basis. There is no emptiness which stands on its own, without a basis of which it is the emptiness. For example, the emptiness of a table depends on the table, which is the basis of that emptiness. The emptiness of the person depends on the person that conventionally exists. The basis of the emptiness and the emptiness of that phenomenon depend on each other; they have the relationship of support (the object) and supported (its emptiness).

There is nothing which is not dependent or related; therefore, everything is empty of true existence. Everything is empty of true existence for the reason that it is dependent and related. That reason is called the king of reasons, the logic of dependent and related. All phenomena in samsara and nirvana do not exist from their own side. The fact of being dependent and related is non-deceptive because it can be realized by valid cognition. When existence from its own side is negated, implicitly it can be ascertained that phenomena are dependent and related. This is one way we can meditate on emptiness when we come across the phrase "Everything becomes emptiness" in our meditation practices.

When we make offerings, we should think that three things—the giver, the recipient, and the gift—do not exist from their own sides and are established through being dependent and related. Then our offering is said to be "held by the mind reflecting on the emptiness of the three spheres." The benefits of making offerings in that way are enormous. Similarly, thinking that the prostrator, the object prostrated to, and the action of prostrating, are not truly existent and are merely established by relying on their parts and on each other makes the practice of prostrations very powerful. The same applies to any virtue.

Thus we can think all phenomena are empty because they are dependent and related, and because they cannot be found when searched for in their basis of designation. But if we do not analyze, and merely leave things as they appear, they do exist and are conventionally able to perform a function. If someone says, "Where is the watch?" we can say it is here and give it to him. That way a watch can be found. However, this is different from when we are searching for a truly existent watch among its parts. Such a truly existent watch cannot be found.

Contemplating that an object is not found when searched for in its basis of designation is one way of getting into the understanding of emptiness, and it is applicable to all phenomena. When it is applied to the person as a basis, we are thinking of the selflessness of the person. When we are thinking of phenomena other than the person, such as the aggregates and so on, we are thinking about the selflessness of phenomena. According to Nagarjuna, after understanding that phenomena are empty of independent existence, if we also know how to posit at the same time action and agent, cause and effect, and dependent and related, it is really fantastic.

The selflessness of persons

There is a person who came to this life from past lives and goes from this life to future lives, a person who accumulates various virtuous and non-virtuous karmas, and who experiences their results of happiness and suffering. The person is the experiencer and the aggregates are what are experienced. When a meditator investigates emptiness, he or she first examines the person and then the aggregates to see if they are truly existent; that is, first one realizes the selflessness of persons and later the selflessness of phenomena. That is the order, and it does not vary from one meditator to the other.

Of the two, persons and phenomena, it is easier to ascertain the emptiness of the person. The meditator first reflects that she herself circles in cyclic existence. She asks how this occurs and what the main cause for it is. In this way, she comes to know that the conception of a self is the root of cyclic existence. That conception is an incorrect mind, and she investigates whether the object of the conception of "I" exists in the way that it is held by that mind to exist. In this way she comes to an understanding that the referent object of the conception of I—an inherently existent I—does not exist. If she realizes the emptiness of the person, has she also realized the emptiness of all phenomena? No, not yet, but the realization of emptiness of other phenomena will not need a lot of effort. It can be realized by merely recollecting the same reasons and examples, and thus can be generated easily.

To make this clearer: to the innate conception of I, which thinks "I," there is an appearance of an I which exists from its own side, and that conception grasps, apprehends, or conceives of that I as existing from its own side as it appears. The meditator investigates whether that I exists in the way that it is conceived of as existing; i.e., she investigates whether its referent object—an I existing from its own side—exists or not. Through her investigation she comes to ascertain the non-existence of that referent object, and thereby ascertains emptiness.

Therefore, when we begin to meditate on emptiness, we should first think about it in relation to the person, asking ourselves, "Is the ignorance which acts as a root cause of circling in cyclic existence a correct or a false mind? Does its object exist in the way it holds it or not?" We may wonder, "How can the person not be truly existent since it appears to be truly existent?" Because something appears to exist in a certain way, that does not mean it in fact exists in that way. For example, the reflection of a face in a mirror appears to be a real face, a mirage appears to be water, and an echo appears to be a real voice, but all of these are known as false to the world. They can be used to illustrate the point that things don't have to exist as they appear.

If we realize that the person, the experiencer, lacks self-existence, we can realize easily that its objects of experience, the aggregates, lack self-existence as well. For example, if we know that a barren woman doesn't have a child, we will easily know that there is no nose on the child's face. We can realize it easily by using that same reasoning. That is one reason for meditating first on the selflessness of the person and then on that of phenomena. The other reason is that the meditator first must recognize the nature of the I that circles in cyclic existence.

If this explanation is clear to you now, that is wonderful. But if it is not so clear, it will gradually become clearer if you carefully and repeatedly listen to and think deeply about explanations given by qualified teachers. Whatever you learn will not be totally clear when you first hear it. But with constant reflection, it will gradually become clear. We should never give up just because we don't understand something at the beginning, because then we would have no way to arrive at a correct understanding. We need to study and keep going in order to come to a clear understanding. If we reach a fairly clear understanding of emptiness on the level of correct belief, even though it is not the actual realization, it will be very satisfying and helpful in our lives.

Freedom from one or many

Many lines of reasoning can be used to refute the object of negation, true existence. Of these, one which is quite straightforward and not very complicated is called the reasoning of freedom from one and many. In addition to this, there is the reasoning refuting production from the four extremes—self, other, both, and without causes—which Chandrakirti uses in his *Supplement to the Middle Way* when he explains the selflessness of phenomena. His explanation clarifies the non-production from the four extremes mentioned by Nagarjuna. This line of reasoning was originally taught in the Perfection of Wisdom Sutras and is more extensive. Also, if we wish for a more extensive reasoning to refute a self of persons, we can use the reasoning of unfindability through the sevenfold analysis, which was also taught by Chandrakirti. If summarized, the meaning of these latter two reasonings is the freedom from being one or many. Lama Tsong Khapa explains this reasoning in his various Gradual Path texts because it is the easiest to understand. If we ascertain the four essential points well and follow up with meditation on them, we will become closer to emptiness. Even if we are not able to meditate in depth, we will definitely have something to think about regarding the subject of emptiness.

The Gradual Path explains the reasoning of freedom from one and many via a meditation called "the four essential points":

1. Ascertaining the object of negation, a truly existent object

2. Ascertaining the pervasion that if something were truly existent as it appears to be, it would have to be findable either among its parts or separate from them, i.e., it would have to be one with its parts or different from them. There is no other possibility aside from these two.

3. Thinking of the faults that would follow if it were one with its parts, i.e., investigating and not finding it among the parts

4. Thinking of the faults that would follow if it were unrelatedly different from its parts, i.e., investigating and not finding it separate from its parts

The first, ascertaining the object of negation, means getting an idea of what the object of negation would be like if it were to exist. It is necessary to know this because before we can state the reason, "because of not being one or many," we need to know what is to be refuted. To go through the other three points, we have to first identify the object of negation. This is the most important and essential point for realizing emptiness. It might well be that we won't realize emptiness in this life, but we can leave good imprints on our mindstream by identifying the object of negation. Once we have a good understanding of the first point, it is said that ascertaining the emptiness of self-existence itself is quite easy. Our problem is that we do not really understand the self which is to be negated. We do not know how that self appears to our mind, how it is grasped, or how to search for it. Because of not knowing these, we have not been able to realize emptiness. For example, if someone stole something and we can only identify the thief as a European, it will be almost impossible to catch him. On the other hand, if we can give a detailed description of the thief and where he lives, it will be possible to seize him. In the same way, if we want to meditate on emptiness, we definitely have to ascertain the object of negation first, or we will get nowhere.

If, before identifying the object of negation, we simply think, "The object of negation, true existence, does not exist," it is like shooting an arrow at a target we cannot see. Therefore we need to ascertain the object of negation. If we understand what true existence is, we will know what to search for, and our meditation on emptiness will go well. Many past lamas who realized emptiness say that if we can ascertain the object of negation properly, the realization of emptiness will come soon. Of course, true existence cannot be ascertained by valid cognition because it does not exist. But we can know, "If there were true existence, it would have to be like this." In this way, we can ascertain what the object of negation is.

There are three kinds of mind apprehending the I: one focuses on the I and grasps it as truly existent, one focuses on the I and grasps it as non-truly existent, and one focuses on the I and does not grasp it as either truly existent or non-truly existent. The latter is, for example, a mind that thinks in an ordinary way without any special emotion, "I am going. I am eating." This is not the innate I-grasping. The innate I-grasping which is the root of cyclic existence is the first type. It apprehends the person as truly existent when its referent and aspect are clear. Its referent, or what it refers to, is the I. Its aspect, or how it relates to that, is to grasp it as truly existent. The way the inborn I-grasping apprehends is clear when we make it arise by thinking, "*I* am respected," "*I* have been badly harmed," "*I'm* falling from a cliff," or "Something is going to happen to *me!*" The times when the referent and aspect of the innate I-grasping are clear are very short. When they manifest, we should use the opportunity to look at how the I appears, because usually the referent and aspect of the innate I-grasping are mixed with others, and therefore are not clear. So, when we are very angry, jealous, proud, or attached and our I-grasping is manifest, we should try to pause for a moment and observe what our sense of I is. How does the I feel then? How does it appear to exist?

The object of negation is an I which does not depend on anything at all. While meditating we have to investigate, "How does the I appear to my innate self-grasping?" First, we sit in the eight-point posture of Vairochana. Then, we go for refuge, generate bodhichitta, and contemplate the four immeasurables in such a way that they merge with our mind. We visualize the gurus of the close lineage of blessings—from the Buddha to Manjushri to Lama Tsong Khapa and down to our root guru on top of our head—and request their inspiration to understand the object of negation exactly as it is. After that, we should generate the I-grasping in our continuum. Right now it is latent; it is there, but not in an obvious way. We do not have a strong feeling of I at this moment. But if we think, "My friend was so kind to *me*," an I will appear which does not seem to rely on anything at all. Or, if we recollect, "This person harmed or insulted *me* so much!" an independent I appears. Similarly, if we walk along a narrow, precipitous mountain path, we have a strong thought, "*I* might fall," and have the appearance of an I which seems quite solid. It is at times like these that the way the I appears to the innate I-grasping is clearest. The I seems to exist obviously from its own side without depending on anything else.

When the innate I-grasping has arisen, let it be there, and with a small part of your mind check how the I appears to that innate I-grasping. We will see that the I appears to our innate I-grasping mind to exist without relying on anything. This innate I-grasping is the ignorance which is the root of cyclic existence, the innate self-grasping of the person, grasping at true existence, and the ignorance which is the first of the twelve links. It is all of these. Based on this, inappropriate attention arises, followed by other disturbing attitudes such as attachment. We then accumulate various karmas and thus wander in cyclic existence as described by the twelve links.

The second of the four essential points is to establish the necessity that if the I existed from its own side as it appears to the innate I-grasping, then it must either exist as one or as many. "One or many" has two meanings: the I must be either one or more than one, or it must be either exactly the same as the aggregates or completely different from them. These two meanings of one or many come to the same point. When we think "I," there is an appearance of a truly existent I upon the aggregates. If that I existed from its own side as it appears, it would have to exist by being either inherently one with the aggregates or inherently different from them. This is called a "pervasion" because it has to be either one of these two, there is no other possibility. If the I were found to be one with the aggregates, it would have to be inseparably one with them, and if it were found to be different from the aggregates, it would have to be totally unrelated to them and exist independently. This is the second essential point.

The third essential point is: if the I existed from its own side and were one with the aggregates, it would have to be inseparably one with them. If that were the case, certain faults would follow, and therefore it cannot be one with the aggregates.

If a truly existent person were inseparably one with the aggregates, then the person would be inseparably one with the form aggregate, for example. In that case, since the form aggregate—the body—consists of various shapes and colors and is visible to the eye, the person would also have to be visible to the eye. However, the person is not an object of the eye consciousness because it is a non-associated compounded phenomenon (this is one class of impermanent phenomena that are neither form nor consciousness). It is true that when we designate names, we say, "I see Sam. He is here," because we see the colors and shape of his body. But in fact the person is not his body; the person is a non-associated compounded phenomenon and is not visible to the eye because the visual consciousness can only apprehend colors and shapes. Also the form aggregate is a collection of many atoms, and the person is not. If the person were inseparably one with the form aggregate, the I would have to be a collection of many atoms, which is not the case.

Similarly, a person would have to be inseparably one with the four mental aggregates:

1. Feeling, which is the experience of pleasant, unpleasant, and neutral
2. Discrimination, which discerns "This is blue. This is an animal," and so forth
3. Compositional factors, which are various other mental factors, attitudes, and emotions
4. Consciousness, which refers to the five sense consciousnesses—visual, auditory, olfactory, gustatory, and tactile consciousness—and the mental consciousness

If the I were inseparably one with one of the aggregates, then it would have to be unrelated to all the others. Or, if the person were one with each of the five aggregates, then there would be five I's all existing at the same time, and that is not the case. In general there is no fault in asserting many persons, because there are in fact many persons. For example, considering the continuum of one person, there is the person of the past life, the person of this life, and the person of the future life. Nor is there a fault in describing the person of the present life as multiple, because that also is a fact. Regarding the continuum of one person, there are the persons of yesterday, today, tomorrow, and so on. However, if the person where inherently one with each aggregate, then since the person who exists at one o'clock has five aggregates, there would have to be five persons at that very moment. That fault would arise if the person were inherently one with the aggregates.

In addition, if the I were one with the aggregates, the person would be subject to production and disintegration in exactly the same way as the aggregates. That would mean that the person would arise and cease in exactly the same way as the form aggregate. When the body is cremated and becomes non-existent after death, we would have to say that the person also becomes non-existent and does not go on to the next life. In addition, the person would be formed when the sperm and the egg unite, which is when the body is formed. These faults would arise, contradictory to our experience which makes it clear that the person is not one with the aggregates.

Initially this way of thinking may seem strange to us, and we may not immediately understand the purport of these reasonings. This is because we are not familiar with examining things in this way. If we continue to learn and to think about these arguments, we will find that they make us examine our deeply held belief that the I exists as it appears to us.

There is a particular relationship between the person and the aggregates—that of designated phenomenon (the person) and the basis of designation (the aggregates). If the person were truly existent, it would have to exist as one with its aggregates. It would have to be found as one, existing from its own side, upon the aggregates. Furthermore, if the person were inherently existent, it would have to be inseparably one with and utterly undifferentiable from the aggregates which are the basis of designation. In that case, all the various classifications of the aggregates would have to be the divisions of the person, and whatever could be said of the aggregates would have to be said of the person, and vice versa.

If the person were inseparably one with the aggregates, then since the person came from past lives to this one and goes from this life to future lives, we would have to say that the aggregates also come from past lives to this life and go from this one to future lives. That would mean that our body came from past lives to this life and goes from this life to future lives. But that is not the case, since the body comes about with the merging of the sperm and egg of our parents and it decomposes at the end of this life.

Because of these reasons we know that the person is not inseparably one with the aggregates. We can see that these absurd consequences
would follow if it were, so we can easily conclude that the person is
not one with the aggregates.

The fourth essential point is: if the I existed from its own side and
were inherently different from the aggregates, certain absurd consequences would result, and therefore it is not different from the aggregates. The term "many" which is used in opposition to "one" can be
taken two ways. "Many" may mean that the person is not several truly
existent persons. That is, because there is not one truly existent person, there cannot be several truly existent persons. This must follow
because for there to be several, there first has to be one, and in the
third point we refuted this possibility.

Another and more common meaning of "many" is that the person is
not inherently separate from the aggregates. In the third point, we refuted that the person was inherently the same as the aggregates. Here,
we are examining whether the person is inherently different from them.

If the person were completely different from and unrelated to the
aggregates, then if we were to take the aggregates away one by one,
the person could still remain; but this is not the case. For example, a
cup and table are unrelatedly different; if we take the cup away, the
table remains. Similarly, if the person were unrelatedly different from
the aggregates and each aggregate were taken away one by one, a
person would still remain. But this is not the case. When the aggregates are missing, we cannot identify the presence of a person. Simply
put, if the person and the aggregates were inherently separate, our
body and mind could be in one place and we could be in another.

In summary, first we identify the object of negation, an inherently
existent I. Here we do not simply intellectually identify it, but recognize it within ourselves and identify the feeling when the inherently
existent I arises. Then we establish that if such an I were to exist, it
would have to be either inherently the same as the aggregates or inherently different from them. Having investigated both of these op-
tions, we cannot find such an inherently existent I. Therefore, we conclude that such a thing does not exist at all. This is the emptiness of
the I, the selflessness of persons. Having analyzed with the four essential points and reached this conclusion in our meditation, we focus
on this experience of emptiness single-pointedly so that it becomes
firm. In this way, we combine the meditation of special insight with
the meditation of calm abiding.

The relationship between the person and the aggregates

If the person and the aggregates were unrelatedly different, after having taken away the five aggregates, there would have to be a person that could be pointed out. But in fact that is not the case. That is a sign that the two are related. When the arms or legs of a person are in pain, the person says, "I am in pain." This too indicates a relationship between the self and the aggregates. Similarly, when a person sees something, he thinks, "I saw this," because his visual consciousness saw it. This indicates a relationship between the person and the consciousness. Therefore the person and aggregates are not different to the extent that they are totally unrelated.

The basis for designating the word "person" is the mere collection of the aggregates, and the name "person" is designated or labeled in dependence upon them. Although the person is designated in dependence upon the mere collection of the aggregates, the person is not any of the aggregates individually. The form aggregate is not the person, nor are the feeling, discrimination, compositional factors, or consciousness aggregates. Is the mere collection of the aggregates the person? It is not, because if one aggregate is not inherently the person, the collection of them cannot be either. For example, if one orange is not an apple, a collection of oranges will not be an apple either.

The aggregates of the person are controlled by the person, and that is another reason why the collection of aggregates is not the person. They accomplish the wishes of the person and are the possessions of the person. We say, "my body" and "my feelings," showing that those aggregates belong to the self. The person is the agent—the doer of deeds—who uses and controls the aggregates, so it must be different from them. How does the person exist in relation to the aggregates, then? It is merely named, merely labeled in dependence upon the aggregates; it merely exists conventionally in dependence upon the aggregates. But if we look in the basis of designation to find something that is the I, we cannot find it.

For example, a watch is not the dial, nor is it the back, the inside, or the strap. So what is the watch? The watch is what is merely labeled on its parts. When all the parts are assembled together, the name "watch" is designated in dependence upon that mere collection. The watch does not come into existence merely by the collection being assembled. Only when the name "watch" has been labeled is it established as being a watch. Therefore the watch "exists merely by name."

If we look for an inherently existent watch, we cannot find it in its basis of designation. This shows that while the watch is empty and does not exist ultimately, it does exist conventionally.

The more we think about, it the closer we will come to understanding that if we search for an object, it cannot be found. This assertion is unique to the Prasangika Madhyamika system. The systems of the Svatantrikas and below, i.e., all other Buddhist schools of philosophical tenets in Tibet, insist that if we search we will find something. The Prasangika's way of positing a person that conventionally exists in spite of its ultimate unfindability is unique.

It is really quite odd, when we think about it: there is a person who comes, goes, stays, sleeps, and uses things. But this person is not found when we analyze and look for it in its basis of designation. Saying "mere I" means the I is not findable and does not exist from its own side.

There are a number of analogies to help us understand this. Imagine seeing a coiled, striped rope in dim light. This rope appears to us as a snake and we are frightened. There being a snake in that striped rope is only imputed by conception. From its own side there is no snake at all. When there is an appearance of a snake on the striped rope and we think it is a snake, the snake is posited by a mistaken conception. Similarly, the person upon the aggregates is merely designated or posited by conception. There is no truly existent person among the aggregates. The example and the point being illustrated are not the same in every way, however. There is no snake on the striped rope, but there is a person conventionally existing in dependence upon the aggregates, although there is no truly existent person there.

We may strip away the layers of a banana tree in the hopes of finding wood inside. No matter where we look, at the parts of the tree or at the collection of parts, we will not find wood. Similarly, wherever we look for the person existing from its own side, in the parts (the aggregates) or in the collection of aggregates, it can never be found. That is an example of not being found when searched for with analysis.

We may see a mirage from a distance and it appears to be water. If there really were water there in the way that it appears, if we went closer we would see it. But as we go closer, the water vanishes; it was a mistaken appearance. Similarly, if things existed from their own side in the way they appear to ordinary people, the aryas who have realized the nature of all phenomena would see them because they are the ones whose perceptions are closest to the actual way that things exist. But these realized beings do not find truly existent things at all.

Conventional existence

Does the person, who collects various karmas and experiences various resultant feelings of pleasure and pain, exist? Yes, there is a person who does various actions and experiences the results of pain and pleasure. Such a person does exist conventionally. Saying it exists does not mean it exists ultimately or truly. Does the person exist in dependence upon the aggregates? Yes, it does. How? It is merely labeled or designated in dependence upon the aggregates which are its basis of designation. Is there a person that can be found when searched for in the basis of designation, the aggregates? No. If we understand this clearly, we can apply our understanding to all phenomena.

If the I is merely labeled in dependence on the aggregates, what is it, then, that collects karma and goes from one life to the next? The various Buddhist philosophical systems have different assertions. Some say it is the mental consciousness, others say there is a special storehouse consciousness called "mind basis of all." The Prasangikas, however, say it is the mere I, the person itself.

If we think that because there is no person existing from its own side, there is no person at all, no one who accumulates karma and experiences results, we are mistaken. We have fallen to the extreme of nihilism because the extent of our negation has been too great. On the other hand, when positing agent, action, and object, if we think, "Conventionally there is a person who is the accumulator of karma and the experiencer of results. There are also the actions of the person and the objects of those actions. Therefore the person is truly existent and findable when searched for in the basis of designation," this is also mistaken and we have fallen to the extreme of permanence.

The person does not exist ultimately, nor truly, nor is it findable through analysis, but it still does definitely exist. Agent, action, and object can be posited conventionally. If we familiarize ourselves with this, at a certain point our understanding will become firm and we will have realized it. We have not realized it when we have only a picture in our mind. At present we may find ourselves seeing it clearly from time to time, but sometimes our understanding vanishes. When we have the realization, it is constant. That realization comes through familiarization with the clear idea that we have now and results from continuous practice. Just knowing that a given object is not findable when analyzed is difficult, but not amazingly difficult. Je Rinpoche said that what is truly difficult is to be able to think that the object cannot be found when analyzed and at the same time not lose the idea that it does nevertheless exist.

One scripture states that everything in the universe, all that exists from the celestial abodes of the gods to the awful abodes of the lower realms, is merely designated by conception. Saying that all phenomena are merely designated by conception does not mean that they are only made up by the mind and lack the ability to do anything. Things do function and interact. The functioning of agents, actions, and objects works within the fact that everything is merely designated by conception. In fact, because phenomena are merely designated, they are able to do actions, and that ability comes through reliance on causes, conditions, and dependent relationship. That is what we should think when we say that phenomena are merely designated by conception. "Merely" bars existing from its own side.

Thinking about and getting a clear understanding of the Prasangika idea of being merely designated by conception is very important. The lower philosophical systems—the Svatantrika, Chittamatra, Sautrantika, and Vaibhashika—are all unable to grasp this concept. However, studying them leads us gradually to comprehend the most subtle view, the Prasangika.

When our ritual texts say, "All phenomena become emptiness," we should not think that all phenomena do not exist at all. Rather we should think that they do not exist from their own side, without relying on anything. Within that state of being empty, we generate the offerings, the deity, the mandala, and so on. None of these inherently exist. They arise through the assembly of causes, conditions, and other dependent arisings that they rely upon. This is symbolized by first visualizing various syllables or implements and then imagining that the offerings or deities arise from those.

Because all phenomena are empty, they are dependent arisings. They are dependent arisings because of being empty. If they were inherently existent, they could not arise by depending on other factors. When we understand that all phenomena are empty of existing from their own side, we will be free of one misconception, the extreme view of permanence or eternalism. When we understand that everything is established through dependence on other factors, we will be free of another misconception, the extreme of non-existence or nihilism. Through understanding these two, we come to rest in the middle way, free of the two extremes of permanence and non-existence.

There is a great danger of going wrong here. All phenomena exist, but not inherently. We need to differentiate between existent and inherently existent. All phenomena are non-inherently existent, but we should not think that they are totally non-existent. We must also differentiate between non-existence and non-inherent existence. Phenomena do exist because they are all established through dependence. By thinking like this, we purify very powerful negativities and accumulate vast collections of positive potential. Nagarjuna said that an outstanding person is one who knows that phenomena are empty of true existence and who is also able to posit karma and its results, seeing that although nothing exists truly, cause and effect are viable.

Self-grasping of phenomena and of persons

Of the two self-graspings, first the self-grasping of phenomena is produced, then the self-grasping of persons. For the person to appear as an object to the mind, first the aggregates of that person appear as an object of mind. For example, to recognize Henry, first his aggregates have to appear as an object of our mind. Once that has happened, we will think, "Henry is here." When the aggregates of the person appear as an object of the mind, they appear as truly existent, and then a mental consciousness arises which grasps them to be truly existent, just as they appear. Once the aggregates of a person have been grasped at as existing from their own side, we think, "There's Henry," and at that point, the person appears to truly exist and will be grasped as truly existent.

After that, if the person is pleasing, we generate attachment towards him; because of that we act in certain ways, thus accumulating karma through attachment. If the person is displeasing, aversion or hatred will be generated, and motivated by that we will act negatively. These actions leave imprints on our mindstreams and when these ripen, we experience various difficulties in our lives. This is the sequence: the aggregates of a person appear to our mind to be inherently existent, we grasp them to be like that; the person appears to be truly existent and we grasp him to be like that; attachment or anger is generated; we act and accumulate karma; and we experience various unpleasant results.

Did the Buddha create emptiness? Was everything originally truly existent, and then did the Buddha make it all non-truly existent? Not at all. True existence has never existed, but due to our mistaken consciousnesses everything appears to us as if it were truly existent. Phenomena do not exist as they appear. They are similar to illusions. Through using mantra-spells and special substances applied to the audience's eyes, magicians can make pebbles and sticks appear as elephants and horses to the eye consciousness. To those whose eyes have been affected, actual horses and elephants will appear in that place, but these do not exist as they appear. Therefore it is said that phenomena do not exist in the way they appear, just as an illusion, for example, does not exist as it appears.

Dreams are similar. During a dream, there is the appearance of happiness and suffering to the dream consciousness, which is a mistaken consciousness. But these are not real because when we wake up there is no happiness or suffering like there appeared to be to our dream consciousness. Therefore it is said that all phenomena are like a dream. However, saying things are *like* illusions or dreams does not mean that they *are* illusions or dreams. They are simply similar to them in that they do not exist as they appear.

How can we say that nothing is truly existent if everything appears to truly exist? This question may arise when we seriously meditate on emptiness. Although things appear to be truly existent, that appearance is deceptive. These things do not exist as they appear, just like illusions and dreams. All phenomena are a combination of appearance and emptiness.

To put this in the context of a logical syllogism: the subject, the person, is not truly existent, because it is dependent and related, like, for example, the reflection of a face in a mirror. "The person" is the subject; "is not truly existent" is the predicate; "because it is dependent and related" is the reason or sign used to prove it. The example to help us understand this is the reflection of a face in the mirror. This may initially appear to be mere logical form, but when we understand how to work with the syllogism, we find it is in fact quite helpful for meditation.

When a person who understands non-true existence explains it to a person who does not understand it, he gives an example that is easy to understand. The one who does not understand the non-true existence of the person must understand the non-true existence of the example first. Here, he must understand that the reflection does not exist truly as a face, i.e., that the reflection is not a real face. Does that mean that he understands that the reflection is non-truly existent? No, but he understands the idea of not existing truly, or of not being true, i.e., the disparity between the way it appears and the way it exists. Although the reflection of a face appears to be a real face, it is not truly a face. He can then make the connection with the main part of the syllogism by thinking, "It must be that the person appears to be truly existent, but does not exist in the way it appears, just like this example."

The reflection is something commonly known in the world to be false—it appears to be a real face but isn't—and this helps us to think about the main point of the syllogism.

The reflection is equivalent to the person. It does not exist before all its causes, conditions, and other dependent arisings are complete. For example, there is no reflection before the face and mirror, which are the principal causes for the reflection, are brought together. These two must exist and they must meet, and only then will the reflection of a face appear. When they meet, all of the reflection of the face appears as a face. It is not that some of it appears as a face and another part doesn't. Similarly, there is no person before all the causes, conditions, and other dependent arisings are complete. If something is missing or if the causes don't come together, the person will not exist. The person also does not exist when searched for in the basis of designation, in the same way that we do not find a real face when we search for it in the reflection in a mirror. Just as the reflection appears to exist as a face from every part, without being able to distinguish a part which appears as a face and a part which does not, all persons and phenomena appear to the consciousnesses of ordinary beings as if they were existing from their own side, and yet they do not exist from their own side as they appear.

Emptiness is explained by using many examples. We should not think that the examples are unimportant and leave them out. If we do that, we will not be able to gain clarity about the points being illustrated. The examples are easy to understand, and if we think them over well they will help us understand the point being illustrated. Nagarjuna, Chandrakirti, and other masters say that we should think about the examples as well as we can, and it is wise to listen to the advice of these great masters.

Lama Tsong Khapa praised the Buddha for being an astounding and peerless teacher because the Buddha understood the root of his own wandering in cyclic existence and eradicated it by clearly understanding its antidote. Then motivated by great compassion, the Buddha taught this to his followers so that they could do the same. Out of his compassion, the Buddha taught hundreds of reasons and methods so that we can arrive at a clear understanding of non-true existence.

Lama Tsong Khapa also praised the Buddha for explaining how emptiness and dependent arising act as supports for each other. Because it is empty of true existence, any phenomenon definitely has to be dependent and related. There is no other possibility. These two are complementary, not contradictory. Because it is dependent and related, it has to be empty of existence from its own side. If this is clear to us, great, but if it is not that clear, it is important to recognize there is something significant in it. Then we will build up imprints in our mind and because of this familiarity, later our understanding will definitely and gradually grow. We need to learn about and contemplate emptiness, compassion, and bodhichitta, putting as much effort as we can into this. Then our precious human life will become very meaningful, and both in our life and when we die, we will have something valuable to share with others.

All phenomena are empty of true existence, and there is an emptiness of each of them: there is the emptiness of the cup, the emptiness of Susan, the emptiness of Buddhism, and so on. All of these emptinesses are the same in entity in that they are all just emptinesses of true existence. So from the point of view of entity, there are not different categories of emptiness. In that case, why do the texts talk about twenty emptinesses, eighteen emptinesses, sixteen emptinesses, and four emptinesses? Because there are different phenomena that are empty. Nevertheless, there is no difference in entity of the emptiness of each of those phenomena. Each of them is a non-affirming negation which is a mere absence of the object of negation, true existence. The twenty, eighteen, sixteen, and four emptinesses are summarized into the selflessness of persons and the selflessness of phenomena.

What emptiness isn't

Emptiness is not a quality of just some phenomena. (Here "phenomena" includes everything that exists.) It encompasses all phenomena: persons and other phenomena, whether they exist in samsara or in nirvana. Nor is emptiness mentally fabricated, meaning that at first things are not empty but are truly existent, and later, because the mind does not find anything when it analyzes, they become empty. In former times in Tibet, people explained emptiness in many ways. Some said it was partial and applied to only some phenomena, and others said emptiness was fabricated by the mind. Lama Tsong Khapa went to the Prajnaparamita sutras and the texts of Nagarjuna and his spiritual descendants to show that emptiness is in fact neither partial nor mentally fabricated. All things are equally empty and they are empty by nature. What changes is not the phenomena, but our understanding of them. We realize that they are empty, thereby destroying our grasping at true existence. Lama Tsong Khapa quotes the writings of Maitreya, which take the Prajnaparamita sutras as their sources. Maitreya says that it is not that there is first a truly existent object which then is eliminated by the mind. The wisdom realizing emptiness does not make things non-truly existent. Rather, phenomena have never been truly existent, and now the mind realizes this.

The doctrine of emptiness is also not nihilistic. When truly existent phenomena are negated, it doesn't mean cause and effect, or actions, agents, and objects become inoperable or non-existent. In fact, it's just the opposite; because things do not exist from their own side, they can change and affect each other, they can arise and perish. When yogis who have reached a high level meditate on emptiness, their meditation is "held" or supported by the method aspect of the path—love, compassion, and bodhichitta. This implies that emptiness is not nihilistic, because if it were, the meditator would think that such things as actions and agents, or love and compassion did not exist at all.

Emptiness is not something which is not cognizable, knowable, or understandable. Emptiness can be realized first conceptually and then through direct experience or cognition. Nor is emptiness meaningless, because realizing it and accustoming ourselves to it gradually removes the obscurations in our mindstreams and causes us to achieve the enlightenment of any of the three vehicles. This point needs to be explained because in the past some Tibetan scholars thought emptiness meant non-existence or that it was not an object of mind. These are mistaken ideas and there are scriptural sources that can be cited to disprove them.

First, we make the object of negation, true existence, appear to the mind. Then we apply reasoning to refute it. When we do that, it cannot stand its ground, because it does not exist. When we refute it, its non-existence dawns on us. If true existence did exist, it would get clearer when we analyze and investigate. It would be able to remain as it is. However, that is not the case. Its appearance vanishes when we analyze, and we are left with the appearance of its non-existence, an appearance of it being empty. What dawns on our mind is a non-affirming negative which is the mere absence of the object of negation. Nothing else is implied in its stead. When that non-affirming negative dawns on our minds, we should go into that void with mindfulness and alertness.

We who have studied these things believe that all phenomena exist conventionally but do not exist truly. However, when phenomena appear to us, the two—truly existent and conventionally existent—appear mixed, and until we have realized emptiness we cannot separate them. For example, the appearance of a conventionally existent flower is mixed with the appearance of a truly existent one. Although we can separate true existence and conventional existence on an intellectual level—we say the former is non-existent and the latter existent—in our daily life, when phenomena appear to us these two appear together. Until we have realized emptiness, we cannot discriminate the two, existence and true existence, when they appear to our ordinary perceptions.

For example, the meditator investigates whether the person truly exists as it appears. She knows that if it did, it should be either inseparably one with or totally different from the aggregates of body and mind. She realizes that both of these positions have faults, and so the emptiness of the person dawns. Because previously the appearance of the conventionally existent person was mixed with the appearance of a truly existent person, now when true existence is negated, to the mind of the meditator it is as if the person itself had been refuted along with its true existence. Initially, the meditator does not think about how the object does exist, for she is investigating how it does not truly exist. When true existence is negated, the practitioner cannot immediately understand that conventional existence remains. However, she has not realized that the object does not exist conventionally. It is simply that the conventional existence of that object cannot come into the perspective of the mind analyzing emptiness. When we negate existence from its own side, it is only later that we think, "Phenomena are not truly existent, but still they are not totally non-existent; each performs its own function."

What is the object of negation, true existence? Meditators who have realized emptiness say it is exactly what we see with our eyes. In the case of the cup, for example, what appears to us is a truly existent cup. The cup appears as if it were truly existent. It is said, "Leave the vivid appearance as it is." That means it is exactly that vivid appearance right in front of us which is the appearance of true existence. We should not put this vivid appearance aside and look elsewhere for the object of negation. The table itself is not the object of negation, but the vivid appearance right in front of us of a truly existent table is. This is a delicate issue; we cannot put the vivid appearance of the cup aside and look elsewhere for the object of negation. Nor can we say that the cup is to be negated. It is just the vivid appearance of its true existence which is.

Dependent arising

There are various reasons that prove non-true existence. Most reasons, such as freedom from one and many, the sevenfold analysis, negating production from the four extremes, negating production from existence and non-existence, and so on are called "reasons of non-observation of a related object." That means we say, "If there were true existence, it would have to be either like this or like that, and since it is neither, true existence doesn't exist." For example, if the person were truly existent, it would have to be one with or completely different from the aggregates. One and many are the "related objects." But since they are not observed, there is the non-observation of a related object, and from that we know the person doesn't truly exist.

We can also prove non-true existence by stating a reason which involves a contradictory object, in this case "dependent arising." Dependent arising is contradictory to true existence. That is, if things arise dependently, they cannot be truly existent. Thus, proving they are dependent and related is a very powerful way to negate their true existence.

When we think about dependent arising, the entire network of mistaken views in our mindstream is dispelled. Thinking about dependent arising involves understanding non-production from discordant causes (e.g., a rose can't grow from a chili seed), non-production without causes (i.e., something cannot come into existence if there are no causes for it), non-production from one cause (e.g., a creator deity who produced everything), production of each thing from conditions which have the potential to produce it (e.g., a rose seed has the potential to produce a rose), and production from conditions which are all impermanent (i.e., the causes must cease for the result to come into existence). Understanding these aspects well frees our mind from much confusion and many mistaken views.

Dependent arising is not a simple subject which only requires generally thinking about something arising through depending on something else. Understanding dependent arising in the context of compounded or produced phenomena, for example, means identifying the unique perpetuating (or substantial) cause which becomes each object, and its cooperative conditions which are essential for its arisal. For example, the seed is the substantial cause which generates the sprout, and the water, fertilizer, and sunshine are the cooperative conditions which enable the seed to give rise to the sprout.

People who hold other systems of belief cannot understand dependent arising clearly. They do not assert that compounded phenomena are produced from both their perpetuating causes and cooperative conditions, and thus they cannot explain the evolution of cyclic existence and liberation in terms of the four noble truths or the twelve links. For example some people believe that the universe and the beings in it are produced from a creator who is permanent. They do not understand that permanent things cannot change or create something new. Nor do they know how to identify the correct causes that have the ability to produce the universe and its inhabitants.

Others, such as the ancient Samkhya philosophical system, say that everything is produced from the "Principal," a permanent substance which functions and from which everything is made. They too do not understand dependent arising. If we state the syllogism to them, "The subject, cyclic existence, is not truly existent, because it is a dependent arising," they do not understand that cyclic existence is a dependent arising. To do that, they would have to understand how it arises from its perpetuating causes and cooperative conditions, not from some universal and uniform substance. In addition, it is impossible for something permanent to produce anything because by definition permanent things cannot change and change is necessary for something to be produced.

Dependent arising is called the king of reasons because it is able to eliminate the extremes of both permanence (the extreme of "existence" which means true existence) and nihilism (the extreme of total nonexistence) at the same time. It is normally explained that "not truly existent" eliminates the extreme of permanence, and "dependent arising" eliminates the extreme of nihilism. But according to the Prasangikas, "dependent arising" also eliminates the extreme of permanence or true existence. How? If all things are dependent arisings, they rely on causes, conditions, and other factors to exist, and this contradicts truly existent things which should be able to set themselves up without depending on other things. When we understand that something arises dependently, we cannot at the same time think it arises independently because these two are mutually exclusive. If it isn't independent, it can't be truly existent. This is the meaning of the passage, "Appearances clear away the extreme of (inherent) existence," in *The Three Principal Aspects of the Path* by Lama Tsong Khapa. Before Lama Tsong Khapa, most people did not understand that dependent arising could eliminate both the extremes of nihilism and permanence. Lama Tsong Khapa had a direct vision of Manjushri who then taught him this difficult but essential point from the sutras.

The Three Principal Aspects of the Path continues, "Emptiness dispels the extreme of non-existence." When we negate true existence, we do not deny existence in general. Things are not totally non-existent. Being empty of inherent existence means they exist conventionally. Therefore, when we say a thing is empty of true existence, it certainly eliminates true existence, the extreme of existence. In addition, it eliminates the extreme of total non-existence, and leaves conventional existence intact. Thus, when we reason, "the subject, the person, is non-truly existent, because of being a dependent arising," the sign "dependent arising" eliminates the two extremes. So does the predicate, "non-truly existent."

That the Buddha taught that all phenomena are dependent arisings is one of the main reasons the great yogis and scholars over the centuries have praised him. The Buddha has marvelous qualities of body, speech, and mind; he has great compassion, wisdom, and power. Yet these are not the chief things that he is praised for. It is the fact that he taught dependent arising that others find so remarkable and marvelous. For example, at the beginning of *Fundamental Wisdom* Nagarjuna praises the Buddha for having taught dependent arising.

Buddhist conduct is non-violent. The reason for this is connected to dependent arising because according to the view of dependent arising, concordant results arise from concordant causes. Results do not occur in a haphazard manner. This means that from harming others a result will follow which accords with that cause. That is, if we harm others the result will be negative. Thus, because we understand dependent arising, we try to avoid the ten destructive actions.

The world and its inhabitants do not arise without causes. Nor do they come about due to a Supreme Being thinking, "It would be good if this were to happen." They arise depending on causes which are impermanent, and these causes and cooperative conditions are concordant with their result. Something cannot produce just anything; for example, a cup can't produce a pen and a banana tree cannot grow from an apple seed. Causes and results are related. Contemplating this can be very rich and beneficial. When we relate this to the other verses of *The Thirty-seven Practices of Bodhisattvas*, we will understand that qualities such as patience, detachment, generosity, and so forth are emphasized because they bring good results. Ignorance, anger, attachment, pride, and jealousy, on the other hand, bring unpleasant results both now and in the future.

However, although the fact that sprouts arise in dependence on seeds, water, and fertilizer is a correct example of concordant results arising from concordant causes, citing this is not looking at causality in detail and ruling out extreme positions. Just understanding the example of seeds and sprouts does not mean we have understood the full significance and depth of dependent arising. We may still hold extreme positions. The followers of Vishnu, the Samkhyas, and those who accept a creator understand that sprouts grow from seeds and depend on water and fertilizer. However, they do not accept that samsara and nirvana arise depending on concordant causes. They posit causes that are in fact unable to produce those things. Thus when we state to them, "The subject, the person, is non-truly existent because of being a dependent arising," the reasoning does not work for them because they do not understand that the person is a dependent arising. When we talk of the person being a dependent arising, there are various levels of dependent arising that can be known, some more subtle than others. In this context, it means they do not accept that the person is produced in dependence on disturbing attitudes and karma.

One sutra says that everything beautiful, such as the pure lands, as well as everything unpleasant, such as the lower realms, is merely designated and posited by conception. All phenomena rely on the conceptions designating or positing them. It is because an object is posited by the conception designating it that it is said to exist. Does "merely designated by conception" mean that all phenomena are designated at random, such as a snake being designated on a striped rope? Is it acceptable to designate "lion" on the aggregates which are the basis of designation of a dog because everything is merely designated by name and does not exist from its own side? This is not a simple point.

We cannot validly designate "lion" on the aggregates which are the basis of designation of a dog, because those aggregates do not have the ability to perform the function of a lion. Similarly, when "snake" is designated to a striped rope, a mistaken consciousness is thinking, "This is a snake." A valid conception is not making this designation. To be a valid designating conception, there has to be a valid basis of designation. That means that the object must have the ability to perform the function in keeping with the name designated. To do this, neither the object nor its basis of designation have to exist from their own side; in fact, they can't! But the basis of designation must fulfill the definition of the designated object and be able to perform the function of that object. The aggregates of a dog cannot perform the function of a lion. Thus they are not a valid basis of designation of the name "lion," nor is the mind that labels them "lion" a valid designating conception.

According to the Prasangika system, all phenomena are merely designated by conception and name. "Merely" eliminates existence from its own side. It excludes not relying on anything else. It also excludes the possibility of findability through searching in the basis of designation, since that is how it would have to be if it existed from its own side. Each phenomenon is merely designated by a valid designating conception on a valid basis of designation which is able to perform its particular function. They do not have to exist from their own side. For example, for something to be designated "microphone," a valid mind had to designate that name on a valid basis of designation. The table, for example, would not be a valid basis of designation of "microphone," because it cannot function as a microphone.

This is a unique attribute of the Prasangikas, which even the great Svatantrika masters cannot grasp. It is a subtle, difficult, yet essential point, which pertains to dependent arising on a very subtle level. There is quite a bit to think about in connection with this point. All things exist conventionally and are able to function, because each thing has an action which it does, a function which it performs. However, it does not have to exist inherently to be able to do this. In fact, if it existed inherently, it could not perform a function because it would be unrelated to and independent from all other things. There is no contradiction between existing nominally and being able to function. "Merely labeled" indicates that the basis of designation of the name does not exist from its own side. It does not mean that the basis of designation of the name does not conventionally have the ability to function. Rather, each object exists, it exists conventionally, and it is able to perform its function. All phenomena are able to perform all their actions within being merely labeled.

When we use the reason of dependent arising to prove that something does not exist from its own side, we are not specifying either gross or subtle dependence. We are just saying that it exists by relying on other things. Some scientific researchers understand this well. They research and know how things happen through depending and relying on other things. For example, they examine what causes produce a certain illness and what causes can cure it. It is clear to scientists that a combination of many different atomic and sub-atomic particles is necessary for any functioning thing to arise and that by many phenomena combining and transforming, a functioning thing is formed. On a subtler level, to contemplate the subtle theory of dependent arising, we need to think in detail about the twelve links of dependent arising and the finer points of karma and its results.

In the world there are objects which have mind and those which have no mind. The ones with no mind are of many types. If we understand that such objects occur through the transformation of many different types of causes which have the potential to become those objects, we have an understanding of dependent arising. If we think that they are made by a creator who is a permanent functioning thing, or that they are all made from one and the same primal substance, or that they all come from one cause, we do not understand dependent arising. When we look in detail at dependent arising, we become convinced that nothing comes into existence without relying on other things. From this, we see that the view of true or independent existence cannot stand its ground.

Buddha came to the world willingly, to benefit sentient beings, not uncontrollably like us. He came to make spiritually mature those who are not, to liberate those who are mature, and to bring those who are already liberated to the ultimate state of enlightenment. To do this he taught emptiness, and the unparalleled reason proving emptiness is dependent arising. Thus dependent arising is highly praised because it is the indispensable method for attaining liberation and enlightenment.

Any phenomenon which arises through depending on and in relation to others abides in the middle, free of the two extremes of permanence and nihilism. For example, this table does not abide in the extreme of permanence, because if it did it would have to be truly existent. If it abided in the extreme of nihilism, it would have to be totally non-existent. Therefore it abides in the middle, not in the two extremes of permanence and nihilism, which are also called the extremes of existence and non-existence. There is no phenomenon which abides in either of the two extremes.

Sometimes it is said, "Dependent arising is free of the eight extremes." The eight are: production and cessation, coming and going, one and different, and permanent and discontinuing. These are explained in connection with the object of negation. Thus, "not ceasing and not produced" means that there is no truly existent cessation because there is no truly existing production. With cause and effect in general, the effect does not exist at the time of the cause, and the cause has to have ceased at the time of the effect. For example, a sprout does not exist at the time of its cause, a seed, and the seed needs to have ceased in order for the sprout to come into existence. If the cause did not cease at the time its result had been produced, there would be the fault of truly existent production and the fault of permanence. The person does not truly cease, i.e., it does not have truly existent cessation, because if did it would have to have truly existent production, and it does not.

"Not permanent and not discontinuing" has to do with the continuity between cause and effect. When the effect has arisen, the continuity of type similar to the cause is not discontinued; that continuity keeps going on. "The continuity of type similar to the cause" means a result which is a type similar to the cause that produced it. For example, when our next life comes into existence, this life must have ceased. But its continuity does not cease; it carries on and becomes our future life. If the cause of the next life, this life, remained and had not ceased at the time of the effect, it would be permanent. On the other hand, if the continuity completely discontinued and this life had no effect, no continuity in future lives, that would be the extreme of discontinuity.

"No coming, no going" means there is no true coming closer from further away, nor is there true going further away from a closer place. "Not one and not different" means there are no phenomena which are truly different, i.e., truly individual objects, nor are there any which are truly the same, i.e., truly non-individual objects.

Therefore, dependent arisings are free from the elaborations of true existence. The peace of nirvana which is free from the elaborations of true existence is a peace which is constant, indestructible, and unchanging. This is not like the peace we have in samsara. Any peace we experience in cyclic existence is only a temporary and fleeting freedom from some suffering. It is changeable and not constant.

There are two kinds of view of the transitory collection: one focuses on the "I" and one focuses on the "mine." The former focuses on the conventional I which is in one's own continuum; that I is its focal object (Tib. *mig yul*). The view of the transitory collection focuses on the self and apprehends it as existing from its own side, i.e., as truly existent. That truly existent self is the object of the mode of apprehension

(Tib. *dzin wang kyi yul*) or the referent object (Tib. *zhen yul*), and it does not exist. That is because there is no self which exists without relying on causes, conditions, or other factors. The person who acts on the conventional level is the focal object; that is the mere I, the person who accumulates positive and negative karma and who experiences happiness and suffering. Since that person exists, we say the self that is the focal object exists. When we refute the self which is the referent object of the view of the transitory collection, i.e., the inherently existent self, we must be careful not to refute the self which exists conventionally at the same time. If we do so, we will not be able to posit karma and its results, nor agents and actions, because all of them would be non-existent for us.

Not existent and not non-existent

Some say, "All phenomena are neither existent nor non-existent." This is called the view of Hoshang and it occurred in China and spread to Tibet many centuries ago. The Dharma kings of Tibet invited the Indian sage Kamalashila to Tibet to disprove this view through debate. Even today, we may come across the claim that "not existent and not non-existent is the ultimate view" when we read certain books. However, saying that this is the ultimate and pure view cannot stand up to logical analysis. The first part "not existent" means non-existent. The second part "not non-existent" means existent. If it is not existent it must be non-existent, and if it is not non-existent it must be existent. The two are mutually exclusive, so that if one is excluded the other is established. There is no third possibility. Therefore saying "not existent and not non-existent" is contradictory.

The Buddha taught according to the different dispositions, thoughts, and interests of sentient beings, so sometimes he taught a substantially existing self that exists independently of the aggregates, and sometimes he taught that there is no such self. To some people he said there is true existence and to others that there is not. To some he taught that there are externally existing objects and to others that there are not. These were all taught by one person, the Buddha, but they were taught to different people at different times, according to their different minds. They were not taught to one person on the same occasion. If we were to accept something as the ultimate way of being just because Buddha taught it, then since Buddha taught all these, we would have to say that the ultimate mode of existence is that all phenomena are truly existent and that they are non-truly existent, that there are externally existing phenomena and that there are not, that there is self-existence and that there is not.

The Buddha did say, "not existent, not non-existent," and those who propound Hoshang's view take that statement literally. However, the Buddha advised us not to take what he said literally as the ultimate mode of existence, but to analyze its meaning with logic. We should not assume that everything the Buddha taught is literally the final mode of existence. Only through checking can we find out if it is.

When the Buddha taught "not existent and not non-existent," he meant that all phenomena are not truly existent, and are also not non-existent conventionally. That is, they do not exist ultimately, but do exist conventionally. This interpretation makes sense: there is no true existence, because there is nothing which exists without depending on causes, conditions, or anything else. But phenomena are not totally non-existent, because conventionally each has its own action and purpose. If we understand "existent conventionally, non-existent ultimately," we have a good understanding of the Middle Way. Even if we only understand this in a general way, we will accumulate great positive potential and purify vast negativity. How? We have to progress on the path of wisdom and method. When we think that all phenomena are non-existent ultimately, we develop the wisdom side of the path. When we think that they are not non-existent conventionally and do exist conventionally, that is the method side of the path. Here we see that love, compassion, and bodhichitta, for example, have their own actions and functions. In this way, we develop both method and wisdom, steadily progress on the path, and create a peerless cause for attaining liberation and enlightenment.

No phenomenon is found if searched for in its basis of designation. When searched for in the basis of designation, it does not exist. That is the meaning of "not existent." However, when we do not investigate in this way, we see it exists. That is because every phenomenon has its own action which it is able to do. This is the meaning of "not non-existent."

Until they have discovered the view of the middle, that is, until they have realized emptiness, ordinary beings cannot differentiate between true existence and existence established by valid cognition. Nor can they differentiate non-existence and non-true existence. In fact there is a difference between the modes of apprehending existence and true existence, and in the modes of apprehending non-existence and non-true existence. But until we realize emptiness, we are not able to distinguish them clearly.

For example, the non-true existence of a vase is ascertained by a mind analyzing the ultimate, which is a valid reasoning consciousness analyzing the ultimate. However, the vase is not non-existent, and a valid conventional mind analyzing the conventional ascertains that.

According to the Prasangika system, nothing can be found when searched for with a reasoning consciousness analyzing the ultimate. If something could withstand this analysis it would exist from its own side. According to the Prasangika system, if we posit true existence, we will not be able to posit the twelve links or the four noble truths. If the twelve links and four truths truly existed, they would have to be totally unrelated objects and we could not talk of one arising from the other. In fact, the twelve links are discussed in the context of reliance of one upon the other, as are the four noble truths. Therefore, they cannot be truly existent. In *Fundamental Wisdom*, Nagarjuna said that if phenomena were not empty of true existence, we could not posit arising and disintegration, production and cessation, and so on. If we cannot posit these, the four noble truths would become non-existent. In this way Nagarjuna refuted the lower philosophical systems.

For a person who accepts that all phenomena are empty of true existence, everything is suitable. This means that action and agent, cause and effect can be posited. That is because "empty" means empty of existence from its own side, and that means being established through reliance on other factors. Thus everything that exists dependently or conventionally can be posited.

BETWEEN MEDITATION SESSIONS, HOW TO GIVE UP THE BELIEF THAT THE DESIRED AND HATED ARE REAL

Just as with conventional bodhichitta, ultimate bodhichitta needs to be developed during meditation sessions as well as in the time between sessions when we are engaged in the activities of daily life. To maintain the view of emptiness in post-meditation times, we practice overcoming the belief that both objects of desire and objects of aversion are truly existent.

Overcoming the belief that objects of desire are truly existent

23   When you encounter attractive objects,
       Though they seem beautiful
       Like a rainbow in summer, don't regard them as real
       And give up attachment—
       This is the practice of Bodhisattvas.

After Bodhisattvas finish their single-pointed meditation on emptiness, they get up and engage in all sorts of daily actions. Although they have perceived emptiness directly during meditation, due to the force of subtle stains on the mind that have yet to be removed, things still appear truly existent to them as they go about their lives. However, they no longer believe in these appearances. They know things do not exist in the way they appear. In this way, they stop their compulsive reactions to things.

When we come into contact with beautiful objects, nice sounds, relatives, friends, and other things we like, they appear to us as truly existent and we grasp them as existing in that way. Thus attachment, craving, and discontent are fueled in our minds. However, just as a beautiful summer rainbow does not exist as it appears, neither do these objects and people. Similarly, the pleasure and well-being that they give us seem to be self-existent, but they are not so.

Overcoming the belief that objects of aversion are truly existent

24   All forms of suffering are like a child's death in a dream.
       Holding illusory appearances to be true makes you weary.
       Therefore when you meet with disagreeable circumstances,
       See them as illusory—
       This is the practice of Bodhisattvas.

This stanza explains how to abandon aversion to various objects of hatred, such as our enemies, unpleasant sounds, ugly sights, and the various things that cause us suffering. By seeing them as not self-existent, our aversion and suffering are pacified. For example, once a woman dreamt that she married and gave birth to a child to which she became greatly attached. Then in her dream, the baby died. She woke up in tears, so miserable that she was difficult to console. Yet, both the birth and the death of the child in the dream were erroneous appearances, and it is because they appeared real in the dream and she thought they were real that she suffered so. Similarly, the unpleasant appearances that we experience seem to be self-existent, but they are not. The appearance of self-existence is erroneous; it arises due to a mind that is erroneous. Yet we hold them as true, and due to that, suffering comes our way. When we see them as empty of inherent existence, that suffering is pacified.

If our meditation on emptiness is good, then automatically our post-meditation time will go well. Although when not in meditative equipoise on emptiness, phenomena will still appear truly existent to us, we will be able to draw on the wisdom built up during equipoise, and without much difficulty we will see that although things appear truly existent, they are not.

If our meditation on emptiness is not so good, we have to work that much harder in our daily life during the post-meditation time to maintain the correct view. It is similar when we meditate on love, compassion, and so forth. When our meditation is strong, all our actions outside of the session—walking, sleeping, interacting with others—will be supported by the meditation, and they also will go well. If they do not go well, it is a sign that our meditation is weak. Thus, the great masters tell us that when we do retreat, our meditation session should help us to practice during the break time, and our practice during the break time should help our meditation. Thus, the way of familiarizing ourselves with emptiness during our sessions is by meditating on space-like emptiness. During the breaks, i.e., during our daily activities, we should meditate on illusion-like emptiness, seeing that things do not exist in the way that they appear.

In the breaks between sessions of meditation on emptiness, while we practice refuge, actions and their results, love, compassion, and so on, all that appears to our mind on those occasions will appear to be truly existing. At this time, we should think that they do not exist as they appear. In this way we will practice a yoga which combines wisdom and method.

Gaining a perfect realization of emptiness will take time, but it is not that difficult simply to contemplate it. We just need to make the time; it certainly won't make itself! We are usually very busy, we have our jobs and family, but if we want to meditate, we can make the time. After all, there always seems to be time for reading the newspaper, drinking coffee, and chatting with our friends. We should think a little about emptiness, for it is the best way to purify our mind, to liberate ourselves from cyclic existence, and to attain Buddhahood.

CHAPTER FOURTEEN

THE BODHISATTVAS' TRAININGS

PART III: THE VIRTUE AT THE END

The third virtue of the text is the concluding practices. This section principally speaks of the Bodhisattvas' trainings: the six far-reaching attitudes, the four points taught in the sutras, the way to abandon the disturbing attitudes, mindfulness and alertness, and the dedication of positive potential to complete enlightenment. After the verses about the Bodhisattvas' trainings, there are some verses which conclude the root text.

THE SIX FAR-REACHING ATTITUDES

The far-reaching attitude of generosity

25   When those who want enlightenment must give even their
       body,
    There's no need to mention external things.
    Therefore without hope for return or any fruition
    Give generously—
    This is the practice of Bodhisattvas.

The six far-reaching attitudes are the far-reaching attitudes of generosity, ethics, patience, joyous effort, concentration, and wisdom. Only the Buddhas have the actual far-reaching attitudes. Before that stage,

we practice them. Our practice is motivated by the altruistic intention and purified by our understanding of emptiness.

Everyone appreciates generosity, the first far-reaching attitude. When people live together and are generous with each other, the entire society is affected in a positive way. It is important to make our motivation for giving as pure as possible, that is, to give without wishing to receive anything in return in this life, and without hoping to receive wealth in future lives. Motivated by genuine love, compassion, and bodhichitta, our giving will become very beneficial.

Generosity can be spoken of in different ways. For example, there are four types of generosity:

1. The generosity of giving material possessions. This includes giving food, money, medicine, and even our own body. However, until we reach a certain level on the path, we are not allowed to give our body. When we are properly prepared and there is a real need, then it is appropriate to give it. At present, we can "give our body" by using it to serve others.

2. The generosity of giving love includes thinking, "May others be happy," as well as actually caring for them. It is important for us not to get so absorbed in the abstract concept of "all suffering mother sentient beings" that we ignore those around us. We should be warm and take care of those in our immediate environment as much as we can.

3. The generosity of giving fearlessness principally refers to saving the lives of others and freeing them from fearful situations.

4. The generosity of giving the Dharma means sharing the Dharma with others by giving teachings or initiations, for example. The generosity of giving Dharma must be practiced with a motivation that is not mixed with disturbing attitudes. That is, we must take care not to wish for money, appreciation, or reputation in return for teaching the Dharma. The more pure our motivation—the more it is solely to benefit others—the more effective our gift of the Dharma will be. When we become an arya, any teaching we give will be of great benefit to others. We also can give the Dharma in unassuming ways, such as by helping a person with problems by explaining the Dharma perspective to them without using any Buddhist words. For example, if our friend is suffering from anger, we can explain how to look at the situation from a different perspective. We also give the Dharma by reciting our prayers out loud so that the animals and insects in the area hear them.

Generosity can also be of three types, as in the taking and giving practice:

1. Giving our own body
2. Giving our possessions
3. Giving all our positive potential of the three times

There are also three other types of giving:

1. Giving. This includes giving clothes, money, food, drink, and so forth, things which are of short-term benefit.
2. Great giving. This is the giving of such things as houses, jewels, horses, and cars.
3. Thoroughly giving. Here we give our body.

The far-reaching attitude of ethics

26   **Without ethics you can't accomplish your own well-being,**
      So wanting to accomplish others' is laughable.
      Therefore without worldly aspirations
      Safeguard your ethical discipline—
      This is the practice of Bodhisattvas.

Ethical discipline is the basis of all higher qualities and the foundation of a peaceful life. Without keeping pure ethical discipline, we cannot even achieve our own purposes. We will experience many problems in this life and will not have a good rebirth in the future. If we cannot attain even our mundane ends without ethical discipline, then of course without it enlightenment is impossible. In practicing the far-reaching attitude of ethics, our motivation should not be for personal goals, such as a higher rebirth, but to attain enlightenment in order to benefit all sentient beings most effectively.

If we practice generosity without ethical discipline, we will have an unfortunate rebirth, perhaps as an animal. Because of being generous, however, we would be a very rich and comfortable animal, like a pampered pet dog or cat in the West. However, this will consume the good karma we had from practicing generosity, and later when we are again born as a human being, we may be poor. Therefore, it is important for us to practice both generosity and ethical discipline.

There are three types of ethical discipline:

1. The ethical discipline of refraining from negative actions. The basic ethical discipline is that of abandoning the ten negative actions, and

everyone is advised to keep this. On top of that, we should protect whatever precepts we have received in the pratimoksha, Bodhisattva, and tantric ordinations. Also included in the ethical discipline of refraining from negative actions is purifying any transgressions of our precepts that might occur, by engaging in the appropriate procedure for confessing them.

2. The ethical discipline of practicing virtue. Here we practice constructive actions as much as possible. This includes listening, thinking, and meditating on the Dharma, doing our daily meditation practice, and helping others. It refers to even small positive actions, and there are plenty of opportunities to do these with ease in our daily lives.

3. The ethical discipline of achieving the aims of sentient beings. This means to help sentient beings as much as we are able. We practice this when we say in the *Six-Session Guru Yoga*, "I shall completely liberate migrators in whatever way I can." In addition, in our daily life we should help others whenever the opportunity presents itself and we are capable of doing so. It is essential to make sure that our help is indeed helpful. We should avoid forcing our own desires on others under the veneer of being compassionate.

The far-reaching attitude of patience

27   To Bodhisattvas who want a wealth of virtue
     Those who harm are like a precious treasure.
     Therefore towards all cultivate patience
     Without hostility—
     This is the practice of Bodhisattvas.

In the Buddhist scriptures, patience is said to be the best of ascetic practices. Patience is the mind that remains undisturbed when we experience harm or suffering. Enduring harm does not mean gritting our teeth and bearing it, nor does it mean pretending we're not angry when we really are. Rather, patience is an undisturbed and calm state of mind that can tolerate the situation peacefully. We know our patience is increasing when we don't get angry—or get less angry—in situations that previously would have set off our anger or resentment. All of the practices mentioned earlier that involve transforming bad conditions into the path are included under the practice of patience. There are three types of patience:

1. The patience of tolerating harm
2. The patience of enduring hardship and suffering

3. The patience of not being afraid of the profound meaning

The first patience involves restraint from retaliation. There are a number of ways in which we can regard the person who harms us so that our mind remains calm. For example, if we suddenly found a treasure in our house, we would be very happy. Similarly, a harmful being is like a treasure in that she is the basis for our practicing patience. Without that person, we could not create the virtue of patience. Therefore we should practice patience and avoid getting angry at her.

Thinking about the disadvantages of our anger helps us to subdue it. Each moment of anger destroys the positive potential we have built up over many eons. In addition, if we retaliate with anger, we create negative karma which causes us to have an unfortunate rebirth and many difficulties even when we are again born as a human being.

The person harming us is doing so because he is controlled by his disturbing attitudes, possessed by them in a sense, so that he has no clarity of mind. If he were not controlled by his disturbing attitudes, he would not harm us. Thinking in this way enables us to generate compassion for the one harming us, and thus helps us endure the harm.

The patience of putting up with hardships enables us to manage what life brings and continue to practice Dharma without interruption. Sometimes we suffer from heat or cold, hunger or thirst, bad living conditions, illness, or even meditating without receiving the realizations. We must be tolerant. It is helpful to think of the stories of the enormous problems the Kadam masters and other practitioners of the past faced and decide to follow their example.

The patience of not being afraid of the profound meaning refers to being able to meditate on emptiness. Meditating on emptiness cuts through the layers of our misconceptions, and this can initially be unnerving. We have to be able to bear the fact that all phenomena are empty, without falling to the extreme of nihilism.

The far-reaching attitude of joyous effort

28   Seeing even Hearers and Solitary Realizers, who accomplish
       Only their own good, strive as if to put out a fire on their head,
       For the sake of all beings make enthusiastic effort,
       The source of all good qualities—
       This is the practice of Bodhisattvas.

It is said that for the sake of just their individual enlightenment, hearers and solitary realizers make such concentrated effort on the path that they would keep practicing even if a fire were on their head. This example is given to show the strength of their motivation and effort to accomplish their goals. Don't take it literally to mean that they are foolish and let themselves die rather than put out the fire! We, who admire the Bodhisattva ideal and are working for full enlightenment for the sake of all beings, should develop even more effort than the hearers and solitary realizers.

Joyous effort is a mental factor that takes delight in and enjoys virtue. It makes practicing Dharma enjoyable because it delights in any virtuous activity that will benefit sentient beings. From the viewpoint of the Dharma, having energy for worldly things is not joyous effort. We must endeavor to practice the three types of joyous effort without discouragement:

1. Armor-like effort
2. Engaging effort
3. The effort of not being complacent

Armor-like effort thinks, "Until I have placed all sentient beings in the state of enlightenment, I shall never give up my practice of the virtues of listening, thinking, and meditating." The Buddha said we must put on this inconceivable armor of unfailingly working for the benefit of sentient beings until they all are enlightened. Armor-like effort also thinks, "If it would benefit even one sentient being, I shall willingly stay in the hell of unceasing torment for eons and eons." Although such aspirations may seem over our heads at the moment, we can build up to them gradually. When our effort slackens, it is helpful to remember how the Buddhas and Bodhisattvas have practiced and to recall how much we personally have benefited due to their joyous effort.

Engaging effort means to engage our body, speech, and mind in positive actions such as practicing the six far-reaching attitudes. Thinking of acting constructively is very important, but that becomes meaningless if we do not actually do anything. Engaging effort also involves giving up all actions that are motivated by attachment, anger, and ignorance. We could think, for example, "First I will do this and that (worldly) activity, and then I'll practice the Dharma." But while the sun endlessly rises and sets, there is always another day to put off the Dharma, right up to the time we die. Our mind is deceiving us if we think it's fine to procrastinate in our Dharma practice. We need to transform our mind now, while we have the opportunity.

The effort of not being complacent means not becoming self-satisfied by thinking, for example, "I have done retreat and recited 100,000 mantras. I've completed 100,000 prostrations. Now I don't need to do any more." We must be on guard not to become smug, sitting back and taking it easy. Of course, we should rejoice in our own and others' positive actions—that increases our virtue and makes us happy—but we should avoid becoming complacent, for that is self-defeating. Until we become enlightened, we must purify our mind and develop our potential, so we should continue our practice with delight.

If we are lazy, we cannot engage in virtue. We cannot achieve our personal aims, let alone those of others. Our own goals will be out of reach, and enlightenment for the sake of others will be even further. For a lazy person, even getting a cup of tea is difficult, because he does not want to exert the effort to make it.

The opposite of joyous effort is laziness, which is of three types:

1. The laziness of indolence, which is being attached to lazing around, sleeping, and daydreaming, not wanting to help anyone or do anything.

2. The laziness of discouragement makes us think we are too dull, too weak, too full of confusion and negativity, too old to practice, and so forth. With low self-esteem we think, "I cannot become a Buddha. I cannot help others." With this attitude, we put off Dharma practice, and then miss out on all of its benefits and positive results. This kind of negative self-image does not reflect reality and is a huge obstacle to our practice. We must be careful not to believe in it.

3. The laziness that is looked down upon is so-called because holy beings disdain it. It refers to putting great effort into things that have no essence, such as getting back at our enemies, helping our friends, accumulating wealth, and in general making ourselves the busiest of the busy due to being extremely attached to the happiness of this life. It is the cause of nothing but suffering. This laziness makes us attached to the cause of suffering.

Although we might possess wisdom that is sharp at explaining, discussing, and composing, if we have no enthusiasm, we can never finish our work. We are beaten down by laziness and lack energy. Without effort, we cannot fulfill even our worldly aims, let alone attain individual liberation or full enlightenment. To attain them requires effort. They will not arise by themselves.

When our mind is virtuous but lacks enthusiasm, recollect impermanence. That way, the mind will be induced to go to Dharma naturally.

Milarepa said, "When I continually remember death, I see that my body, possessions, and everything is to be given up. They are no use ultimately. They do not bring everlasting happiness." Thinking this way, we will set wise priorities in our life, use our physical, verbal, and mental energy wisely, and will conquer the devil of laziness.

The far-reaching attitude of concentration

29 Understanding that disturbing emotions are destroyed
 By special insight with calm abiding,
 Cultivate concentration which surpasses
 The four formless absorptions—
 This is the practice of Bodhisattvas.

We can cut the root of cyclic existence only by combining calm abiding and special insight. Concentration is the ability to keep the mind on an object of meditation one-pointedly without being distracted, and calm abiding is an extremely stable form of concentration which is able to stay on any object as long as we wish and is sustained by the joy and bliss of physical and mental pliancy. Here, special insight refers to wisdom realizing emptiness. This wisdom can cut the root of cyclic existence, but it is only able to do so when combined with calm abiding. On the other hand, if we only have calm abiding but lack the wisdom realizing emptiness, we could take birth in cyclic existence as a god of the form or formless realms, but we would not be able to free ourselves from cyclic existence. To do this we need calm abiding which rests one-pointedly on a positive object united with special insight, which is the wisdom realizing emptiness.

Although single-pointed concentration alone cannot free us from cyclic existence, it nevertheless is very important. If the mind is under the influence of the disturbing attitudes, we act negatively and will suffer the results. Although we may practice the other far-reaching attitudes, without concentration our mind will wander to external objects and we will not be able to realize emptiness. If we think of the disadvantages of wandering in cyclic existence, we will naturally be interested in developing calm abiding and will undergo the hardships involved in doing so with joyous effort.

In general, calm abiding is best developed during meditation retreat. A peaceful, isolated place is conducive for this. In addition, it is essential that our mind also be "isolated," that is, not have much conceptualization. Conceptualization occurs when our mind is busy thinking all sorts of things, such as, "I need this. I'm going to do that.

He should do this. Why aren't things going the way I want them to?"
We have to train ourselves to abandon all thoughts tainted by the three
poisonous attitudes. In general, we don't have to avoid positive
thoughts, but to attain calm abiding even positive conceptualization
is to be temporarily abandoned. Whether we are in an isolated place
or in the midst of a crowd, we should try to let go of all useless
conceptualization, for then we will able to engage in virtue. If we don't
put a damper on our rambling conceptualization, staying alone in a
place is not much use because we will just sit and think about all sorts
of other things. When doing retreat, it is also important to have few
needs and to be content. This is very important, for without it, our
mind will go to objects of attachment and try to procure them, and we
will not have time to practice the Dharma.

To place the mind firmly and one-pointedly on a positive object
for as long as we wish, we need calm abiding. The way to develop it
is explained in the Gradual Path. Whether we develop it through sutra
or tantric practice, we need to rely on the method outlined there, where
the accomplishment of calm abiding is described in terms of the five
faults, the eight antidotes, the six powers, the four attentions, and the
nine stages of having the mind abide.

The far-reaching attitude of wisdom

30   Since the five perfections without wisdom
      Cannot bring perfect enlightenment,
      Along with skillful means cultivate the wisdom
      Which does not conceive the three spheres [as real]—
      This is the practice of Bodhisattvas.

There are various types of wisdom in the world, such as understanding carpentry, medicine, poetry, and grammar. However, here wisdom
refers to the wisdom that realizes emptiness. Emptiness is initially to
be realized through reasoning. We have to recognize the object to be
refuted—true existence—and then investigate to discover if it exists.
Concentrating one-pointedly on an object may make our mind peaceful and calm, but this alone is not the realization of emptiness. Similarly, simply emptying our minds of all discursive thoughts is not the
realization of emptiness.

Whether we want to attain the full enlightenment of Buddhahood
or the individual enlightenment of the hearers and solitary realizers,
both method and wisdom are needed. However, the method in each

case is different. For a person wishing to attain full enlightenment, the method is love, compassion, bodhichitta, and the first five far-reaching attitudes. Without these as the method, there is the danger of falling to the extreme of peace, that is, being satisfied with one's own liberation from cyclic existence and abiding in peaceful nirvana. Without wisdom, there is the danger of falling to the extreme of remaining in cyclic existence.

The first five far-reaching attitudes alone, without wisdom, will not lead the practitioner to enlightenment, even though they are virtues. Method is like having legs, and wisdom is like having eyes. We need both to go somewhere. The first five far-reaching attitudes are said to be blind, for they lack the eye of wisdom that perceives emptiness directly. Without wisdom, we cannot sever the chains of self-grasping. Without the other five, factors discordant with the practice—miserliness, impure ethical discipline, anger, laziness, and distraction—cannot be subdued. They are eliminated by generosity, ethical discipline, patience, effort, and concentration, respectively. If either method or wisdom is missing, it is difficult to go where we wish.

Practicing a path which unifies method and wisdom is indispensable. Wisdom supported by method means meditating on emptiness with the compassionate motivation of becoming a Buddha to benefit of all beings. Method supported by wisdom is cultivating the virtuous practices of love, compassion, generosity, ethical discipline, and so forth accompanied by the wisdom realizing that they are not inherently existent. We meditate on this wisdom by contemplating the emptiness of the three spheres—agent, action, and object. To do this in the case of generosity, for example, is to see that none of the three—the giver, the action of giving, and the recipient or gift—exists independently. If we give with this understanding, our practice of generosity is supported by the wisdom realizing the three spheres are not self-existent. In terms of compassion, the three spheres are compassion itself, the meditator, and the sentient beings which are regarded with compassion. These three depend on each other; none of them exists inherently.

If we have realized that things do not truly exist, then our practices of the first five far-reaching attitudes are genuinely supported by wisdom. Even if we haven't realized emptiness yet, we can still contemplate in this way so that our practice of method is held by an echo or a reflection of the real wisdom. This is of great benefit.

THE FOUR POINTS TAUGHT IN THE SUTRAS
Check our own faults and give them up

31   If you don't examine your own errors,
        You may look like a practitioner but not act as one.
        Therefore, always examining your own errors,
        Rid yourself of them—
        This is the practice of Bodhisattvas.

This practice is to be done only if we have faults. There is no need to check for faults if we have none! However, if we do not check, we will not see our faults, and we might even think that what actually is a fault is a good quality. This is very dangerous, because what we do will have merely the semblance of Dharma practice. With this delusion, we will engage in many activities, thinking that we are doing quite well, but actually making many mistakes. Others, of course, will see our faults and criticize us. Due to our inappropriate behavior, there is danger that they will lose faith in Buddhism or in the Mahayana. This is very harmful.

Bodhisattvas examine their own minds and actions and are aware of their faults. Similarly, we should continuously check our usual thoughts and activities to see if we are acting in accordance with the Dharma or not. When we notice a fault, we must give it up. If we do not check ourselves, we will become experts at noticing even small faults in others but be totally blind to our own big ones. The Buddha said we should not notice or dwell on the faults of others, but look at and correct our own. The great practitioner Drom Tonpa remarked, "A person who points out his or her own faults has become a great sage." If we observe ourselves, our mistakes will appear clearly. Only by seeing them will we be able to correct them. Whenever we see one of our faults, instead of feeling despondent, we can rejoice, for now we recognize the enemy—self-centeredness—and can dispel it.

Desist from criticizing Bodhisattvas

32   If through the influence of disturbing emotions
        You point out the faults of another Bodhisattva,
        You yourself are diminished, so don't mention the faults
        Of those who have entered the Great Vehicle—
        This is the practice of Bodhisattvas.

As a Dharma practitioner, we should avoid looking at the faults of others and criticizing them. Our perceptions of others are not wholly reliable. We often think we know the reason behind someone's action, when in fact we have no idea. We are simply projecting onto them, thinking our assumptions are reality. We ordinary beings cannot judge others' spiritual level. For example, there are many stories of Vajra Varahi, a female Buddha, who sometimes manifests in an ordinary form, as an old lady, an ogress, or a bar maid in order to benefit others. Also, Naropa was horrified the first time he saw his guru Tilopa, for Tilopa was catching fish, eating them alive, and piling up the bones. His preconceptions were dispelled a moment later when Tilopa grimaced, made some grumbling noises, snapped his fingers, and the fish were restored to life. Since we are unable to tell who is a Bodhisattva and who is not, it's wise if we don't angrily criticize or judge anyone.

Sever attachment to the households of benefactors

33   Reward and respect cause us to quarrel
      And make hearing, thinking, and meditating decline.
      For this reason give up attachment to
      The households of friends, relations, and benefactors—
      This is the practice of Bodhisattvas.

If we have benefactors and friends who are generous and offer us possessions, service, appreciation, or veneration, we may become jealous when they help others. Attached to receiving food, clothing, medical help, praise, and honor, we will argue in order to get *my* this and that. In this way, our virtuous activities of listening, thinking, and meditating will degenerate. If we have few desires and are easily contented, we will not be attached to the households of benefactors and friends and thus will not get entangled in such jealous squabbles.

Refrain from harsh words

34   Harsh words disturb the minds of others
      And cause deterioration in a Bodhisattva's conduct.
      Therefore give up harsh words
      Which are unpleasant to others—
      This is the practice of Bodhisattvas.

If we are not mindful of our speech, we can easily say unpleasant things to others. This disturbs their minds and becomes a great fault on our part. The Buddha said our words should be beautiful like flowers and honey, not useless and disgusting like excrement. He advised that when we are with others, we should speak pleasant words that are suitable for them. First delight them by speaking kindly, then speak of the Dharma. If we speak harshly by criticizing, complaining, ridiculing, or putting them down, instead of our practice benefiting others, it will deteriorate.

THE WAY TO ABANDON THE DISTURBING ATTITUDES

35   Habitual disturbing emotions are hard to stop through
          counteractions.
      Armed with antidotes, the guards of mindfulness and mental
          alertness
      Destroy disturbing emotions like attachment
      At once, as soon as they arise—
      This is the practice of Bodhisattvas.

In our daily lives, episodes of attachment, anger, and confusion start small and gradually grow. We need to counteract them while they are still small, for after they have become big, they are difficult to handle. Therefore, we need to notice them when they first arise. To do this, we rely on two mental factors. The first is mindfulness, which, without forgetting, remembers what to practice and what to abandon. The second is mental alertness, with which we keep checking to see if our actions of body, speech, and mind are positive or negative. Through mindfulness and alertness, if you become aware of attachment welling up, counter it with meditation on the undesirable and ugly aspects of the object. For anger, meditate on love. For ignorance, think of dependent arising. For jealousy, rejoice at the fortune and qualities of others. By knowing the appropriate antidote to each disturbing attitude, we will become like a wise doctor who knows the right medicine for each disease.

TRAINING IN MINDFULNESS AND ALERTNESS

36   In brief, whatever you are doing,
      Ask yourself, "What's the state of my mind?"
      With constant mindfulness and mental alertness
      Accomplish others' good—
      This is the practice of Bodhisattvas.

We should scrutinize the beginning of each action, the action itself, and its conclusion, with mindfulness and alertness. In this way, we will be able to guard our minds from self-centeredness and disturbing attitudes and continue developing the intention to benefit others. Mindfulness and alertness are essential to guard our mind. Without them it will be difficult to develop our positive qualities, and those that we have already developed will degenerate. Although we cannot actually help sentient beings as much as we would like to now, we should never be separated from the wish to benefit them and the wish to attain enlightenment so that we can do so most effectively. If we continuously think, "I must work for enlightenment," all our actions will be held by that thought and will be very good. On the other hand, if we are reckless and do not check our mind by using mindfulness and alertness, we may give up bodhichitta, and that would harm both ourselves and others. The sage Atisha said, "The best quality is the mind wishing to benefit others. The best advice and instruction is to check the mind for faults. The best companions are mindfulness and alertness."

Dedicating the Virtue to Complete Enlightenment

37   To remove the suffering of limitless beings,
      Understanding the purity of the three spheres,
      Dedicate the virtue from making such effort
      To enlightenment—
      This is the practice of Bodhisattvas.

Bodhisattvas dedicate all their virtue to the enlightenment of all sentient beings, and by dedicating it in this way, it is never used up. They complete the dedication by directing their wisdom to the lack of inherent existence of themselves as the agent, enlightenment as the object, and the dedication of positive potential as the action. Although these three are empty, they exist conventionally and are established in dependence upon each other.

Conclusion of the Root Text

      For all who want to train on the Bodhisattva path,
      I have written *The Thirty-seven Practices of Bodhisattvas,*
      Following what has been said by the excellent ones
      On the meaning of the sutras, tantras, and treatises.

      Though not poetically pleasing to scholars
      Owing to my poor intelligence and lack of learning,
      I've relied on the sutras and the words of the excellent,
      So I think these Bodhisattva practices are without error.

However, as the great deeds of Bodhisattvas
Are hard to fathom for one of my poor intelligence,
I beg the excellent to forgive all faults,
Such as contradictions and non-sequiturs.

Through the virtue from this may all living beings
Gain the ultimate and conventional bodhichittas
And thereby become like the Protector Chenrezig
Who dwells in neither extreme—not in the world nor in
   peace.

This was written for his own and others' benefit by the
monk Togme, an exponent of scripture and reasoning,
in a cave in Ngülchu Rinchen.

With these verses, Togme Sangpo concludes the text. Here, he again shows his humility and his respect for the Buddhas and Bodhisattvas. Although he does not claim any credit for composing the text himself, it does not diminish the value of the Bodhisattvas' practices described in it. Instead, he traces their origin to the Buddha's scriptures and encourages us to put them into practice because they are valid teachings coming from the Buddha.

He concludes by dedicating the positive potential so that all sentient beings may develop and complete the two bodhichittas in their minds and thus become like Chenrezig, the Buddha of Compassion, who abides neither in cyclic existence nor in the complacent peace of individual liberation, but works continuously for the benefit of all beings.

For as long as space endures,
And for as long as sentient beings remain,
Until then, may I too abide
To dispel the misery of the world.

—Shantideva

THE THIRTY-SEVEN PRACTICES OF BODHISATTVAS

by Gyelsay Togme Sangpo

> Homage to Lokeshwara
>
> I pay constant homage through my three doors,
> To my supreme teacher and protector Chenrezig,
> Who while seeing all phenomena lack coming and going,
> Makes single-minded effort for the good of living beings.
>
> Perfect Buddhas, source of all well-being and happiness,
> Arise from accomplishing the excellent teachings,
> And this depends on knowing the practices.
> So I will explain the practices of Bodhisattvas.

1   Having gained this rare ship of freedom and fortune,
    Hear, think, and meditate unwaveringly night and day
    In order to free yourself and others
    From the ocean of cyclic existence—
    This is the practice of Bodhisattvas.

2   Attached to your loved ones you're stirred up like water.
    Hating your enemies you burn like fire.
    In the darkness of confusion you forget what to adopt and
        discard.
    Give up your homeland—
    This is the practice of Bodhisattvas.

3   By avoiding bad objects, disturbing emotions gradually
        decrease.
    Without distraction, virtuous activities naturally increase.
    With clarity of mind, conviction in the teaching arises.
    Cultivate seclusion—
    This is the practice of Bodhisattvas.

4   Loved ones who have long kept company will part.
     Wealth created with difficulty will be left behind.
     Consciousness, the guest, will leave the guest house of the
          body.
     Let go of this life—
     This is the practice of Bodhisattvas.

5   When you keep their company your three poisons increase,
     Your activities of hearing, thinking, and meditating decline,
     And they make you lose your love and compassion.
     Give up bad friends—
     This is the practice of Bodhisattvas.

6   When you rely on them your faults come to an end
     And your good qualities grow like the waxing moon.
     Cherish spiritual teachers
     Even more than your own body—
     This is the practice of Bodhisattvas.

7   Bound himself in the jail of cyclic existence,
     What worldly god can give you protection?
     Therefore when you seek refuge,
     Take refuge in the Three Jewels which will not betray you—
     This is the practice of Bodhisattvas.

8   The Subduer said all the unbearable suffering
     Of bad rebirths is the fruit of wrong-doing.
     Therefore, even at the cost of your life,
     Never do wrong—
     This is the practice of Bodhisattvas.

9   Like dew on the tip of a blade of grass, pleasures of
          the three worlds
     Last only a while and then vanish.
     Aspire to the never-changing
     Supreme state of liberation—
     This is the practice of Bodhisattvas.

10   When your mothers, who've loved you since time without
          beginning,
     Are suffering, what use is your own happiness?
     Therefore to free limitless living beings
     Develop the altruistic intention—
     This is the practice of Bodhisattvas.

11   All suffering comes from the wish for your own happiness.
     Perfect Buddhas are born from the thought to help others.
     Therefore exchange your own happiness

For the suffering of others—
This is the practice of Bodhisattvas.

12   Even if someone out of strong desire
Steals all your wealth or has it stolen,
Dedicate to him your body, possessions,
And your virtue, past, present, and future—
This is the practice of Bodhisattvas.

13   Even if someone tries to cut off your head
When you haven't done the slightest thing wrong,
Out of compassion take all his misdeeds
Upon yourself—
This is the practice of Bodhisattvas.

14   Even if someone broadcasts all kinds of unpleasant remarks
About you throughout the three thousand worlds,
In return, with a loving mind,
Speak of his good qualities—
This is the practice of Bodhisattvas.

15   Though someone may deride and speak bad words
About you in a public gathering,
Looking on him as a spiritual teacher,
Bow to him with respect—
This is the practice of Bodhisattvas.

16   Even if a person for whom you've cared
Like your own child regards you as an enemy,
Cherish him specially, like a mother
Does her child who is stricken by sickness—
This is the practice of Bodhisattvas.

17   If an equal or inferior person
Disparages you out of pride,
Place him, as you would your spiritual teacher,
With respect on the crown of your head—
This is the practice of Bodhisattvas.

18   Though you lack what you need and are constantly
        disparaged,
Afflicted by dangerous sickness and spirits,
Without discouragement take on the misdeeds
And the pain of all living beings—
This is the practice of Bodhisattvas.

19   Though you become famous and many bow to you,
And you gain riches to equal Vaishravana's,
See that worldly fortune is without essence,

And be unconceited—
This is the practice of Bodhisattvas.

20   While the enemy of your own anger is unsubdued,
Though you conquer external foes, they will only increase.
Therefore with the militia of love and compassion
Subdue your own mind—
This is the practice of Bodhisattvas.

21   Sensual pleasures are like saltwater:
The more you indulge, the more thirst increases.
Abandon at once those things which breed
Clinging attachment—
This is the practice of Bodhisattvas.

22   Whatever appears is your own mind.
Your mind from the start was free from fabricated extremes.
Understanding this, do not take to mind
[Inherent] signs of subject and object—
This is the practice of Bodhisattvas.

23   When you encounter attractive objects,
Though they seem beautiful
Like a rainbow in summer, don't regard them as real
And give up attachment—
This is the practice of Bodhisattvas.

24   All forms of suffering are like a child's death in a dream.
Holding illusory appearances to be true makes you weary.
Therefore when you meet with disagreeable circumstances,
See them as illusory—
This is the practice of Bodhisattvas.

25   When those who want enlightenment must give even their
          body,
There's no need to mention external things.
Therefore without hope for return or any fruition
Give generously—
This is the practice of Bodhisattvas.

26   Without ethics you can't accomplish your own well-being,
So wanting to accomplish others' is laughable.
Therefore without worldly aspirations
Safeguard your ethical discipline—
This is the practice of Bodhisattvas.

27   To Bodhisattvas who want a wealth of virtue
Those who harm are like a precious treasure.
Therefore towards all cultivate patience
Without hostility—
This is the practice of Bodhisattvas.

28 Seeing even Hearers and Solitary Realizers, who accomplish
Only their own good, strive as if to put out a fire on their
head,
For the sake of all beings make enthusiastic effort,
The source of all good qualities—
this is the practice of Bodhisattvas.

29 Understanding that disturbing emotions are destroyed
By special insight with calm abiding,
Cultivate concentration which surpasses
The four formless absorptions—
This is the practice of Bodhisattvas.

30 Since the five perfections without wisdom
Cannot bring perfect enlightenment,
Along with skillful means cultivate the wisdom
Which does not conceive the three spheres [as real]—
This is the practice of Bodhisattvas.

31 If you don't examine your own errors,
You may look like a practitioner but not act as one.
Therefore, always examining your own errors,
Rid yourself of them—
This is the practice of Bodhisattvas.

32 If through the influence of disturbing emotions
You point out the faults of another Bodhisattva,
You yourself are diminished, so don't mention the faults
Of those who have entered the Great Vehicle—
This is the practice of Bodhisattvas.

33 Reward and respect cause us to quarrel
And make hearing, thinking, and meditating decline.
For this reason give up attachment to
The households of friends, relations, and benefactors—
This is the practice of Bodhisattvas.

34 Harsh words disturb the minds of others
And cause deterioration in a Bodhisattva's conduct.
Therefore give up harsh words
Which are unpleasant to others—
This is the practice of Bodhisattvas.

35 Habitual disturbing emotions are hard to stop through
counteractions.
Armed with antidotes, the guards of mindfulness and mental
alertness
Destroy disturbing emotions like attachment
At once, as soon as they arise—
This is the practice of Bodhisattvas.

36   In brief, whatever you are doing,
      Ask yourself, "What's the state of my mind?"
      With constant mindfulness and mental alertness
      Accomplish others' good—
      This is the practice of Bodhisattvas.

37   To remove the suffering of limitless beings,
      Understanding the purity of the three spheres,
      Dedicate the virtue from making such effort
      To enlightenment—
      This is the practice of Bodhisattvas.

      For all who want to train on the Bodhisattva path,
      I have written *The Thirty-seven Practices of Bodhisattvas,*
      Following what has been said by the excellent ones
      On the meaning of the sutras, tantras, and treatises.

      Though not poetically pleasing to scholars
      Owing to my poor intelligence and lack of learning,
      I've relied on the sutras and the words of the excellent,
      So I think these Bodhisattva practices are without error.

      However, as the great deeds of Bodhisattvas
      Are hard to fathom for one of my poor intelligence,
      I beg the excellent to forgive all faults,
      Such as contradictions and non-sequiturs.

      Through the virtue from this, may all living beings
      Gain the ultimate and conventional altruistic intention
      And thereby become like the Protector Chenrezig
      Who dwells in neither extreme—not in the world nor in
            peace.

      This was written for his own and others' benefit by the
      monk Togme, an exponent of scripture and reasoning,
      in a cave in Ngülchu Rinchen.

This translation was prepared by Ruth Sonam and published in The 37 Practices of Bodhisattvas, *an oral teaching by Geshe Sonam Rinchen (Ithaca, NY:
Snow Lion Publications, 1997). It is reprinted with her permission.*

OUTLINE OF *THE THIRTY-SEVEN PRACTICES OF BODHISATTVAS*

The text is divided into three parts:
1. The virtue at the beginning—the introduction
2. The virtue in the middle—the main part of the text
3. The virtue at the end—the conclusion

1. The virtue at the beginning—the introduction

1.a. Stating the name of the text
1.b. Offering of praise
1.b.1. A brief explanation
1.b.2. An extensive explanation
1.c. Promise to compose

2. The virtue in the middle—the main part of the text

2.a. The preliminary practices (verses 1-7)
2.a.1. The difficulty of gaining a life with freedom and fortune (verse 1)
2.a.2. Giving up one's native land (verse 2)
2.a.3. Relying on solitude (verse 3)
2.a.4. Being mindful of impermanence (verse 4)
2.a.5. Giving up bad company (verse 5)
2.a.6. Relying on good friends (verse 6)
2.a.7. Taking refuge (verse 7)

2.b. Explanation of the paths of the three levels of practitioners

2.b.1. How to train in the path of the initial-level practitioner (verse 8)

2.b.2. How to train in the path of the middle-level practitioner (verse 9)

2.b.3. How to train in the path of the advanced practitioner (verses 10-24)

2.b.3.a. Generating the altruistic intention (verse 10)

2.b.3.b. Becoming familiar with and applying the altruistic intention

2.b.3.b.1. The all-obscured mind: conventional bodhichitta (verses 11-21)

2.b.3.b.1.a. Meditating on equalizing and exchanging self and others during meditative equipoise (verse 11)

2.b.3.b.1.b. Transforming unfavorable circumstances into the path during post-meditation (verses 12-22)

2.b.3.b.1.b.1. Transforming distressing events into the path (verses 12-15)

2.b.3.b.1.b.1.a. Loss (verse12)

2.b.3.b.1.b.1.b. Suffering (verse 13)

2.b.3.b.1.b.1.c. Blame (verse 14)

2.b.3.b.1.b.1.d. Criticism (verse 15)

2.b.3.b.1.b.2. Transforming difficulties into the path (verses16-17)

2.b.3.b.1.b.2.a. Ingratitude (verse 16)

2.b.3.b.1.b.2.b. Derision (verse 17)

2.b.3.b.1.b.3. Transforming wealth and ruin into the path (verses 18-19)

2.b.3.b.1.b.3.a. Ruin (verse 18)

2.b.3.b.1.b.3.b. Wealth (verse 19)

2.b.3.b.1.b.4. Transforming the desired and hated into the path (verses 20-21)

2.b.3.b.1.b 4.a. The hated (verse 20)

2.b.3.b.1.b 4.b. The desired (verse 21)

2.b.3.b.2.Ultimate bodhichitta (verses 22-24)

2.b.3.b.2.a. How to meditate on space-like emptiness during equipoise (verse 22)

2.b.3.b.2.b. How to overcome the beliefs that the desired and hated are real between meditation sessions (verses 23-24)

2.b.3.b.2.b.1. Overcoming the belief that objects of attachment are truly existent (verse 23)

2.b.3.b.2.b.2. Overcoming the belief that objects of aversion are truly existent (verse 24)

3. The virtue at the end—the conclusion

3.a. Engaging in the trainings of bodhichitta (verses 25-37)

3.a.1. The six far-reaching attitudes (verses 25-30)

3.a.1.a. The far-reaching attitude of generosity (verse 25)

3.a.1.b. The far-reaching attitude of ethical discipline (verse 26)

3.a.1.c. The far-reaching attitude of patience (verse 27)

3.a.1.d. The far-reaching attitude of joyous effort (verse 28)

3.a.1.e. The far-reaching attitude of concentration (verse 29)

3.a.1.f. The far-reaching attitude of wisdom (verse 30)

3.a.2. The four points taught in the sutras (verses 31-34)

3.a.2.a. Check our own faults and give them up (verse 31)

3.a.2.b. Desist from criticizing Bodhisattvas (verse 32)

3.a.2.c. Sever attachment to the households of benefactors (verse 33)

3.a.2.d. Refrain from harsh words (verse 34)

3.a.3. The way to abandon the disturbing attitudes (verse 35)

3.a.4. Training in mindfulness and alertness (verse 36)

3.a.5. Dedication of virtue to complete enlightenment (verse 37)

3.b. Conclusion of the root text

Glossary

Please note: the following definitions give the general meanings of terms and not the detailed explanations found in the philosophical texts. In general, the meanings are in accordance with the Prasangika Madhyamika tenet system.

Aggregates: the parts on which "I" is labeled. There is one physical aggregate (the form aggregate) and four mental aggregates (feeling, discrimination, compositional factors, consciousness).

Altruistic intention (Skt. *bodhichitta*): the mind dedicated to attaining enlightenment in order to be able to benefit all sentient beings most effectively.

Analytical meditation: thinking about the topics of the Gradual Path by using logical reasoning and scriptural quotations, and by understanding their application to our lives.

Arhat: a person who is free from cyclic existence, but who is not necessarily fully enlightened.

Arya: any person who has direct non-conceptual realization of the nature of reality, the lack of inherent existence.

Attachment: an attitude that exaggerates the good qualities of a person or thing and then clings to it.

Basis of designation: the parts or attributes upon which something is labeled. In the case of the I, it is the aggregates.

Bodhichitta: see altruistic intention.

Bodhisattva: a person who has developed spontaneous bodhichitta.

Great resolve: determining to take the responsibility upon oneself to bring about the happiness of sentient beings and to eliminate their suffering.

Hearers: those who follow the path to liberation from cyclic existence and become arhats. They are so-called because they hear the Buddha's teachings and teach them to others.

Heart-warming love: wanting all sentient beings to be happy, based on seeing them as lovable.

Impermanent: changing moment to moment. All produced things are impermanent.

Individual vehicle (Skt. *hinayana*): the path to one's individual liberation.

Inference: an infallible conceiving cognition that arises in direct dependence upon the basis of a correct reason or a consequence. This mind is a valid cognition.

Inherent or independent existence: a false and non-existent quality that we project onto all persons and phenomena; existence independent of causes and conditions, parts, or the mind conceiving and labeling a phenomenon.

Innate self-grasping: the inborn, spontaneous grasping at self-existence that all beings in cyclic existence have.

Intellectually acquired self-grasping: self-grasping learned through studying wrong philosophies.

Karma: action. Our actions leave imprints on our mindstreams and later bring about our experiences.

Liberation: the state of having removed all disturbing attitudes and karma that cause us to take rebirth in cyclic existence, together with their imprints.

Love: wishing sentient beings to have happiness and its causes.

Mantra: a series of syllables consecrated by a Buddha and expressing the essence of the entire path to enlightenment. They can be recited during meditation to purify and calm the mind.

Meditation: familiarizing ourselves with positive attitudes and accurate perspectives.

Meditative equipoise on emptiness: the time of single-pointedly meditating on emptiness.

Nirvana: the cessation of suffering and its causes; freedom from cyclic existence.

Non-abiding nirvana: full enlightenment in which one does not abide in either cyclic existence or the self-complacent peace of an arhat's nirvana.

Non-affirming negative: the mere absence of the object of negation. Nothing positive is implied in its stead and one is left with a mere absence.

Object of knowledge: that which is suitable to serve as an object of an awareness.

Object of the mode of apprehension: the main object with which a consciousness is concerned.

Object of negation: what is to be negated or proven non-existent in the meditation on emptiness, for example. It is essential to identify this properly before meditating on emptiness.

Obscurations to omniscience: the imprints left on the mindstream by the disturbing attitudes. These prevent us from attaining Buddhahood.

Occasionally produced: produced only when its causes and conditions have been assembled.

Permanent: not changing moment by moment. Permanent phenomena are not necessarily eternal. Many do not exist forever.

Permanent, single (or partless), and independent self: in this context, permanent means not arising and not perishing; single means not relying on parts; and independent means not depending on causes and conditions. That the person exists in this way is to be negated.

Perpetuating (substantial) cause: the main thing that produces something else, e.g., the seed is the perpetuating cause of the sprout.

Person: the mere I which is designated in dependence upon any of the five aggregates.

Phenomena: that which holds its own entity. In general, this is synonymous with object of knowledge and refers to all existents. In the context of the self-grasping of persons and of phenomena, however, "phenomena" refers to all existents other than persons.

Positive potential: imprints of positive actions, which will result in happiness in the future.

Prasangika Madhyamika: a proponent of non-inherent existence who does not assert that phenomena exist by way of their own nature even conventionally. Tibetan Buddhist scholars consider this the most exact and highest school of philosophical tenets.

Pure land: a world established by a Buddha where all conditions are conducive for practicing Dharma and attaining enlightenment.

Realization: a deep understanding that becomes part of us and changes our outlook on the world.

Referent object (Tib. *zhen yul*, conceived object) of ignorance: the truly existent object which appears to ignorance and which the latter grasps or conceives as existing.

Sangha: any person who directly and non-conceptually realizes emptiness. In a more general sense, sangha refers to a community of at least four ordained monks and nuns.

Selflessness: see emptiness.

Self-sufficient substantially existent person: a person existing without depending on the aggregates. This is to be negated.

Self-existent: being able to exist without depending on anything, be it causes and conditions, parts, or the mind that conceives and labels it. This type of existence is negated for all existents, both persons and other phenomena.

Sentient being: any being with a mind who is not a Buddha. This includes ordinary beings as well as arhats and Bodhisattvas.

Self-grasping: grasping at phenomena as existing completely independently of anything else. This is a form of ignorance.

Solitary realizers: those who, in their last lifetime before becoming arhats, practice in solitude at a time when no Buddha has appeared in the world.

Subsequent attainment: the mind of a practitioner who has arisen from meditative equipoise on emptiness and is engaging in other activities.

Suffering (Skt. *duhkha*): any unsatisfactory condition. It doesn't refer only to physical or mental pain, but includes all problematic conditions in cyclic existence.

Sutra: a teaching of the Buddha which is not a tantric teaching; Buddhist scripture.

Taking refuge: entrusting our spiritual development to the guidance of the Buddhas, the Dharma, and the Sangha.

Tantra: a scripture taught by the Buddha describing the Vajrayana practices.

Three higher trainings: the higher trainings of ethics (Skt. *shila*), meditative stabilization (Skt. *samadhi*), and wisdom (Skt. *prajna*).

Three Jewels: the Buddhas, the Dharma, and the Sangha.

True cessation: the state of some or all of the disturbing attitudes having been abandoned; the extinguishment of true sufferings and true causes.

True existence: the objective existence of phenomena through their own entity without being posited by thought.

Truth body (Skt. *dharmakaya*): in general, the Buddha's mind. This includes both the ultimate nature or emptiness of this mind and the wisdom of a Buddha.

Uninterrupted path: a consciousness realizing emptiness directly that eliminates some of the disturbing attitudes forever.

Universal vehicle (Skt. *mahayana*): the path to full enlightenment in order to benefit all beings.

Vajrayana: a branch of the universal vehicle in which the practitioner engages in tantric practice.

Valid cognition: a consciousness that knows its object without mistaking it; an incontrovertible cognition.

View of the transitory collection: a viewing consciousness which, having apprehended the nominally existent "I" or "mine," conceives them to truly exist. "I" refers to the person; "mine" refers principally to the person's aggregates and also includes one's possessions.

Wisdom realizing emptiness: an attitude which correctly understands the ultimate or final manner in which all persons and phenomena exist, i.e., the mind realizing the emptiness of inherent existence.

SUGGESTED READING

Advice from a Spiritual Friend. Geshe Rabten and Geshe Ngawang Dhargyey. Boston: Wisdom, 1977.

An Anthology of Well Spoken Advice. Geshe Ngawang Dhargyey. Dharamsala: Library of Tibetan Works and Archives, 1985.

Awakening the Mind of Enlightenment. Geshe Wangchen. Boston: Wisdom, 1987.

Awakening the Mind, Lightening the Heart. H. H. the Dalai Lama. New York: HarperCollins, 1995.

Bodhicitta: Cultivating the Compassionate Mind of Enlightenment. Ven. Lobsang Gyatso. Ithaca: Snow Lion, 1997.

The Door to Satisfaction. Zopa Rinpoche. Boston: Wisdom, 1994.

Enlightened Courage. Dilgo Kyentse Rinpoche. Ithaca: Snow Lion, 1993.

Essential Teachings. H. H. the Dalai Lama. Berkeley: North Atlantic, 1995.

Kindness, Clarity and Insight. H. H. the Dalai Lama. Ithaca: Snow Lion, 1988.

Liberation in our Hands: Part One, The Preliminaries. Pabongka Rinpoche.Howell, NJ: Mahayana Sutra and Tantra Press, 1990.

Liberation in our Hands: Part Two, The Fundamentals. Pabongka Rinpoche. Howell, NJ: Mahayana Sutra and Tantra Press, 1995.

Liberation in the Palm of Your Hand. Pabongka Rinpoche. Boston: Wisdom, 1991.

Meditations on the Path to Enlightenment. Geshe Archarya Thubten Loden. Melbourne: Tushita, 1996.

Mind Training Like the Rays of the Sun. Nam-Kha Pel. Dharamsala: Library of Tibetan Works and Archives, 1992.

Open Heart, Clear Mind. Thubten Chodron. Ithaca: Snow Lion, 1990.

A Passage from Solitude. Alan Wallace. Ithaca: Snow Lion, 1992.

Path to Bliss. H. H. Dalai Lama. Ithaca: Snow Lion, 1991.

The Path to Enlightenment. H. H. Dalai Lama. Ithaca: Snow Lion, 1995.

The Path to Enlightenment in Tibetan Buddhism. Geshe Acharya Thubten Loden. Melbourne: Tushita, 1993.

The Principal Teachings of Buddhism. Tsongkapa. Howell, NJ: Mahayana Sutra and Tantra Press, 1988.

Taming the Monkey Mind. Thubten Chodron. London: Tynron Press, 1990.

Thirty-seven Practices of Bodhisattvas. Geshe Sonam Rinchen. Ithaca: Snow Lion, 1996.

Training the Mind in the Great Way. Gyalwa Gendun Druppa. Ithaca: Snow Lion, 1993.

Transforming Problems. Lama Zopa Rinpoche. Boston: Wisdom, 1993.

The Way to Freedom. H. H. Dalai Lama. New York: HarperCollins, 1994.

What Color Is Your Mind? Thubten Chodron. Ithaca: Snow Lion, 1993.

The Wheel of Sharp Weapons. Dharmaraksita. Dharamsala: Library of Tibetan Works and Archives, 1976.